BY APPOINTMENT TO
H.M. QUEEN ELIZABETH THE QUEEN MOTHER
CHEESEMONGERS
PAXTON & WHITFIELD LTD

PAXTON & WHITFIELD'S
FINE CHEESE

BY APPOINTMENT TO
H.M. QUEEN ELIZABETH THE QUEEN MOTHER
CHEESEMONGERS
PAXTON & WHITFIELD LTD

PAXTON & WHITFIELD'S

FINE CHEESE

MAGGIE BLACK

Webb & Bower

MICHAEL JOSEPH

First published in Great Britain 1989 by
Webb & Bower (Publishers) Limited
5 Cathedral Close, Exeter, Devon EX1 1EZ
in association with Michael Joseph Limited
27 Wright's Lane, London W8 5TZ

Published in association with the Penguin Group
Penguin Books Ltd, Registered Offices: Harmondsworth, Middlesex,
England
Viking Penguin Inc, 40 West 23rd Street, New York, New York 10010, US
Penguin Books Australia Ltd, Ringwood, Victoria, Australia
Penguin Books Canada Ltd, 2801 John Street, Markham, Ontario,
Canada L3R 1D4
Penguin Books (NZ) Ltd, 182–190 Wairau Road, Auckland 10, New Zealand

Designed by Ron Pickless

Photography by Charles Parsons

Maps by Malcolm Couch

Production by Nick Facer/Rob Kendrew

British Library Cataloguing in Publication Data

Black, Maggie
    Paxton & Whitfield's fine cheese.
    1. Cheese
    I. Title
    641.3′73   SF271

ISBN 0-86350-105-2

Typeset in Great Britain by
Keyspools Ltd, Golborne, Lancashire

Colour reproduction by Peninsular Repro Service Ltd, Exeter, Devon

Printed and bound in Great Britain by BPCC Paulton Books Limited
The text is set in 10/11½ pt Plantin Light

CONTENTS

INTRODUCTION: Cheesemongers By Appointment   6

A Note to the Reader Concerning the Recipes   8

PART I

What is Cheese?   9

Cheese in the Past   11
How Europe's Cheeses Got Going

The Uses and Care of Cheese   13

PART II

Know Your Cheeses   21
Profiles of selected fine cheeses;
what to drink with them, and recipes
using them.
1 British and Irish Cheeses   21
2 French Cheeses   48
3 Other Cheeses: Swiss, Italian, Dutch,   81
Danish, German and Mediterranean Cheeses

PART III

Glossary of Cheeses and Cheese Terms   116

List of Cheese-Making Terms   139

Index   142

Acknowledgements   144

INTRODUCTION

CHEESEMONGERS BY APPOINTMENT
(The Story of Paxton and Whitfield)

In about 1740, a young but far-sighted Suffolk cheesemonger called Stephen Cullum decided to chance his luck in London, and leased a corner shop in the notoriously rough Clare Market. By the time he had trained his elder son, John, in the cheese business, he was prosperous enough to buy his first branch store at 24 Surrey Street nearby, and install John as manager.

Then it was his younger son's turn.

Young Sam Cullum had sniffed the aroma of cheese with his first breath – the best possible start for a cheesemonger. He learned his trade well and quickly. So in 1772, his father set him up in business, under Sam's own name, in Southampton Street off London's famous Strand.

London was spreading year by year, drawing crowds of small businessmen who saw her as a golden Mecca. To man the new factories, thousands of poor folk turned off the land were crowding into London – a huge new market for cheaper cheeses. Stephen and his son John took a partner, and moved their headquarters to John's branch at Surrey Street.

The new partner's name was Paxton!

Sam Cullum, now independent, had grander ideas. He saw the fine houses which the wealthy were building around Mayfair and Piccadilly, and saw another new market to be tapped.

Better transport was now making richer cheeses well known beyond their home valleys. Sam Cullum opened a new cheese store at 37 Swallow Street, near Piccadilly, in premises owned by one Anthony Bruce. It was a smart area where a few select shops catered for the upper end of the market. Sam did so too. He prospered, almost certainly helped by becoming close friends with Anthony Bruce Junior, his landlord's son. Anthony ran, with his father, a high-class provision store frequented by the royal family, and Sam wisely put money into the business.

In spite of the Napoleonic Wars and rising costs, the Prince Regent set a standard of opulent living which all London's elite copied. As its social scene grew more glittering, its servants more numerous and its meals more lavish, the Cullums' volume of business grew. It was too much for one man or family to cope with, and sharing with partners was the best way to handle it – and to expand still more.

Sam prospered most because he had chosen to sell high-quality products and refused to handle second-rate ones. The farmers from whom he bought rich cheeses and pure butter had to meet his high standards. His society customers appreciated quality, and he would not fob them off with anything less than the best. It paid off because they knew they could rely on it.

As a result, when old Mr Bruce died, Sam was able to take a much larger financial stake in young Anthony's provision business. Since it was thriving and bringing in good dividends, he was soon well on his way to being a wealthy man. When peace came with France in 1816, the business boomed because the restrictions on continental trade were eased.

Sam still had close links with the partnership which his father and brother had formed with their friend Paxton in Surrey Street. Perhaps because of it, he took into partnership in 1826 a younger Paxton, Harry, to help him run his many interests. Soon after, he added to these by buying a named partnership in the firm of an old friend, John Whitfield, at 44 Old Bond Street. Whitfield's firm thus became called *Cullum and Whitfield*.

However, Sam Cullum was now an old man. By 1832, he had been in the cheese and provision business for sixty years. When he heard that his Swallow Street offices were to be demolished in the building scheme for Regent Street, he decided to 'call it a day'. He realised most of his business assets and retired, leaving Harry Paxton to carry on his business.

Harry Paxton had all Sam's energy, and similar close links with other London cheesemongers. By 1835, he had found new premises at 18 Jermyn Street. After a short interlude, John Whitfield's younger grandson, Charles, joined him there as his partner, and the firm became *Paxton, Whitfield and Sam Cullum* until Sam died in 1837.

Paxton & Whitfield's quality products have been sold from the same premises for more than a generation.

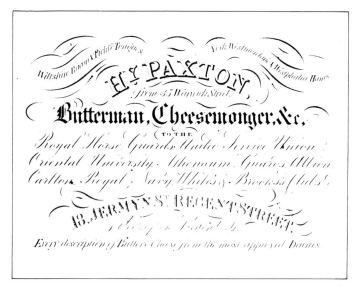

These trade cards from the early years of the nineteenth century demonstrate the high class society which Anthony Bruce and Harry Paxton served.

Not long after, Charles Whitfield went off to help run his own family's firm, so his name as well as Sam's disappeared from the register for the Jermyn Street shop – for a full eighteen years. Then in 1853, when he rejoined Harry Paxton at 18 Jermyn Street, the firm's name was changed again, to *Paxton and Whitfield*, the name it bears today!

Charles had already become a well-known cheesemonger when he rejoined Harry Paxton. In the years which followed, his repute grew still more. He came to serve the wealthiest in the land, culminating, in 1870, with the honour of being appointed 'Cheesemonger to Her Majesty'.

By that time, however, the history of *Paxton and Whitfield* was no longer the story of either a family or partners, but of the company they had formed and its customers, and of how its products changed to meet new conditions.

Through wise buying, judgement and its century-long personal contact with good farmers, the firm maintained and increased both its clientele and its repute; so it was easily able to get extra financial backing from a Mr James Best who became a 'sleeping partner' in 1856.

However, between 1875 and 1880, all English cheese prices slumped. This hit the farmhouse cheese-makers and the retailers who bought from them hardest. 'Paxton's', whose repute rested on its farmhouse cheeses, suffered more than most. The firm also suffered an unexpected decline in trade because of a marked change in British eating and drinking habits in the later part of the century. New, smart hotels like the Savoy fostered the view that champagne was the 'in' wine to drink at meals – and champagne is one of the few wines which only really goes with light, creamy French cheeses. English cheeses were relegated to servants and labourers – for whom creamery-made cheap cheese 'would do'.

Although its steady customers remained, *Paxton and Whitfield* was in such a bad way by 1887 that it could not even pay the rent. The large house at 18 Jermyn Street with its high overheads was too costly, but the lease, with only nine years to run, was not saleable to another retail business.

The firm's owners used those few years well. They saw, for instance, that although the middle-class mass had deserted them, their wealthy and gourmet clientele remained. They pinned their faith to it, and decided to stick to their farmhouse and the best of the factory cheeses, not to traffic in the cheaper, bulk-produced products; people who wanted first-class, individual quality cheese would pay to get it. Besides, they still held the Queen's Royal Warrant, and must fulfil the promise of high quality which it implied.

Acting on this decision, they first re-assessed society's eating habits – its late dinners and suppers, balls and soirées, the Season's events, and all-male military, livery and club dining. They sought the custom of the smart hotels and restaurants, and of exclusive men's clubs with a gourmet reputation, establishing links with them which have lasted to this day. They also revitalised their foreign contacts, and imported new high-quality French and Italian cheeses to match society's other food and wine tastes.

They were well on their way to renewed prosperity when they had to move to new premises in 1896. They could afford to remain in the smart West End street where the firm had now been for sixty years, moving to 93 Jermyn Street – an old house built in 1674 and scarcely altered since.

So, the firm of *Paxton and Whitfield* entered this century much as we know it now, with its present name, in its present premises, and with the same policy of maintaining high quality in both traditional and modern cheese for a discriminating clientele.

Inevitably, there were still some great changes to come. Changes of ownership, for instance, after Harry Paxton and Charles Whitfield gave up the reins. Luckily, in 1929, Fred Moore, a retired businessman with all old Sam Cullum's shrewd foresight, energy and business flair bought it and increased its already secure reputation as the supplier of fine cheeses – even to regaining the Royal Warrant in 1932, until his death in 1951.

It had not been easy to supply those cheeses and maintain the firm's reputation throughout the 1914–18 war and its aftermath. When Fred Moore took over, in the worst year of the Depression, it would have been all too easy for him to turn *Paxton and Whitfield* into just another supplier of mass-produced cheeses to the mass population. It took far-sighted courage to resist the temptation as the situation in the '30s grew increasingly difficult; it says even more for Fred Moore's ability that he managed, during those years, to make the firm steadily more successful without lowering its standards – a new and flourishing section of his trade coming from the growing stream of business visitors and tourists flocking to London as Hitler tightened his grasp on Europe!

Then came the shortages, dangers and disasters of World War II. Number 93 Jermyn Street survived the bombs, but suffered several fires, in the worst of which all its records, files and other documents were destroyed. With eggs, butter, cheese and bacon 'on coupons' and severely restricted in type as well as supply, 'Paxton's' became an ordinary grocer's shop 'for the duration'.

With peace, it reverted to selling mainly the high-quality dairy foods, hams and bacon for which it had gained such high repute. Although Fred Moore died in 1951, his son, Archie, carried on in the true Cullum family tradition. He maintained the confidence of all his 'regulars', from the Palace downward, until in 1972 the Royal Warrant, which had lapsed on his father's death, was renewed. By that time, age having told on him in his turn, he had taken as partner Dermot Adamson of John Adamson and Co, a firm of cheese factors established since the turn of the century and by this time highly experienced in the cheese import and export market.

The current of a family tradition runs strong in 'Paxton's' and, when Archie Moore died in 1974, Dermot Adamson brought his own family into the business – perhaps to celebrate the renewed grant of the Royal Warrant.

Cullum, Whitfield, Moore, Adamson – they have forged a strong tradition of family dedication to their firm, and they have been well served in the making of it by their managers and staff.

A NOTE TO THE READER CONCERNING THE RECIPES

Most of the recipes in this book were devised for the *Paxton and Whitfield Cheese Club*. Every so often, the club members were offered a choice of speciality cheeses by mail order; and with each cheese they got a 'potted' biography of that cheese, and a recipe using it.

This means that a good many dishes in the book are made with quite unusual cheeses, some of which may be hard to obtain. Do not despair of being able to use the recipes for this reason. Many cheeses, although not all, are interchangeable. Most creamy Brie-style blue cheeses are similar, for instance, and so are mild, fresh goats' cheeses.

One way to find a substitute cheese is to read the paragraphs in the book about the cheese you *cannot* get; note, especially, its texture, type of flavour and any herbs or spices it contains. Then find a similar cheese among those you know well, and try to imagine how it will taste in the dish you want to make.

Another way is to see how the unobtainable cheese is used in the recipe. If it is grilled (broiled) for instance, find another recipe which uses an available cheese in the same way. Check whether the two cheeses are alike in other ways, and how they differ. Also check the cost of the other recipe ingredients. Do not risk spoiling fillet steak or foie gras, but if the dish consists mostly of potatoes or pulses, be bold and try making it with the alternative cheese. Who knows – your 'invented' dish may be much better than the original.

Let me make one other point about these cheese recipes to encourage you. Even if you use the same type of cheese as I have done, your cheese will probably not be identical to mine. It will taste stronger or milder, be creamier or flakier, simply because any cheese except a 'stabilised' – that is mummified – processed product is a living, changing organic food.

A few words about measures. You can choose to use metric or imperial measures (ie kilos and litres or pounds and pints), which are given in one column, or you can opt for American cup and spoon measures given in a second column. Select which set of measures you like in making any recipe, but do *not* mix them. The measures in the three columns are not equivalents. Elsewhere in the recipes, the American measures or terms are given in brackets after the metric/UK ones.

The teaspoons and tablespoons used are the British standard 5 ml and 15 ml spoons. Always measure the contents level with the rim unless a rounded or heaped spoonful is specified.

PART I

WHAT IS CHEESE?

When you go into a speciality cheese shop such as *Paxton and Whitfield*, you are faced by shelves crowded with, literally, dozens of different cheeses. It may seem impossible at first to reduce them to any sort of order, or to arrange them in groups or classes so that you can pick a suitable type of cheese for your needs now or later.

A good cheesemonger will always be as helpful as he can. But he may have a queue of customers, and, in any case he cannot let you taste the ready-wrapped small cheeses. To a large extent, you are likely to have to make your own choice. So, besides describing what goes to the making of a cheese, this first chapter provides a few guidelines to identifying the main types of cheese.

All cheeses are made from some form of milk which has been curdled. New milk, free from decay-making bacteria, is soured after a time by the milk's own bacteria. They produce enzymes which change the milk's sugar (lactose) into lactic acid; then when the milk reaches a certain degree of acidity, it separates into solid curd and watery whey.

The curd can be made to come (solidify) faster by adding an acid to the milk, and it can be made firmer by heating it gently. Then the liquid whey can be drained off, and the solid curd can be eaten at once while fresh and glossy like very soft cheese. But it cannot be made into true cheese by being cured or ripened (left to develop its own special flavour and then to mature) because it contains no means of fighting decay-making bacteria. It goes bad within a day or two.

All true cheeses are made with renneted milk. Rennet comes from the fourth stomach of any suckling animal which eats grasses, and it has two vital functions in cheese-making. First, it changes the make-up of the milk more radically than when the milk sours naturally or with the help of acid; it makes the protein and butterfat in the milk draw together into a more solid curd. Second, it develops enzymes in the curd which delay or prevent it going bad. So most renneted cheeses can be given a curing or ripening period in which to gain the best flavour and texture their making allows.

It is the cheese-maker's craft which determines what kind of cheese will emerge from the processes to which he or she subjects the milk curds. It has done so ever since cheese was first discovered thousands of years ago; although many other, variable factors such as the local climate and pasture, the type of milk and its quality have influenced every cheese-maker in deciding what processes to use to make a new cheese or improve an old one.

One modern process has led to the creation of a good many new cheeses and to new methods of making old ones: the heat treatment of the milk which we call pasteurisation. This treatment destroys certain potentially harmful bacteria in the milk, but it also eliminates the curdling bacteria and the ones which help to form a cheese's particular texture and flavour. Pasteurised milk for cheese-making, therefore, usually has a culture of cheese-making bacteria, called a starter, added to it before use.

Pasteurisation, together with other factors such as the regular use of mixed milk from many sources, has made it much easier to produce stable, uniform, modern cheeses for the mass market, although the cheese-maker's skill is still needed to regulate the making of the cheeses.

The steps in making any renneted cheese are the same whether pasteurised or unpasteurised milk is used. After a solid curd has formed, it is sliced or cut into cubes to release the whey, the liquid part of the milk, which is then drained off. The curd may then be heated, then cut again, coarsely or finely, or put through a mill to shred it. The temperature and the amount of whey drained out, quickly or slowly, determine the texture of the completed cheese.

Curd for soft cheeses is put into moulds to drain, and is then salted. The curd for more compact cheeses is put into moulds after it is salted, and it is then pressed, lightly or heavily, and for as long as the particular kind of cheese requires. Most blue cheeses, for instance, are only lightly pressed, if at all, because air paths for the blue mould spores must be left in the cheese paste. The longer a cheese is pressed, the more condensed it will be and the longer it will take to ripen or mature.

After they are made, all new cheeses are ripened in curing rooms called cellars at a carefully controlled temperature. (Most cheeses used to be cured in cool cellars; air conditioning makes it unnecessary, but the curing rooms are still called cellars.) Some cheeses need a damp atmosphere or a cool draught to make them ripen properly. Most must be turned over regularly to make them ripen evenly all through. Some need to be washed with brine or to have their rinds brushed or treated with oil or wine. All must be watched with care until they reach their peak of flavour and are ready for sale.

When the cheese-maker decides they are at their peak, some cheeses must be marketed and eaten quickly because they will 'go off' rapidly. The simplest and mildest true cheeses contain very little rennet so their curds do not get very firm. After being partly drained, they may be lightly pressed, but even then they still contain a good deal of whey, which is where decay-making bacteria grow. These cheeses must, therefore, be eaten fresh within a day or two of being made because they go bad almost as soon as non-renneted, clotted cream.

Ordinary cottage cheese is one of these lightly renneted, barely ripened cheeses.

More heavily renneted soft cheeses can be ripened and so get a stronger flavour while still good to eat. Some types get it not only from the curing process but because mould spores are sprayed or smeared on their surfaces, or get there from the air and walls in the curing cellar. Two groups of cheeses are surface-ripened and flavoured in this way. First, cheeses like Brie are sprayed with *Penicillium* mould spores after being shaped, and develop a white powdery down on the outside; they then ripen from the surface inward quite quickly, so that the outside layer next to the rind may go bad before the centre strip. Second, there is a group of smallish, strongly-flavoured cheeses such as Pont l'Évêque and Livarot which develop amber or russet rinds and then strong flavour because bacteria of a type called *B. linens* are applied to their surfaces; they are then brushed or washed, usually with brine. These cheeses are ripened for a bit longer than the Brie-style cheeses, and they keep longer as well.

Some of the milder, small soft cheeses get a special aroma and taste, not from a mould but because they are cured on reed mats or wrapped in leaves, and pick up their flavour. Herbs, seeds or spices, if added to the paste, also give cheeses their own distinctive character which may be as marked as in some mould-flavoured cheeses.

This seems a good moment to mention goat's and sheep's milk cheeses. Most goat's milk cheeses are soft cheeses, while sheep's milk cheeses are on the whole firmer; the most famous sheep's milk cheese is the French blue cheese, Roquefort. Both goat's and sheep's milk cheeses are made in the same ways as cow's milk cheeses – in fact, some cow's milk cheeses were at first made from sheep's milk or mixed milks.

Penicillium moulds also flavour the blue-veined cheeses. Again, there are two types. The traditional 'blues', such as Stilton, Roquefort and Gorgonzola, are usually cylindrical, drum-shaped, semi-hard cheeses which vary in flavour with the making method and their age. Then there is a modern, international family of soft, creamy white-mould cheeses with streaks or 'eyes' of blue mould in their paste.

The mould for the traditional blue cheeses used to be grown on bread, leather or other materials, and was sprinkled on the unripened cheese curd before it was put into its hoop (the casing in which a cheese ripens until it is firm enough to stand alone). Today, a bottled extract of the mould spores is mixed into the milk before it is curdled. During the curing time, the mould spreads naturally along thread-like air pathways in the developing cheese; as a result the ripened cheese is aromatic and strongly flavoured.

Most modern, soft blue cheeses are also 'blued' by mould spores being added to the milk before it is curdled; but their condensed, creamy paste is only lightly 'blued'. Sometimes, white-mould spores are sprayed on the new cheeses. All these cheeses taste quite mild and keep longer than surface-ripened, white-mould cheeses like Brie because of the way they are made.

Any firm or hard cheese can also develop blue-mould streaks if the right spores invade it while it is being cured and its acidity and composition encourage them. Among English cheeses, some red Cheshire and white Wensleydale cheeses are deliberately encouraged to become respectively blue Cheshires and blue Wensleydales for their superb flavour. But the international crowd of assorted plain, pressed cheeses are the ones we know best. These cheeses vary greatly but one can make a few broad divisions to help identify the various types and textures of the plain parent cheeses.

There are smooth, yielding cheeses like Edam, sometimes with small 'eyes' or 'teardrop' holes in the paste like Samsøe or Esrom. There are Swiss cheeses, and others like them, with distinct, sometimes large holes – Gruyère, Emmental, Jarlsberg. There are semi-hard crumbly cheeses like Caerphilly or white Lancashire, and condensed hard ones which flake when dry such as mature Cheddar or Double Gloucester. Finally, there are hard cheeses like Parmesan, which if left to mature long enough become rock-hard, grainy and very strong-tasting indeed.

Cutting across these divisions, some of these cheeses are made with skimmed or partly skimmed milk and are very low in fat; a domed, semi-hard French Gaperon, for instance (freakish in shape and highly flavoured with garlic and herbs). Others are 'cooked', that is the curd is heated after being partly drained – Gruyère is the best known example. One must remember too, that some so-called 'hard' cheeses traditionally made for ageing, such as Cheddar and Gouda, are now mass-produced, usually in rindless, rectangular blocks, for quick eating; they are pliable cheeses, uniformly mild in flavour, which will never change with keeping except to go hard or sour.

Mild or strong, every cheese has its own flavour. However, if one must generalise, it seems fair to say that the smooth, pliable cheeses, as a group, have the least personality. The 'holey' Swiss and similar cheeses have flavour enough, but it is subtle rather than determined. Semi-hard, crumbly cheeses are generally distinctly stronger, and sometimes slightly acid, especially if made with skimmed milk. Hard, mature cheeses have a full, rich, generous flavour; and for concentrated punch on one's palate (or pasta) an aged, grainy Parmesan is unbeatable – which is why it is matured for so long.

This description is only a skeleton guide to help you start tasting individual cheeses. Choose which to try first by reading the rest of the book, and picking a selection which appeals to you. Then go out and buy them by name, and eat them. There is no substitute for this; because the best answer to the question, 'What is Cheese?' is that it is one of the most exciting eating experiences you can have.

CHEESE IN THE PAST

HOW EUROPE'S CHEESES GOT GOING

Ancient Cheeses

Our first written records of cheeses being made are references in ancient Sumerian and Egyptian texts. The Egyptian ones seem to be a soft curd cheese and a hard cheese called 'Cheese of the North' and 'Cheese of the South'.

Biblical references are not much clearer. The earliest are in the story of David; first when his father tells him to take food to his brothers in King Saul's army and ten cheeses to their commanding officer, and later when 'cheese of kine' is mentioned among his supplies. Job gives us another reference; the last three lines may refer to a pressed or even a ripened hard-pressed cheese:

> Remember, I beseech thee, that thou hast
> made me as the clay;
> and wilt thou bring me into dust again?
> Hast thou not poured me out as milk,
> and curdled me like cheese?
> Thou hast clothed me with skin and flesh,
> and hast fenced me with bones and sinews.
>
> (Job 10)

We are on much safer ground when we consider who ate cheese, and what kind of cheeses they ate, in ancient Greece. Ripened and matured cheeses seem to have been known very early in Greek history. Homer describes how Polyphemus, the one-eyed giant in the *Odyssey*, made sheep's cheese by curdling the milk of his flocks, draining it in baskets and moulding it. We know from later writings, too, that the Greeks preferred olive oil to butter for cooking so that most of the milk from their sheep and goats was turned into cheese – soft, rich fat cheeses for the wealthy, hard but sustaining cheeses for the poor. The island of Samos, for instance, renowned as the centre of Ionian culture, science and art, was also notable for its luxurious cuisine, including honey-sweetened hot cheesecakes. Hypata in Thessaly was famous for its fresh cheeses, and Roman cheese factors later made special journeys there to buy them.

The Romans valued cheese both as a nutritious food and as a delicacy. Town as well as country households made many and varied cheeses, in assorted shapes and sizes. In the first century BC, Varro wrote for his wife a recipe for making cheese with hare's rennet or fig juice, told her when to make it (from May to July, preferably from morning milk) and described the effect of different milks – asses' milk, hare's milk and so on – on the bowels. Columella, a hundred years later,

filled in a lot more detail and gave a detailed method for making exportable cheese; in essentials, his method of curdling, draining, salting, re-draining in moulds, and pressing the cheese has hardly changed today. He gave three other recipes as well: for fresh cheeses, brine-washed, lightly smoked cheeses, and for a wine-soaked year-old sheep's cheese.

Sophisticated Romans knew and enjoyed a wide variety of imported as well as Italian cheeses, debated their merits and had them served in many different dishes from salad dressings to breads and cakes. Athletes, too, were given cheese in their diet, and soldiers probably got it in their rations.

Not everyone approved of cheese, however; old cheese in particular was thought indigestible and constipating by some writers, although one suspects they 'asked for it' when they ate dishes such as smoked pigs' knuckles topped with sizzling melted cheese and with extra cheese in honey sauce 'on the side'. Equally eccentric, at least to our palates, was a mixture of chopped and mashed meats and 'innards' with varied spices, raisins, honey and toasted cheese.

Early French Cheeses

Cheeses from the Black Sea area, Dalmatia and Gaul were the favourite imported cheeses in Imperial Rome. Cantal is said to have been one of them, and Roquefort, praised by Pliny the Elder in the first century AD had probably been made even before the Romans got to Gaul.

After they left, cheese-making continued uninterrupted, especially in Christian monasteries after the Frankish king Clovis was converted to Christianity. The sixth-century diet 'Rules of St Benedict' for monks and nuns, forbade them four-footed flesh and more than two meals a day; and although the Rules would be relaxed later, the need for sustaining, palatable and varied food led, early on, to a great tradition of expert monastic cheese-making in French abbeys. Roquefort is said to have been Charlemagne's favourite cheese, while Munster is said to have been developed by seventh-century monks; the word Munster itself comes from the Latin *monasterium*. Maroilles, first made about AD 960 by the monks of the abbey of Thiérache, is another very early, dated French cheese.

Some farm and village cheeses as well as monkish ones are probably as old or older. Pont l'Évêque and Livarot are both ancient, derived directly from the medieval golden-crusted Angelot cheeses. St Nectaire and St Marcellin are both believed to be medieval cheeses.

French monks are also said to have taken their cheese-making expertise to England after the Conquest, and to have stimulated the farmhouse making of simple soft and hard cheeses. In Yorkshire they also started, so folktale maintains, the making of blue-veined Wensleydale in the great abbeys of the North Riding.

Early British Cheeses
We have no hard evidence that any British cheese was exported to Rome although our earliest recorded cheese, Cheshire, mentioned in the *Domesday Book*, may well have been eaten by the Roman legions stationed around Chester. Certainly, archeologists have found remains of cheese presses and wrings on several Romano-British sites, indicating that hard or semi-hard cheeses were made, and it is thought that fresh soft cheeses flavoured with herbs were also made, being set and drained in shallow pottery bowls with spouts.

Early Swiss and Dutch Cheeses
Swiss farm cheese-makers had prospered as early as their French confrères, and specialised in making cheeses for export. Ancestral Swiss cheese was carried to Rome by Caesar's legions, according to Pliny, and was admired there because it was made for long keeping with a rind like leather. 'Swiss' – that is Emmental – has been exported ever since; it is now made with the size of holes each recipient country likes, and is aged for the time it prefers.

The Netherlands had a thriving cheese-making industry and export business early in the thirteenth century; a dairy market and trade centre was set up at Haarlem in 1266, while Gouda had a half-yearly market where foreign merchants came to buy cheeses. There were also town weigh-houses where cheeses were inspected for quality as well as weighed. Specially-pressed Edam cheeses with cloth-bound rinds were made for export; in the sixteenth century, an English writer called Barnaby Googe rated 'Holland' cheese, together with young Parmesan, above any English cheese. A hundred years later, King William III did the same (but then, he was a Dutchman!).

Two Famed Italian Cheeses
Surprisingly, most Italian cheeses do not seem to derive directly from Roman ones, in spite of the many models. However, some are very old, and two in particular have always been esteemed as exports.

The great grana cheese we call Parmesan is thought to have been re-developed in the tenth–eleventh century from an ancient Etruscan recipe dating back to before the Roman Empire. By the fourteenth century, it was so popular in Italy that Boccaccio included it in his description of a land of plenty in the *Decameron*. Two hundred years later, the famous sixteenth century papal chef Fr Bartolomeo Scappi called it 'the best cheese on earth', and it was reputed the favourite cheese of at least two popes, and of Leonardo da Vinci. It also played a part in creating a national cuisine in France when Catherine de Medici took her Italian chefs there on her marriage; and in England it was admired for four centuries as the finest foreign cheese to use, from the time of Barnaby Googe to that of Mrs Beeton.

Gorgonzola, with its delicate green veining, can also be dated back to the tenth century. It, too, became an inveterate traveller; so much so that London's green-marbled Stock Exchange was once nicknamed Gorgonzola Hall.

Danish Newcomer
At the other end of Europe, Denmark has joined the traditional European cheese exporters, France, Switzerland, Holland and Italy. Her own, known cheese production seems to have been started by medieval Cistercian monks, thought to have developed the use of herbal rennets for their strictly meatless diet. Danish cheese-making evolved rapidly and cheeses even became a form of currency for paying taxes, but an export business only really developed in the eighteenth and nineteenth centuries when Danes, stimulated by a great woman cheese-maker called Hanne Nielsen, formed large-scale co-operatives and were pioneers in the use of modern equipment.

This outline of how European cheeses 'got going' has done no more than indicate the longevity of some of them, their variety and capacity for travel. Fuller biographies of the outstanding ones and paragraphs about many others are given later in this book.

THE USES AND CARE OF CHEESE

Cheese as a food supplies concentrated nourishment in a compact, lightweight form which is clean and easy to carry and to use. Since it is also safe and easy to store, it is especially useful for busy people and for pensioners who may not be able to shop often. As nourishment, it is an excellent source of protein as well as fat, and provides good supplies of the vitamins A and D, of calcium and of phosphorus. Hence, it is a valuable food for children who need to establish strong bones and teeth as well as for adults, especially nursing mothers and the elderly.

Another merit of cheese is that it is one of our most adaptable, all-purpose foods. One can eat it raw or cooked, and at any kind of meal from a mid-day snack to the main course of a family dinner, or a frivolous savoury to complete a dinner-party menu. It never becomes boring because there are so many different varieties of cheese. Leftovers need present no problems, because they can be used in dozens of different ways, and meanwhile take up very little space in the larder or refrigerator; nor do hard cheeses lose food value while stored or become unsafe to use.

For the elderly, cheese is easier to cut up than bread or meat, and easier to process; a less sharp knife is needed, and only minimal cooking heat. Cheese is also easier to chew than meat; and it is easy to digest if eaten grated, in small mouthfuls or mixed with other foods. It adds intriguing instant flavour to otherwise plain dishes; and its first-class food value makes even a little of it satisfying . . . and therefore economical.

CHOOSING THE RIGHT CHEESE – IN THE STORE

You may buy cheese for many different reasons; from a gourmet delight in fine flavour to a housekeeping need for protein food to keep in stock. Both the type and age of the cheese you buy will vary with your needs or preferences.

One thing does not vary, however. Whatever cheese you buy, get first-grade cheese. This is much easier to do if you buy from a supplier who sells cheese by weight, not merely pre-packaged cheeses. There are three reasons for this. First, the supplier is investing regularly in large cheeses, and he must therefore know and care more about the quality of cheeses he buys than if he simply orders packets from his wholesaler. Second, you can assess the unpackaged whole cheeses by eye, and ask to taste them if you propose to choose among them; even cheeses of the same type and quality have an individual character, and a good supplier will encourage you to taste to find out which suits your purpose and your palate best. Third, if you buy unpackaged cheese, you can buy as much or as little as you want. In a speciality cheese store, the supplier or salesman will also take pains to guide you by his knowledge of the cheeses, including the pre-wrapped ones.

Assessing the quality and condition of the cheeses in an unfamiliar provision store or delicatessen is more difficult. You obviously cannot taste any pre-packaged cheese – nor, in fact, unpackaged ones if the staff are busy (as they should be in a store with a good turnover). You will have to judge by the way the cheeses are presented, and by the appearance of the unwrapped ones. Here are a few guidelines.

Cheeses should always be on a separate shelf or in a different part of the chilled cabinet from other foods; and different types of cheese (especially strong-flavoured ones) should not jostle each other or be piled one on another. All the cheeses should look in trim condition. Cheese with a sweaty or cracked surface or in a dented or dirty package has almost certainly been lying around too long unsold, and is likely to be in poor condition. A strong, musty aroma around the cheese counter is an even surer danger signal.

Unwrapped hard and semi-hard cheeses

Cheeses such as Farmhouse Cheddar, Double Gloucester and Leicester can be judged by the condition of their cut surfaces. These may be slightly flaky, but they must not be cracked. A darker colour near the rind hints that the cheese is past its best, while a blue sheen or dusting of white flecks denote mould – and criminally careless grooming by the cheesemonger.

A few cheeses, notably Italian Parmesan, become almost rock-hard with age, and the craggy, chiselled surfaces are grainy. Any grana cheese, but especially Parmesan, is best bought in the piece before it reaches this stage; grate it and store it at home. Cartons of ready-grated Parmesan have a harsh flavour by comparison.

Semi-soft to firm (yielding) cheeses

Cheeses such as Port Salut and Edam have a higher water content than hard cheeses, and a plastic, slightly rubbery texture which yields a little when pressed. Any cut surfaces visible (wedges of Dutch cheeses are often sold in transparent film) should be velvety and cream-coloured all over.

Surface-ripening cheeses

Brie and Camembert, with their velvety-white or russet-flecked rind, are our most popular unwrapped foreign cheeses, but they also have a very short shelf life, so it is especially important to be able to assess their condition in the store. The top surface of an unwrapped Brie, may be bumpy and streaked with russet, while a creamery-made wheel is flat

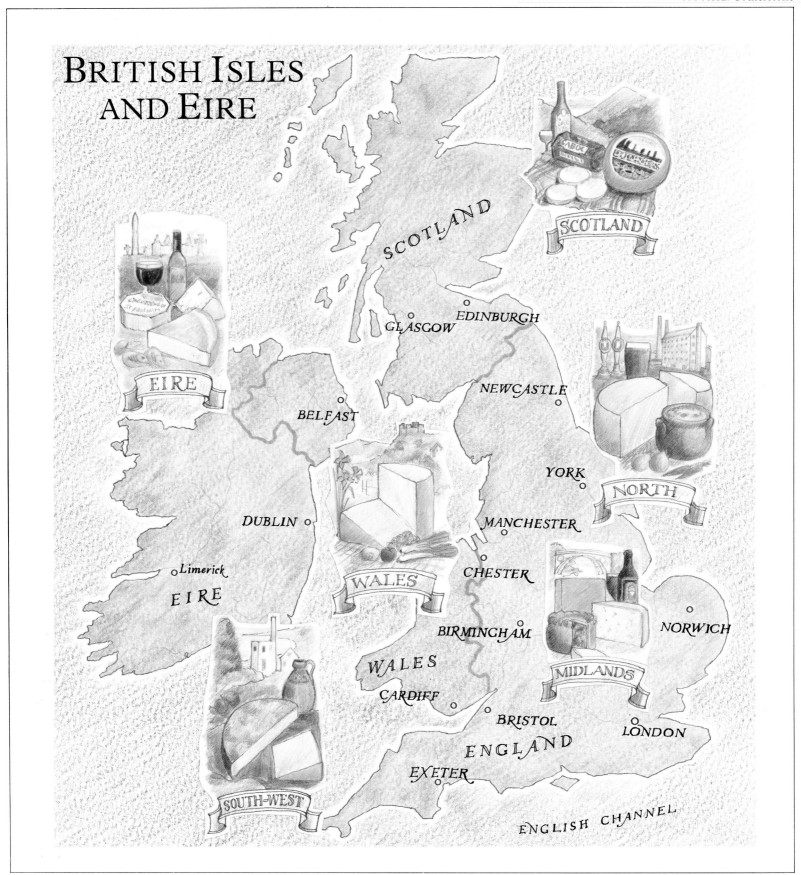

BRITISH ISLES AND EIRE

SCOTLAND

SCOTLAND

EIRE

EDINBURGH

GLASGOW

NEWCASTLE

BELFAST

NORTH

YORK

DUBLIN

MANCHESTER

Limerick

CHESTER

EIRE

WALES

NORWICH

BIRMINGHAM

MIDLANDS

WALES

CARDIFF

BRISTOL

LONDON

ENGLAND

SOUTH-WEST

EXETER

ENGLISH CHANNEL

and snow-white, but this is not important for keeping quality. The crucial test is the smell. Even the faintest whiff of ammonia as you approach the cheese indicates that it is already 'over the top' and will almost certainly be unfit to eat by the time you get home. If the wheel has been cut, the surface of the paste is an even surer guide to its condition. If the cheese has a white cake-like layer in the centre, this centre strip is unripe and is unlikely to ripen before the rest of the cheese goes off. On the other hand, if the paste is seeping out from under the rind as if melted, it will be too far gone to eat within 24 hours. The ideal choice is a wedge which is cream-coloured and glossy all through but still keeps its shape when cut. A whole small Camembert should yield to finger pressure enough to indicate that it will cut in the same way.

Richer, surface-ripening cheeses, such as a russet brine-washed Pont l'Évêque or Livarot, may be aromatic or even strong-smelling but the aroma should be 'clean' and pleasant. Any surface-ripening cheese, including the very rich double and triple-cream cheeses, should be plump with a fairly firm paste which fills the rind when it is cut.

Soft cheeses
There are dozens of soft small cheeses made from cow's or goat's milk, and even more fresh (ie unripened) so-called 'cream cheeses', curd cheeses and cottage cheeses of various kinds. Most of these can be eaten with a spoon and all have a very short shelf life; they go bad – and smell putrid – within a few days of purchase. Since most of them are sold in packages or cartons, the wisest way to make sure you get a good one is usually to check the 'sell by' date on the container. A soft cheese such as Ricotta sold unwrapped should be compact but without any dryish yellowing edges or tendency to crumble into fragments when cut.

Blue cheeses
Any blue cheese is likely to taste sour or harsh if overripe, so buy with care. Choose a cheese which looks moist rather than 'cakey' and greyish. The paste, which may vary from pale cream to gold, should generally be an even texture and colour throughout except for the blue veins. It should never be cracked, or have dull, dark streaks or patches. The blue veins may be pale branching sprays or a dark close-set network, depending on the type of cheese. Most cheeses have only a light rind, even Stilton these days, but avoid any cheese with a seeping rind. (Rindless cheeses will be moist when unwrapped.)

Packaged cheeses
The majority of cheeses, especially small ones and pre-cut pieces, are sold wrapped in paper packaging, boxes, vacuum packs or foil wrappings. Even high quality foreign cheeses are often sold packaged for carriage, and may be hard to distinguish from mass-produced, almost anonymous cheeses until you open them. Here again, a knowledgeable cheese-monger will be your best guide; it will be in his interest to advise you well as soon as you indicate that you care about the quality of the cheese you serve and eat.

If you have to choose for yourself, note how the various cheeses are presented, and the condition of their wrappings. Any cheese should be dry, and fill out its wrapping. Never buy a torn, seeping or wrinkled package or one with a grubby label and avoid any which lie in a jumbled pile of variously-priced pieces; they have probably been handled over-much. Open and examine any packaged cheese as soon as you can after buying it. If it smells sour or looks deteriorated, return it to the retailer at once if possible. A wise supplier will be glad, in case he has similar cheeses in his stock which may contaminate others of good quality.

When they are sold, packaged cheeses are always ready to eat and as good as they will ever be. Some unwrapped cheeses, noticeably higher-grade surface-ripening and blue cheeses may however be sold before their flavour develops fully. If you find it easier to buy cheeses, say for a dinner-party, ahead of time, a reliable supplier should be able to advise you on which to buy.

CHOOSING THE RIGHT CHEESE – IN THE KITCHEN

You may buy several cheeses at a time, but when you choose them, you should know what role you want each to play in your meal-making. Are you picking it to eat as part of a cheeseboard choice or for a packed lunch; or will you use it in a recherché cooked dish such as a soufflé, as a grilled topping on fish or vegetables, for flavouring a savoury sauce or as a ready-to-use protein snack food? The types of cheese you choose, their texture and strength of flavour will depend on your purpose.

Some choices are obvious. A mild loaf Cheddar will suit children's taste as a snack food, but is too bland and also too 'gummy' to grate for storage. Blue Stilton is a regal cheese, but hardly acceptable at breakfast to most people; on the other hand, mild Edam, thinly slivered as the Dutch use it, makes a nourishing, light breakfast on toast or crispbread. Cheeses for a particular type of meal always need to be chosen with some care.

Choosing cheeses for a dinner menu can be tricky because you have to select ones which will complement, not dominate, the flavours of other menu items. Remember, too, that cheese is a filling protein food. Although small cheese biscuits make pleasant cocktail snacks, cheese cubes, especially with onion or pineapple, will take the edge off your guests' appetite and spoil their palates.

Cheese should only feature in one dish in the dinner apart from a cheese choice at the end of an English-style meal. (It is a very old tradition going back to medieval times, to round off a meal with cheese; it was thought to seal in and mop up the alcohol consumed.) There are some suggestions for suitable cheeses to put on your cheeseboard later in this section. It is the right place to offer interesting and flavoursome (even strong) cheeses; there is no longer any risk of spoiling anyone's appetite or palate, as there is earlier in the meal.

Cheese is not often served as a 'starter' course at dinner for this reason, although much depends on what the following courses contain, and a creamy Stilton or other cheese soup can be a welcome beginning to a winter meal. A marinated, chilled Camembert is a well-known 'starter' but is probably best served as the first course of a summer lunch menu, say with cold salmon salad and fresh fruits as the following courses.

There are occasionally times when you can make cheese the main feature of a three-course menu. An informal dinner for six to eight people could consist of a salad 'starter', followed by a Swiss cheese fondue, and then by fresh fruit. This is a pleasant way to entertain vegetarian (although not vegan) friends. A more formal vegetarian menu might have a cheese roulade or soufflé (made with any quick-melting cheese) as its main dish; a mildly-flavoured vegetable soup could precede it, to let the main-course cheese make its full impact, and a baked or cold fruit dessert could follow as the last course.

Much more often, if cheese features in a main course at all, it is just a flavouring ingredient of a meat or fish dish or of a coating sauce. The type of cheese is then dictated by the recipe you use; and the only decision you have to make as far as the cheese choice is concerned is to make sure that your cheeseboard does not contain the same cheese or one like it.

You can serve a cheeseboard after the main course in the French fashion if you wish, rather than at the end of the meal. It is often a good idea if red wine has accompanied the main course and is still being drunk. However, if you want to serve a cheese savoury instead of a cheeseboard, the dessert should always be served straight after the main course, leaving the cheese dish to complete the meal. There is one other option. You can choose a dessert containing cheese – there are some delicious ones. Again, serve it straight after the main course – but follow it with a last-course savoury which does NOT contain cheese.

Your cheeseboard choice for a conventional dinner menu calls for real decision-making. Ideally, it should consist of three, or at the most four, cheeses; one should be mild, one tasty but not strong, and one can be richly aromatic and flavoursome. They should also vary in texture. If you are serving the usual cosmopolitan-style menu, choose a mild semi-soft cheese such as Port Salut, a surface-ripening cheese such as Somerset Brie or Carré de l'Est, and a blue cheese, perhaps Pipo Crem'. If you want a fourth cheese, you could add an English or French soft goat's milk cheese. This choice, or one like it, will cater for everyone's taste around the table. Vary it if you are serving an Italianate meal by using Italian cheeses of similar types, say Provolone, Taleggio and Gorgonzola; or if you offer traditional English food, remember that there are now several interesting compound products

(cheeses with additions) as well as the time-honoured hard ones and fine new soft cheeses.

At a dinner party, serve only medium-sized pieces of cheese. No one will eat much after a filling main course; 25 to 50 g/1 to 2 ounces per person is ample. Serve each cheese with its own knife to prevent cross-flavouring, and cut it yourself if possible, to save yourself being left with odd-shaped pieces to repackage. Some people have a compulsive tendency to cut the corners off a wedge or block of cheese.

At a buffet party or a wine and cheese party, you will obviously serve a wider variety of cheeses, and can give your own interest in cheese more scope by offering lesser-known ones. However, do not serve too many. It is better to offer a few dramatically large pieces than a whole lot of little ones which inevitably end up as a smeary, messy collection of bits too small to save.

Storing Cheese

Any cheese is best stored loosely wrapped in greaseproof paper, foil or polythene: clingfilm is only suitable for a short time, up to 24 hours. Leave a little air space inside any wrapping, and puncture it with a few tiny holes so that the cheese can 'breathe' and does not become sweaty or mouldy. Keep the cheese in a cool larder or in the least cold part of your refrigerator. Bring it to normal room temperature an hour or two before you want to use it, to let it recover its full flavour; it will have been dulled by the chilling.

Vacuum-packed cheese should be stored at a slightly cooler temperature than unwrapped cheese. If its surface is wet when you unwrap it, let it dry off naturally before you serve it.

If you will be serving several cheeses together, say at a buffet meal or on a dinner-table cheeseboard, keep the cheeses loosely covered with an old net curtain or soft paper until you are ready to serve them, and if possible keep them at cool room temperature near, but not *in*, the room where you will be eating. You do not want a pervasive, cheesy smell to fill the room throughout the meal.

If a hard, semi-hard or semi-soft cheese stays unused until it becomes sharp in flavour or begins to grow a mould, do not throw it away out of hand. Only throw away at once (before they cross-flavour nearby foods) soft cheeses such as Camembert which develop an ammonia-like smell. A light mould on any harder cheese can be scraped off; then use the rest at once for cooking. If hard cheese becomes dry with age, grate it. You can then store or freeze it to use later.

Freezing Cheese

Most natural, plain cheeses with 45 per cent butterfat or more can be frozen if absolutely necessary; the richer the cheese, the less it will be affected. Low-fat cheeses and any with a high water content, such as cottage cheese, usually go 'grainy' in storage; so may some hard-pressed cheeses.

On the whole, freezing is usually less deleterious to very

Lancashire

PAGE 22: *Left to right*: Red, White and Blue Cheshire

OPPOSITE: White Wensleydale and Blue Wensleydale

PAGE 23: Sage Derby and plain Derby

good quality cheeses. On no account freeze poor-quality or dull cheese; it will not improve, and it will not make a good dish if you cook with it. By the same token, even freezable cheese will not mature any more; an underripe wedge of Brie will go bad rather than ripen when you thaw it. Washed-rind cheeses should never be frozen.

Herbs or nuts in a cheese or on its surface may deteriorate in storage, besides tending to cross-flavour other foods; so may alcoholic or other flavourings, sometimes added to cheese in manufacture. It is wise to make a flat rule not to freeze such compound products. Leaves or seeds used as coverings may be damp or flavourless when thawed, and are also best not frozen at home, although cheeses with seeds in the paste, such as Leiden, freeze satisfactorily. So does Morbier with its strip of ash through the centre (see page 65).

Unless it is already sliced, cut any cheese into small blocks or wedges weighing 175 to 225 g/6 to 8 ounces before freezing. Wrap them closely in foil or freezer wrap, and seal them carefully to prevent cross-flavouring. Any aromatic cheese, especially blue-veined cheese, presents hazards in this respect. (Interleave cheese slices with freezer wrap before packaging.)

Grated cheese freezes well. Freeze grated hard cheese in a polythene bag. The shreds remain separate, so you can shake out as much as you need, and return the rest to the freezer. Seal the cold bag carefully. Spilt grated cheese in the freezer is an unholy nuisance to clear up.

Thaw all cheeses in opened wrappings for two to three hours at room temperature. They will flavour other foods if you thaw them in the refrigerator. Hard cheeses tend to crumble when thawed, so if you need to cut them, do it before they have fully thawed out. They also tend to lose quality and flavour sooner than softer cheeses in the freezer. No cheese should be frozen for more than two months.

Cooking With Cheese

Whether thawed, taken from store or straight from the shop, cheese is rewarding to cook with. It makes delicious, nourishing dishes in a few moments, and adds panache to otherwise bland fish, grains and vegetables. Cooking with cheese is also easy if you understand how cheese behaves when heated.

In general, cheese should be cooked slowly, over very gentle heat, just enough to melt it. The reason for cooking cheese gently is to prevent it becoming rubbery. The solid part of cheese consists of tiny particles of milk solids surrounded by fat globules. When cheese melts, the particles burst in the heat and mix with the fat. In many cheeses, however, the fat globules melt easily and may run off before the milk solid particles burst. This means that the cheese, instead of becoming a creamy mixture, turns to a ropey mass of solids with separate globules of fat.

This is not difficult to avoid with a little care. It you want to cook with a cheese which becomes ropey easily, either grate or crumble it first and mix it with breadcrumbs, flour, ground nuts or a little extra fat. Any of these ingredients will combine with the fat of the cheese itself, absorb some heat when cooking, and so prevent the fat running off before the solid particles burst.

Another way to melt cheese safely is to cut it into slivers and put it in a basin over a saucepan of simmering water. Yet another way is to put grated or crumbled cheese into a hot mixture; for example, add the cheese to a sauce after the sauce is completed, or sprinkle it into an omelette just before you fold and serve it.

It is worth remembering that well-ripened hard and semi-hard cheese melts and blends more easily with other ingredients than younger cheese, and you usually need less of it because it has a stronger flavour. Farmhouse and mature cheeses are, therefore, particularly good for cooking as well as eating, and worth using even though more expensive than milder types. (Processed cheese also melts easily but its flavour is often so bland that it adds none to the dish.)

You need not worry about the cooking heat if you use cheese in a casserole or pasta dish such as lasagne which is cooked at a moderately high temperature, because the other ingredients layered with the cheese protect it from excessive heat. However, if you want to grill (broil) cheese, take care to keep it 10 to 15 cm/4 to 6 inches from the heat and keep the heat low. If using it as a topping, grate it and mix it with crumbs or ground nuts before sprinkling it on the dish, or mix it with a basic coating sauce. Here is a basic recipe using an English white sauce as foundation.

Cheese Sauce (pouring sauce for mixing with macaroni, etc)

butter or margarine	25 g/1 ounce	2 tablespoons
flour	25 g/1 ounce	4 tablespoons
milk, warmed	575 ml/1 pt	2½ cups
seasoning and flavouring (depending on type of cheese)		
grated, crumbled or creamed cheese without rind	as recipe requires (if using Cheddar, 100 to 225 g/4 to 8 ounces, depending on flavour of cheese)	1–2 cups

Melt the fat gently, stir in the flour and cook for two minutes without browning. Remove from the heat, and stir in the milk gradually. Blend in thoroughly. Return to low heat, and bring to simmering point, stirring constantly. Cook for a few minutes, still stirring, until the sauce thickens. Beat well, and add seasoning. Remove from the heat, and stir in the cheese a little at a time.

PART II

KNOW YOUR CHEESES

BRITISH ISLES AND EIRE
NORTH (EAST AND WEST)

WENSLEYDALE
BLUE AND WHITE

One of the established English cheeses, Wensleydale has two unique features in its past. First, we know that until about 1300 it was made wholly of ewe's milk. Second, it was, as far as we know, the first English monastery cheese. The local lore about its early days is backed by documents. Among French monks there had been skilled cheese-makers since very early times, and no doubt those who emigrated to benighted Britain in the wake of the Conqueror included some of them. Land was allotted to these French monks in Wensleydale, first at a place called Fors where we know they made cheese in 1150, and after fifteen years at Jervaulx where the remains of their great abbey still stand. These monks were Cistercians, a reforming order, who believed fervently in those days that *qui laborat orat*, ie that work was a fine form of prayer, especially agricultural work; and so the discovery of mould-spores in cellars under the stony slopes at their new home must have reminded them of the cheeses in France, and excited them to action. They had plenty of ways of finding out how the greatest of French cheeses, the ewe's milk, blue Roquefort, was made; monks were frequent travellers and had contacts in many monasteries. At Jervaulx therefore, we are told, local 'blued' cheeses came to be made too. They were matured at first in the abbey's own cellars, and later on farms which the monks leased to lay farmers, whom they taught to make the cheeses – which then became part of the farmers' rent. This cheese-making system went on, unaffected by the fact that around 1300 cow's milk began to be used instead of sheep's milk as more and more lambs were kept and reared for their wool.

When the monastery was dissolved between 1536 and 1540, the farmers – or rather their wives – carried on the cheese-making, helped, we are told, by ex-monks and by the landlord of the local inn who had been given the recipe. Cow's milk was mostly used with a small proportion of ewe's milk added to keep the cheese's open-textured character, 'blueing' capacity

and fine flavour, which made Edward Bunyard in 1937 refer to Wensleydale as one of the most subtly flavoured of all the cheeses, and as 'the ideal which Stilton set out to follow'.

Blue Wensleydale cheeses were still the rule in 1840 when they were labelled as such at local cheese fairs.

Summer cheeses, loose in texture, were the best 'bluers'; they were shaped like Stiltons and matured for up to six months, for instance for Christmas. Whole evening milk, unpasteurised of course, was ripened to mix with whole morning milk and was curdled with locally made rennet. The young cheeses were salted by brining as a rule, which was thought to produce softer and stronger cheeses than salting the curd.

The small, isolated upland farmers bartered their cheeses for groceries, but the quality was inevitably uneven. Equally inevitably, a few dissatisfied grocers decided in the 1880s to make their own cheeses, buying the milk from the farmers instead of the made cheeses. This led to the start of creamery, ie factory, production and this in its turn led to standardisation, and to the making of one-milking, curd-salted, more firmly pressed cheeses in the interest of keeping quality. But firmly pressed cheeses do not 'blue' readily because there are few air-ways along which mould spores can grow within the cheese. So eventually most of the mass-produced creamery cheeses succumbed to the pressure for quick sale, and were marketed unripened, slightly sour and snow-white at around three weeks old. Only the cheeses bought by family grocers or interested factors were carefully chosen, nurtured and left for six months to 'blue'.

Shopping with my mother in the 1930s, I remember blue and white Wensleydale on the grocer's counter side by side. The white kind was the one I associated with the old couplet:

An apple pie without its cheese
Is like a kiss without a squeeze,

but I liked them both. I knew nothing of the care needed to make them, using completely fresh milk, turning the curd to drain it, and pressing it after it had been bound in calico – and on top of that the extra time and care needed to 'blue' some of them in the traditional way. Given this care, it was not surprising that wartime brought the cessation of blue Wensleydale making 'for the duration'.

Sadly, however, even after cheese rationing finished in 1954, regulations concerning the sale and usage of milk and the low 46 per cent moisture content insisted on by the Ministry of Food, prevented the revival of the pre-war moist blue cheeses. Even today, most Wensleydale cheeses sold are

EIGHTEENTH CENTURY POTTED CHEESE   **Snack**

Fills one 225 g/8 ounce (½ pound) pot

Red Cheshire cheese	150 to 175 g/5 to 6 ounces	1¼ to 1½ cups
softened unsalted butter	40 g/1½ ounces	3 tablespoons
salt to taste		
ground mace	large pinch	pinch
Bristol cream or other rich sweet sherry	2 tablespoons	2 tablespoons
melted clarified butter to cover		

Modern recipe Shred the cheese. Process about one-third of it with the unsalted butter in a food processor or blender. When the mixture is smooth and pasty, blend in the remaining cheese gradually with the salt, spice and sherry.

Press the cheese paste into a small decorative pot, tapping it on the table-top several times to knock out any air-holes. Leave at least 1 cm/½ inch headspace. Smooth the top surface. Chill until firm, then cover with clarified butter. Chill again. When the butter topping is firm, cover with a second coating of butter to seal any cracks. Refrigerate until needed. Keeps for 4 to 6 weeks. Serve with freshly made hot toast.

Red Cheshire seems better suited than White Cheshire to this version of the old dish, with its dark sherry flavouring.

Here is *the original recipe*. Slice one pound of old Cheshire cheese finely into a mortar and to it add an ounce of beaten mace, 8 ounces of butter, a glass of sack and grind all this together. Put it into pots and leave until required, then serve in slices.

Here is another old version for which White Cheshire would be suitable. This recipe, which was said to 'excel the best cream cheese made' used 1.5 kg/3 pounds cheese, 225 g/8 ounces butter, 125 ml/4 fl oz (½ cup) white wine, and 15 g/½ ounce ground mace. Take your choice.

SAGE DERBY DOUBLES   **Snack**

Makes 12 sandwich biscuits (savory cookies)

Sage Derby cheese, grated	50 g/2 ounces	$\frac{1}{2}$ cup
plain (all-purpose) flour	50 g/2 ounces	$\frac{1}{2}$ cup
softened butter	100 g/4 ounces	$\frac{1}{2}$ cup
beaten egg	2 tablespoons	2 tablespoons
salt to taste		
grinding of white pepper (optional)		
finely chopped (minced) parsley	2 teaspoons	2 teaspoons
finely chopped (minced) sage leaf	1 (small fresh or $\frac{1}{2}$ large one)	1

Combine the grated cheese, flour, 50 g/2 ounces ($\frac{1}{4}$ cup) of the butter and the beaten egg in a bowl. Season. Beat thoroughly until blended to a paste. Sprinkle the paste with a little extra flour, and chill until firm.

Roll the chilled paste into 24 equal-sized small balls. Place well apart on an ungreased baking sheet. Flatten slightly with your hand. Bake at 180°C/350°F/Gas 4 for 12 to 15 minutes until lightly coloured. Cool on the sheet. While cooling, combine the remaining butter with the chopped parsley and sage. Sandwich the cooled biscuits (cookies) with the herb butter.

Freezing Freeze unbaked dough for up to 2 months, baked biscuits (cookies) without filling for up to 1 month. Sandwich with herb butter after thawing.

of the young white type. They are excellent cheeses with a ripe buttermilk flavour and a smooth texture, but they are not all that the famous ancient cheese-making region of Wensleydale still has to offer.

Wensleydale is now sold in dry-rinded cylinders about 4.5 kg/10 pounds in weight. Closely wrapped, a white Wensleydale will keep in a cool larder for two weeks provided it is in fair-sized sections. Drink a dry English white wine with it if you can get one, or – remember the apple pies – Bulmer's Number 7 extra dry cider.

The rare blue Wensleydale deserves a rare wine, perhaps even one from the original home of the old French monks at Savigny in Burgundy or at least nearby. A Beaune, perhaps, of whatever quality your pleasure in eating good cheese merits.

LANCASHIRE (TRADITIONAL AND ACID CURD)

Traditional Lancashire is England's most unusual cheese. Indeed, it is unique because it it made from the blended curds of two days' – even, sometimes, three days' – milking, using less 'starter' than other cheeses. As a result, and because the making method is more complicated, it takes more space and more time to make than other cheeses.

Due to this, less of it is being made now than at almost any time since the Railway Age began, and it is rarely found outside its home county. Only four farms and six creameries were still making it in 1988, producing about 1900 tonnes/tons a year – and only 15 per cent of that was sold beyond the county border. Lancastrians eat their fine cheese themselves.

It is a cow's milk, soft, dry-rinded cheese, with a 48 per cent fat content, made from unpasteurised milk said to taste of pastures impregnated with wind-blown salt from the Irish Sea. It is softer and whiter than the other English regional (territorial) cheeses: softer because it is neither heated much nor heavily pressed, and its two-day-old curd content gives it a crumbly texture; whiter because the older the curd, the more tangy and whiter it becomes.

The flavour of this cheese strengthens progressively with age. It is called 'creamy' while young, and it is just that; soft and mild with a last hint of acid when two to three months old. When older, approaching maturity, it is sometimes called the 'Leigh Toaster' after a little town between Liverpool and Manchester famed for its 'toasted cheese' in the past. If the cheese used at Leigh was the long-kept, close-textured Lancashire made up to 1913, a deft cook might have been able to roast it on each side in front of the fire as in the early recipes before laying it on toasted bread. But if it was like the post-1913 cheese, as quick-melting and open-textured as the traditional cheese is now, it must have been more like Mrs Beeton's Welsh Rarebit in 1861, a slice of barely toasted bread with melted, mustard-seasoned cheese on top – or just the cheese alone in little silver pans, served with fingers of toast. It

would be a dextrous cook indeed who could toast even a thick slice of this soft cheese, then turn it and re-process it still in one sizzling piece.

Until 1913, all Lancashire cheese was made on farms, often in the kitchen. The method has not changed much. Cooled overnight milk (including, since 1910, a mere smidgeon of 'starter') is added to warm morning milk, and renneted to make the curd. The curd is cut with hand-held knives, then allowed to settle so that its fat will not seep away with the whey as it drains. Now comes the troublesome part. As Patrick Rance ably describes it, the curd is pressed in cloth-lined tubs, then cut and broken by hand, re-pressed and re-cut at least three times before it is mixed with the previous day's curd. The two curds – sometimes after a waiting period – are then salted, milled and re-milled before being put into muslin-lined moulds and left to dry and mature. In the past, anywhere in the farmhouse might be used for storing the cheeses, even the bedrooms if the temperature was right, so the whole farmhouse smelt of cheese.

After 1913, the cheese-makers in dairies used the same basic method as the farmhouse makers (although, of course, they standardised and modernised the conditions). By the time World War II broke out, farms and dairies were making about 4800 tonnes/tons of traditional unpasteurised Lancashire cheese between them.

Some of this was, and is, the delicious but rare Sage Lancashire cheese and even rarer Lancashire with walnuts. Some of the sage cheese is made with fresh sage finely chopped, but more and more of it is made with dried sage. It tastes better! 110 g/4 ounces of sage is added to each 18.14 kg/40 pound cheese, which is ready for sale in two to three months; the herbs taste too strong later. Smaller 9 kg/20 pound cheeses are also made. The weights of the plain, traditional Lancashires are as a rule 21 kg/46 pounds, 9 kg/20 pounds and 1.4 kg/3 pounds. They are cylindrical in shape with rounded edges to the flat tops, or are very slightly conical. In the past they were greased or buttered, but they are now waxed to foil air attacks.

After World War II, traditional Lancashire making was started again, but the burst of revival did not last and the number of traditional cheeses being made has dwindled sadly.

The creameries and their plant have not, however, stood idle. They have been used to make a different type of cheese, called at first New Lancashire, and since 1980, Single Acid Lancashire. The acid content of this cheese is high, to hasten the making, and it is made from the pasteurised milk of one day only. Sold at only four weeks old, it has a sharp, biting flavour quite different from the older cheese. It is made in the same sized cylinders and also in 4.5 to 5.5 kg/4 to 5 pound blocks.

This single curd cheese is probably best used for cooking; use one of the modern variations on Welsh Rarebit such as a Three-Cheese Rarebit made with a 'sandwich' of mild

Cheddar, Acid Lancashire, mild Cheddar; or a Ham Rarebit containing chopped ham, green pepper and onion crumbled with the cheese. Beer is a suitable drink. Traditional cheese is worth enjoying on its own, perhaps if you like with pickled onions or other saladings, and with crusty bread or oatcakes. If eaten like this, drink with it a young, well-rounded red wine – a Côtes de Bergerac could be successful.

Store the cheese, if you must, in the bottom of a refrigerator, closely wrapped to prevent it drying out. As usual, bring it to room temperature in ample time to let it recover its senses and appeal to yours, and do the same to the wine.

BRITISH ISLES AND EIRE
MIDLANDS

FARMHOUSE WHITE CHESHIRE AND RED CHESHIRE

Plain Cheshire, unveined and undyed as far as we know, is the oldest recorded English cheese, since it is mentioned by the Norman invaders in the *Domesday Book* of 1087. The French have been keen on this one English cheese ever since, having christened it after the region's main town, Chester. Indeed they have gone so far as to try to make Cheshire – sorry, Chester! – themselves, in south-western France.

What is remarkable about this aged cheese is the unswerving devotion its flavour and quality have commanded through the ages since. In the last quarter of the twelfth century, the busybody chronicler Giraldus Cambriensis, congratulated the Countess of Chester on the cheese she was making from her cows. In the sixteenth century, the historian John Speed attributed both the quality and quantity of the milk to the 'divers sweet-smelling flowers' and the quality of the pastures. From 1669, when Sir Kenelm Digby was quoted as calling it 'quick, fat, rich, well-tasted cheese', to 1888 when Isabella Beeton's book called it, overall, the most esteemed English cheese for cooking, it was generously lauded as an eating cheese as well.

One reason (besides the hardy cows and salty pasture) must have been that the traditional general method of making the cheese hardly changed from the beginning of the eighteenth century, when the first recipe was recorded, until the introduction of modern mechanised methods. Its main features seem to have been the unique 'Cheshire' method of making rennet, and a long hand-squeezing and heavy pressing of the curd to expel the whey. By 1750, the large cheeses, which might weigh as much as 50.8 kg/112 pounds, were made wholly of new milk and some, too, it has been said, were impregnated with the aroma, or even the drippings, of sherry-style white wine or sack in the curing cellars.

The Cheshire cheese-making method was used in a larger area than Cheshire itself, including parts of Staffordshire, and notably in Shropshire around Whitchurch. A large proportion of the cheeses, big or small, were coloured sunrise-red (in fact peach-coloured). This feature of Cheshire cheese-making goes way back into history. Annatto has been used to tint the cheese since the late eighteenth century, but carrot juice is said to have been used before that from medieval times onward. The colouring is used now on most of the summer-made cheeses which are drier and are matured for longer than the ones made in spring.

Traditional farmhouse Cheshire cheese-making has been somewhat modernised now, but not so much as to lose (as in the mass-production cheese) the product's real personality. Real farmhouse Cheshire, usually red, is still a full-cream cheese made from unpasteurised milk and well-drained, small-cube scalded curd, well pressed and cured. It can be ripened for twelve to eighteen months, but is usually prepared for sale at only three to six months old. It has a dry rind, is made in the shape of a drum or cylinder, and has a fat content of 48 per cent.

The texture of this cheese is crumblier and less moist than Cheddar, and its flavour is very slightly sharper, although just as rich. The cut surfaces of a drum or portion tend to dry and flake quite soon, so the cheese should be closely wrapped in foil and kept in a cool larder or refrigerator salad compartment. Luckily, even when dry, it is still a fine cooking cheese, just as it was when Mrs Beeton used it more than a hundred years ago.

DERBY AND SAGE DERBY

Cheese was being made in Derbyshire in fair quantity at least as early as 1750, because it was being carted to London for sale then, along with other Midlands cheeses. The early Derbyshire farmhouse cheeses were reputed 'full of meat and wholesome' although deemed farmers' and workers' fare rather than for connoisseurs. This was hardly surprising because they were probably meant primarily to feed the local coal and lead miners and other labourers rather than their masters among the gentry.

The Derbyshire farmers, whose maids had developed this definable Derbyshire cheese-making method by the 1850s, were commercially-minded men, probably because of their close contacts with mines and factories and the markets they provided. Before 1850, a dairymaid might well kneel on a board, carefully balanced on the curd, to squeeze out the whey. By 1880, curdbreakers were commonplace, modern cheese presses were in use, and – most important – their pioneer cheese-factory production was already ten years old.

26

Derbyshire farmers working together had been the first to get it going in Britain, in 1870.

Natural Derby cheese was still being made on quite a large scale in the mid 1960s, but it has since become a very rare treat. It is sold for eating when a month old, but it is still, then, a very young, rather acid cheese; it should really be matured for three to four months at least, to gain character and to yield its most satisfying, full-bodied flavour. A Côtes de Beaune Villages or similar red wine complements it perfectly.

Sage Derby cheeses are made now, as they have always been, from Derby cheese curd. Soft curd cheeses flavoured with herbs, like herbal coagulents, were known to both the ancient Greeks and Romans, and perhaps to the peoples of northern Europe as early as the European Bronze Age. The belief that sage cures a wide variety of ailments is also very old, going back to the teachings of the famous medical school at Salerno, and it is more than likely that it was added to cheeses in the Middle Ages as a prophylactic. Hard cheese was widely thought to cause colic in sedentary stomachs, and sage was considered a potent protection against indigestion and wind (as well as against some kinds of sepsis and putre-faction).

Originally most of the Sage Derby cheeses were made in late spring to be ready for eating during haymaking and at Harvest Home. Patrick Rance has described vividly how such cheeses were made. Two-fifths of the milk, vatted separately from the rest, was flavoured with the juice of pulped fresh sage leaves and coloured with spinach or some other vivid green vegetable juice. When both the unflavoured and flavoured curd had been milled and salted, they were moulded in five alternate layers, with plain white curd at the bottom, top, and in the centre of the cloth-lined hoops. The resulting cheese was a stubby, barrel-shaped little fellow weighing about 6.3 kg/14 pounds.

Today, layered composite and other cheeses are common enough, but in the past the broad green stripes across the paste of a cut Sage Derby must have looked dramatic. I do not remember those, but I do remember more than one honey-coloured Derby drum with a single bright green strip 2.5 cm/1 inch wide right through the centre because, by this time, the system of steeping the sage in chlorophyll had come in.

T A Layton, cheese 'master' and restaurateur, pronounced Sage Derby to be one of his favourite cheeses but laid down that it must be eaten 'fresh' – which means before the herb flavour sharpens and makes the cheese 'biting'. It is less true now than when he wrote in 1967, but it is worth remembering that, whether you believe sage has healing powers or not, Sage Derby is a quite different cheese from natural Derby with a perky flavour of its own which needs no maturing to give it character.

I am told that Sage Derby goes well with a sparkling white wine or apple juice. Bulmer's Number 7 cider would be my own choice.

LEICESTER

In 1722, Daniel Defoe called Leicestershire a county 'taken up with country business' such as wool spinning and weaving, and cattle breeding and feeding. But the only mention he makes of cheese is a reference to a 'great cheese fair' held at Atherstone on the Staffordshire border from which the major cheese factors carried 'vast quantities of cheese' to Stourbridge Fair at Cambridge to be resold to all East Anglia. At the fair itself, or on their journey to Cambridge, they must have gathered up the deep orange Leicestershire cheeses which traditionally came from Hinckley, Lutterworth and Market Bosworth, all near the border.

Those cheeses were already well known locally by 1700. Ambrose Heath says that their fame spread to London at the same time as Stilton's cheeses and Melton Mowbray's pork pies. By the 1790s, some cheese-fanciers preferred them to Stilton. Certainly local patriots did; the Town Crier of Leicester was required to call the penalties against those who sold short-weight or adulterated cheese. Farmhouse Leicester's devotees considered it even better than Lancashire (the 'Leigh Toaster') for making Welsh Rarebit.

No matter what other cheeses this Leicester might compete with, the farmers of the area were only just behind the Derbyshire men in turning over to 'factory' production in 1875. Farmhouse Leicester diminished in quantity and quality; by 1912, it was mostly being made just with the surplus milk from Stilton in summer; very little milk from natural pasture was available in winter. Partly due to this, by 1939 there was no farmhouse making at all. Then came World War II. The long-traditional, deep orange colouring was forbidden until the war ended, so a whole generation had to relearn the signature of Leicester cheese. As supermarket sales expanded, more and more of it consisted of pre-packed slabs cut from rindless block cheeses, inevitably from pasteurised milk as such cheeses have to be.

Some creamery Leicester (and one farmhouse revival) is today made in the traditional grindstone shape. This modern Leicester is a rich russet colour, flaky when cut from a fully matured wheel, aged for two to three months. Such a cheese has a satisfying flavour. It is even better, according to some experts, if matured for longer, but it is then, of course, a rarity, especially from a farm. The bandaged farmhouse cheese is a 30 cm/12 inch cylinder, 12 cm/4½ inches high, weighing 10 kg/22 pounds. The creamery grindstone is 20 cm/8 inches in diameter, 10 cm/4 inches high, and weighs 4.5 kg/10 pounds.

Either the farmhouse or a creamery, well-matured piece of custom-cut Leicester is good with lunch ale or with a light red wine, say from Hungary. Several areas make pleasant wines from the Kadarka or the Pinot Noir grape.

SHROPSHIRE BLUE

The first Scottish-born king of England bore the name of Stuart. Three hundred and seventy-seven years after James

Stuart showed himself to the English people as their new king, a 'new' cheese bred in Scotland at the Castle Stuart Dairy, Inverness, also moved south, and was presented in public for the first time by a well-known Blue Cheshire maker. It had been named Blue Stuart for a time although John Adamson and Co had always sold it as Shropshire Blue in Scotland.

The pleasant co-operation which characterises most cheese-makers was displayed to the full in the production of this cow's milk cheese. A Scots Stilton maker had originally got it going in Scotland and the Inverness dairy manager was now able to advise the new English maker and his employer when they got their new cheese under way. Using unpasteurised milk from two Cheshire herds, they produced, so they believe, a firmer easier-to-handle batch of cheeses than the Scottish ones. Heavily tinted with annatto from the start, the cut cheese cylinder could be said to resemble a fiery setting sun, streaked with wisps of cloud. More prosaically it was, and is, a lightly pressed, dramatically coloured but otherwise typically English Stilton-style 'blue'.

Paxton and Whitfield's interest in the cheese has never faltered. When the English maker, Elliot Hulme, and his craft cheese-maker Harry Hanlin, found it impossible to carry on, 'Paxton's' persuaded Long Clawson Dairy to take on the manufacture. Their cheese still came from the same dairy when this book went to press, although its popularity has led to its being made in others.

Shropshire Blue is made from full-cream, pasteurised cow's milk with some extra cream. It is made in a cylinder 20 cm/8 inches in diameter and 30 cm/12 inches high. This size weighs about 7 kg/15 pounds. Some 2 kg/5 pound cheeses and packaged portions are also available. The large cylinders take about four months to mature.

For some reason – its colour perhaps – this strikes me as a particularly good sportsmen's cheese, or one for serving at a men's club or livery company. It also takes kindly to two very different drinks – the rich fortified wines (as Stilton does) and good English brown ale.

BLUE CHESHIRE

Blue Cheshire is a good modern example of how a fine cheese may be born, develop and become established as a secure favourite. Our descendants in 100 years' time will be able to confirm its final status.

The old white and red Cheshires occasionally 'blued', being a welcome haven for what Patrick Rance calls 'many a roving mould spore'. The cheese-makers, looking for marketable whites and reds, discarded what they called the 'green fade' cheeses, except for a few found (empirically) to have healing properties, and some sold cheap in local markets. But then folks began to like these cheeses. So farmer-cheesemakers began to encourage the making of lightly-pressed cheeses containing a little day-old curd which, hopefully, might 'blue'. This was just before the turn of the century.

By 1911, the *Encyclopaedia Britannica*, mentioned 'blueing' in Cheshires as a characteristic development of eighteen-month-old cheeses; but cheeses which 'blued' successfully were comparatively rare, and got rarer as red and white Cheshire-making became more standardised. They might easily have disappeared altogether.

The dedicated pioneer who acted as nurse to this infant cheese and brought it to adolescence was Geoffrey Hutchinson. He discovered that 'blueing' took place in particularly moist, rich, flaky cheeses, and proceeded to select, ripen and encourage his Cheshire cheeses to 'blue' – especially after he started storing his cheeses in cellars at Whitchurch where natural mould flourished. But Blue Cheshires were still 'accidental' even when, after 1961, the cheeses were pricked at two to three months old to encourage mould development. (By that time, the Milk Marketing Board owned Geoffrey Hutchinson's business and the cellars.)

The second major name in the development of this fine cheese is that of Mrs Hutchinson-Smith, graduate agricultural scientist and hereditary cheese-maker. She maintains that the Milk Marketing Board's research workers, the Ministry of Agriculture's laboratory assistants at Crewe and their dairy husbandry advisers all helped to create the formula which led to her creation of a purpose-made, consistent new blue cheese. But undoubtedly her own enthusiasm and skills, patience and persistent experimentation have contributed most to the establishment of this rich good cheese.

The cheese made in Mrs Hutchinson-Smith's farm dairy is an annatto-coloured, more acid and flaky product than the usual Cheshire; it is milled by the traditional method, and is very lightly pressed in the final calico binding by vertical presses for two days. The cheeses are pressed enough to make them develop a skin, and spring cheeses are pressed slightly more than others because they are tricky to drain, but as a general rule the pressure is as light as possible. Skin formation takes two weeks under damp conditions in a special room kept at just over 16°C/60°F, and the cheeses then get three weeks in a cool cheese room. The next stage is piercing by compressed-air jets. Then, three weeks to a month or so later, you can have your cheese – eating it eight to nine weeks from the time it is made. Fast going.

It will go fast too, because it is very good to eat. If proof is needed, it lies in the fact that other, later makers of Blue Cheshire are using the Hutchinson-Smith method or one very similar. The cheeses are full-fat, with a buttery texture, and according to Mrs Hutchinson-Smith a mild, nutty flavour, although it also has body enough to stand up well to a good claret. Try a quality St Emilion, or, for a wider choice, an Australian Coonawarra Shiraz.

STILTON

Britain's most regal and best known cheese has no clearer pedigree than other long-standing British cow's milk cheeses.

SOMERSET FRUIT BOWL

Dessert

Serves 4 to 6

White Lymeswold cheese	275 g/10 ounces	$1\frac{1}{3}$ cups
double (heavy) cream	150 ml/$\frac{1}{4}$ pint	$\frac{2}{4}$ cup
caster (fine white) sugar	50 g/2 ounces	$\frac{1}{4}$ cup
sponge cake or cake crumbs	50 g/2 ounces	1 cup
ground almonds	25 g/1 ounce	$\frac{1}{4}$ cup
fresh, cooked or canned fruit of your choice	about 1 pound	about 1 pound

Pare all the rind off the cheese, leaving about 200 g/7 ounces paste. Cream it with the back of a spoon until smooth. Whip (beat) the cream until it holds soft peaks, then beat in the sugar and the cheese in small portions until completely blended in. Mix in the cake crumbs and ground almonds.

Line an 850 ml/$1\frac{1}{2}$ pint (4 cup) glass dessert bowl with the cheese paste. Chill it for 6 to 8 hours. Prepare the fruits so as to prevent discolouration, or drain them thoroughly if cooked or canned. Pile the fruit in the cheese bowl just before serving. Serve with cream or with any juices from cooking or draining the fruit. (A sprinkling of a suitable liqueur is delicious for a party.)

The cheese bowl loses its light texture if frozen.

Note: choose vivid or dark-coloured fruit. If using canned fruits, remember to allow for the weight of the juice in the can.

CURWORTHY CHICKEN

Main dish

Serves 4

young chickens, about 450 g/1 pound weight each	2	2
rashers (strips) of unsmoked bacon without rind (skin)	4	4
brandy	2 tablespoons	2 tablespoons
softened butter	2 tablespoons	2 tablespoons
sprigs of parsley	4	4
Stuffing		
Curworthy cheese with rind removed	75 g/3 ounces	scant $\frac{1}{2}$ cup
soft white breadcrumbs	50 g/2 ounces	1 cup
dried mixed herbs	$\frac{1}{2}$ teaspoon	$\frac{1}{2}$ teaspoon
ground nutmeg	small pinch	dash
salt and white pepper to taste		
beaten egg	2 tablespoons	2 tablespoons
melted butter	2 tablespoons	2 tablespoons

Make the stuffing first. Cream the cheese with the back of a spoon. Set 25 g/1 ounce aside. Combine remaining cheese with the breadcrumbs, herbs and nutmeg. Season well. Use the beaten egg and melted butter to bind the mixture, blending thoroughly. Divide the stuffing between the birds, then truss the stuffed birds securely. Cut the bacon strips in half across and lay them over the birds' breasts.

Place a trivet or rack in a large stewpan. Pour in just enough boiling water to cover the rack. Place the birds on the rack, breast side up. Cover the pan. Bring the water to a boil. Reduce the heat and simmer for 35 minutes.

Remove the birds (still on the rack) to a roasting pan. Take the bacon off the breasts and set it aside. Warm the brandy in a ladle, and light it. Pour it over the birds. When the flames die down, cover the breasts with the softened butter. Place in the oven at 180°C/350°F/Gas 4, and roast for 30 minutes or until the birds are cooked through and the breasts are browned; baste 2 or 3 times while roasting. Ten minutes before the end of the cooking time, cover the breasts with the reserved cheese, and place the bacon on the rack to crisp it. Serve half a bird to each person, garnished with parsley and a bacon strip.

Freezing The birds can be frozen for up to 3 weeks after being flamed and before roasting; freeze the reserved cheese and the bacon separately. Oven-cook them from frozen for 40 minutes or until they test done; add the thawed cheese topping and bacon, and complete the dish.

Note: this is a good way to cook elderly game birds.

Vulscombe DEVON GOAT CHEESE with fresh herbs

At the end of the eighteenth century, the reputable writers William Marshall and John Nichols competed to suggest that the cheese, originally called Lady Beaumont's or Quenby cheese, had first been made either by Elizabeth Orton, née Scarbrow, once housekeeper to the Ashby family at Quenby Hall near Leicester, or by her daughter Mrs Paulet. One of these ladies, it was said, came to supply her cheeses to Cowper Thornhill, landlord of the Bell Inn at Stilton in Huntingdonshire (now Cambridgeshire), thirty miles from Quenby.

Certainly the Stilton innkeeper spread the fame of the cheese he sold, largely by supplying travellers on the nearby Great North Road who ate at his inn. Just when he started doing so, and where he got his cheeses from are more doubtful. Mrs Orton only started making cheese, we are told, about 1730, and Mrs Paulet (still living in 1790) cannot have started earlier. Yet by 1736 three published references to Stilton indicate that it was already renowned. Daniel Defoe's *Tour Through the Whole Island of Great Britain* (1724–27) contained a famous passage about the cheese coming to table 'with the mites or maggots round it so thick that they bring a spoon for you to eat the mites as you do the cheese.' Alexander Pope wrote a couplet about it in his *Imitations of Horace* (1733–38). Most telling, perhaps, Richard Bradley, first professor of Botany at Cambridge, published a recipe for the cheese in 1726 which he repeated or adapted in his later writings, calling it an old receipt and lamenting that the cheese was now made less well than formerly.

The dates of these references suggest that the cheese (possibly enriched with cream as Bradley states) was already known widely as a Stilton speciality when Mesdames Orton and Paulet started making it. Major Rance's modern research has shown that Quenby Hall fell into neglect around 1730, so it seems plausible that Elizabeth, who is known to have seen the cheese receipt at Quenby Hall, gained the help of one daughter or two to take over making the cheeses which had hitherto been supplied to Cowper Thornhill from the Hall.

It is a pity that Bradley's recipe does not give us more detail about these original cheeses. He indicates that the curd was 'broken as small as for Cheese-Cakes' and that the new cheeses were scalded in boiling hot whey after a first two-hour pressing. The scalded cheeses were then pressed again, bound for a fortnight in linen rollers, and turned twice daily for the first month on the curing shelves. Unfortunately, however, we are not told how long they were matured for thereafter, nor whether they were sometimes or always sold while still white, or only when 'blued'.

One undoubted fact is that the cheese, having acquired fame, never lost it. Defoe's nickname, 'the English Parmesan', was still being used in the third edition of Mrs Beeton's mammoth compilation when she referred to it as being 'generally preferred to all other cheeses by those whose authority few will dispute'. In the *Epicure's Companion* of 1937, Edward Bunyard goes further. He says: 'There are, of course, we know, those who prefer other cheeses . . . but we wait with a serene confidence for the day when they shall see the error of their ways. When . . . they do so, they can join the elect by all means . . . at the end of the queue. They must not however expect a welcome . . . their final conversion we took for granted long ago'. He goes on to recommend joining a gentleman's club, preferably two or three, to be sure of always getting Stilton at its best. For eating at home, he says the cheese must be matured in bulk; so the small consumer, especially, must await his chance, usually after Christmas, to find a piece fitting for his needs, 'at the moment of perfection'. It would be interesting to hear his comments on the modern pre-packed Stilton portions on our supermarket shelves.

Modern Stilton is Britain's only protected cheese. And it deserves its status. Although it is no longer made on farms, all but one of the dairies making it are clustered around its birthplace; the pastures from which its milk comes are there, and every cheese is still made largely by hand and, although individual, is of acceptable quality.

In 1910, Stilton-makers formed themselves into an association to improve their methods of making which had hitherto been sadly hit-or-miss. They defined the character of their cheese and where it might be made, and openly admitted the more or less secret current recipe. Dairy cheese-making began in the 1870s, but by and large respected the Stilton Maker's code. However, to deal with mavericks, the Association obtained a High Court judgement in 1969 which laid down certain fixed criteria for Stilton cheese. It must be a white or blue-veined cheese made from full cream milk without applied pressure (what would Professor Bradley say?). It must be cylindrical in shape, with its own natural crust, and be made from pasteurised or unpasteurised milk produced in a certain well-defined Midlands area.

The only break with these standards that I know of is that, these days, all the young 'green' cheeses are scraped to seal the outside before maturing; much skill is needed to seal them properly without forming a thick crust which consumers resent paying for. (Cheese matured in jars for speciality sale are naturally rindless, and so are pre-packed portions.)

A Stilton, then, is a cylinder of cheese with a white or blued, semi-hard, unpressed paste under a slightly crinkled rind. A whole cheese is about 20 cm/8 inches in diameter, 30 cm/12 inches high and weighs about 7 kg/15 pounds. Smaller cheeses weigh 2 kg/5 pounds, and there are pre-packed portions varying in weight. The cheeses' fat content is 48 per cent, derived from whole cream milk enriched with some extra cream. The texture varies, depending on how tightly the cheese curd is pressed down in the hoop (the casing in which it is moulded).

White Stilton, ie the cheese before it has the chance to grow mould, is a slightly sharp, refreshing, luncheon cheese. It is sold after only three to four weeks' ripening and is unashamedly immature, but none the less well worth eating. It is good in scones or sandwiches instead of butter, with a mild chutney as a second 'filler', perhaps eaten with salad as part of a picnic or point-to-point lunch. Drink a Muscadet with it, or a light Danish lager if you prefer.

Blue Stilton is a different cheese – the one we usually just call Stilton, meaning no disrespect. Ripening times have shortened considerably from the original eighteen months, due to modern methods of temperature and humidity control. Perfectly 'blued' Stiltons can – although not with 100 per cent success – be turned out for sale after four months' maturing. A perfect blue cheese has branching, greenish-blue veins, a fairly evenly cream-coloured paste (never white!) and no signs of darkening towards the crust.

If you buy a whole drum of cheese, say for Christmas, cut off the top crust evenly and with care; do not break it. Keep it aside, while you cut off a whole, round, evenly thick slice about 5 cm/2 inches in thickness from the top of the cheese. Cut this slice into wedges for serving, and replace the top crust until you have finished them. This is the best way to keep your cheese fresh and moist. (Cover the cut side of a half drum with a circle of greaseproof paper instead of the missing top crust.)

If you are the proud possessor of an antique cheese scoop, you may prefer to follow the old-fashioned method of serving a drum or half-drum of Stilton by digging a piece out of the centre after the top crust is cut off. There is no reason why you should not do so if you wish, except that it is wasteful of a fine cheese; the outside paste near the rind becomes dry, dark and sourish before you get near eating it. What you *must not* do is trickle port or any other red wine into the centre hole if you make one. It tastes, smells and looks horrible. Drink your port or a fine Madeira *with* your cheese, rather, or at lunch-time partner it with Burgundy.

BRITISH ISLES AND EIRE
SOUTH WEST

CHEDDAR – FARMHOUSE, MATURE (AND OTHERS)

'Cheddar is a name covering a multitude of cheeses which have undergone the "Cheddaring process".' So André Simon wrote in *A Catechism Concerning Cheeses* in 1936. Today he would cast his net even wider. But this multitude of cheeses under the Cheddar logo are a different product from the traditional cheese pictured in our imaginations and in advertisements for pub lunches. One essential characteristic of a

'true' Cheddar cheese is lacking – the slowly matured, long keeping quality which eats well after a year to eighteen months or even more.

This traditional Cheddar is a wholly British cow's milk cheese, hard pressed and uncooked, made in a cylinder about 38 cm/15 inches in diameter and height. Originally the milk came from Shorthorn cattle grazing on rich Somerset and nearby pastures, but Friesians have now replaced Shorthorns, and some very good farmhouse Cheddars come from Wales. The milk is still used raw by some specialist farm cheese-makers, and the method of processing it still retains the basic features which make Cheddar cheeses quite different from, say, the Gloucester cheese group.

The cheese is made with fresh, warm morning milk mixed with the previous evening's supply. Added rennet makes a soft flocculent curd. This is allowed to set, and after being cut into cubes, it is heated and held at a temperature just above blood heat for thirty to fifty minutes. It is then allowed to settle, and to drain. When it is firm enough to be turned without breaking, it is 'cheddared' or matted; that is, it is cut into slabs, which are turned and doubled up or stacked until enough whey has been discharged to leave them condensed and firm, ready for milling, salting and pressing in cloth-lined metal 'hoops'. The final steps in the process are curing and maturing the cheese at a temperature usually between 45° and 60°F for, at the very least, sixty days; more often for about ten months. Large, fine cheeses may be matured for as much as a year to eighteen months. (*Paxton and Whitfield*'s cheeses are normally sold at something over a year old.)

To watch today's farmhouse cheese-making is a fascinating experience. The up-to-date, gleaming, stainless steel vat, long and narrow with rounded ends, is used with hand tools which have not changed in shape for more than a hundred years. From cutting the curd to hand-packing in the cloth-lined moulds, the method is virtually unchanged too; and in the store, the solid, almost black cheeses weighing about 27.5 kg/60 pounds each look as enduring as mounting blocks – and probably would be if cheese fanciers among retailers did not buy, unwrap, cut up and sell them all. There is always a demand for the full, concentrated flavour of the rare and fine, long-matured cheeses.

Such cheeses are now for connoisseurs. The labour-intensive cost of making and storage pile up their price. In creameries where Cheddar is mass-produced, a good part of the cost is avoided by automation. New techniques include cheddaring the curd in a column or tower in which up to 13,600 kg of cheese can be 'cheddared' in two hours. The curd can be vacuum pressed in the mechanism, and each block is pushed out into a bag, which is then emptied of air and heat-sealed more or less ready for curing. Long-term research in recent years is also likely to result very soon in the acceleration of Cheddar ripening by means of enzymes.

Processes like these are used to make the rindless blocks of

Cornish Yarg

Cornish Fish Pasties		**Light dish**
		Makes 8 pasties
puff pastry, thawed if frozen	450 g/1 pound	1 pound
fresh mackerel fillets	400 g/14 ounces	14 ounces
medium-sized shallots	4	4
chopped (minced) parsley	1 teaspoon	1 teaspoon
thick white sauce	3 tablespoons	3 tablespoons
Cornish Yarg cheese with rind removed	100 g/4 ounces	¼ pound
salt to taste		
grinding of black pepper		
egg, beaten	1	1

Roll out the pastry, 'rest' it and cut out eight 15 cm/6 inch rounds, using a small plate as a guide. Rinse and dry the fish fillets and chop them into small pieces. Finely chop (mince) the shallots. Combine the fish, shallots, parsley and sauce. Dice and add the cheese. Season lightly. Divide this filling between the pastry rounds, placing it on one half of each round. Brush the edges of the pastry with beaten egg. Fold over the pastry, enclosing the filling, and press the edges together to seal them. Brush the tops of the semi-circular pasties with beaten egg, then make 3 small slits in the top of each. Place on an ungreased baking sheet. Bake at 230°C/450°F/Gas 8 for 10 minutes. Reduce the heat to 180°C/350°F/Gas 4 for another 25 minutes. Cover loosely with foil if the pasties seem likely to overbrown. Eat hot or cold.

Freezing The pasties can be frozen for up to 2 weeks if reheated and served warm.

Note: make a double quantity for a party.

mild or 'mature' (strong) cheese designed for sale in packaged portions. 'Mature' blocks are sold after six to ten months in the store. Low-fat and sundry shapes and sizes of cheeses with various additions are also made, by and large, in blocks.

Some creameries, of course, make traditionally shaped Cheddars by only semi-automated methods, which require longer storage for thorough maturation; and equally some farmhouse making is thoroughly modern in style. In 1988, there were twenty-eight such farms in the Milk Marketing Board's Farmhouse Cheese-Makers' Scheme in England and Wales, offering Cheddars graded by the Board. Scottish Cheddar-makers were all members of the Company of Scottish Cheese Makers Ltd which graded their products; their 'choicest' grade is first grade cheese capable of being kept in peak condition for a year.

The National Dairy Council's Quality Selected Cheese Mark has, since July 1983, been awarded to English and Wales creamery Cheddars which meet the Council's high standards, including its demand for lasting quality; and this is double-checked by a large consumer panel at the point of sale.

Similar modernisation, sales-catching variation and market expansion, along with general quality improvement, has been taking place in the many countries outside Britain which make Cheddar. But few, if any, as far as I know, make traditional, hand-made and patiently matured farmhouse Cheddar as they make it in the south-west of England.

Eat the 'everyman's, everyday cheese' with bread and pickles, or in sandwiches with lettuce and a smear of mustard. Drink lager, beer or cider as you will. Pay a fine farmhouse Cheddar the compliment of fresh-baked bread as a 'carrier' and crisp celery, watercress and apple wedges 'on the side'; and drink with it a well-aged Côtes du Rhône or red Burgundy.

GLOUCESTER CHEESES (SINGLE AND DOUBLE)

Cheeses have been made and marketed in and around the county, once called Glowecestrescire, for upward of a thousand years. Perhaps longer! The area's surviving folk customs of cheese-rolling and parading decorated cheeses at church may well be remnants of early common law practice and first-fruits festivity, or even of earlier sun-worship.

In the Middle Ages, sheep were milked as well as cows, but the great flocks on the uplands were kept for their wool, so when large-scale cheese-making developed in the sixteenth century, it was in the wide lowland valley of the River Severn, using the milk of the ancient local breed of Gloucester cattle. The rich lowland pastures were in the Vale of Berkeley (a wide strip on the southern bank of the Severn estuary) and the Vale of Gloucester, a roughly triangular area to the north of it.

Except that the cheese-makers cooled and thinned the new milk with water in the Vale of Berkeley, much the same cheese-making method was used in both vales right up to the 1800s. The dairymen of adjoining North Wiltshire also used the Vale of Gloucester method and called their cheeses Gloucester cheeses as the Gloucester men themselves did – Single Gloucesters if made from skimmed, ripened evening milk and full-cream morning milk (that is, using only one lot of cream) and 'best making' if made just from one full-cream milking. But what about Double Gloucesters? Patrick Rance in *The Great British Cheese Book* explains that, by 1772, the rich full-cream cheeses had come to be made from evening plus morning milk, both of them unskimmed just as they came from the cow; he says that purists believe these cheeses (which contained the cream from two milkings) were originally called Double Gloucesters for this reason. Not all authorities hold this view, however, as Major Rance says. Some maintain that a single Gloucester, having had half its fat and some of its milk solids skimmed off, was a thinner cheese in size as well as in richness; the fatter Double Gloucester was therefore named for its avoirdupois in every sense.

Right up to the 1880s, this Double Gloucester weighed 10 to 11 kg/22 to 24 pounds, and was 10 to 13 cm/4 to 5 inches thick. Single Gloucester weighed 6.3 to 7 kg/14 to 15 pounds but was only about 6.5 cm/2$\frac{1}{2}$ inches thick. Both cheeses were 39 to 40 cm/15$\frac{1}{2}$ to 16 inches in diameter (presumably made in the same moulds). Double Gloucester was therefore a thicker wheel; and the curd was probably cut more finely than for Single Gloucester to give it a closer texture.

The depth of flavour of the cheese also distinguished it. Single Gloucester was only matured for two months so was quite mild, whereas Double Gloucester needed three months maturing and could happily wait much longer without becoming bitter. This did not mean, however, that Single Gloucester was a feeble cheese. The luxuriant pastures and splendid cattle made the best Single Gloucesters as good as whole milk cheeses from other areas, according to the expert William Marshall in 1706.

Less important although more noticeable, the spry local dairymen coloured the cheese paste of their Double Gloucesters with annatto, to deepen their golden tint, and later painted their cheeses as a kind of trademark as well (although this rebounded because other makers copied them).

Both Single and Double Gloucesters had become so highly reputed by the 1770s that many were sold to factors who visited the farms or who bought blind, and demand outran supply of the gaily painted wheels of cheese at the region's large, bustling twice-yearly fairs. Then, quite suddenly, a decline in popularity set in, and production dropped from near 8000 tons in a season in 1779 to less than 2000 tons in 1849, most of it made in the Vale of Berkeley.

The Vale of Berkeley dairymen referred to their cheeses as Single and Double Berkeley until they disappeared, seemingly forever, in the 1930s; and in 1939 when World War II stopped farmhouse production, only a few farms, it seems, were making any Gloucester cheese at all. Factory production, which had started in 1875, had more or less taken over.

It had become inevitable, really, when the Gloucester cheese-making method came to be used to make variously-named cheeses in several other areas. When, in Gloucestershire itself, the fine milch cows of the old breed had become virtually extinct, there seemed to be nothing special about Gloucester cheeses any more. Certainly not when wartime rationing reduced all the cheeses to depersonified blocks!

Post-war developments have proved, however, that the cheeses were too good to be totally lost. Since the war, slowly, the old Gloucester breed of cattle is increasing in numbers again, and a few devoted cheese-makers have started making, first Double, and then a small amount of Single, Gloucester on a farmhouse pattern.

The modern cheeses are made by renneting the curd before the fresh morning milk has cooled. Temperatures are carefully controlled; and instead of the hard, polished or painted rind the cheeses are washed in brine and dipped in lard to prevent any air penetration. Some makers, such as *Paxton and Whitfield*'s supplier, now produce both Single and Double Gloucester in whole cloth-bound cylinders – much thicker than the old-style wheels – which are matured for six to ten weeks. The Double Gloucester made from whole milk has a 48 per cent fat content. The Single Gloucester, as tradition dictates, has had a quarter of the cream skimmed off, and is made without any annatto staining; its texture is crumbly and its colour is a pale peachy gold.

An experimental modern cheese called Double Berkeley, with an annatto-marbled paste, had just come onto the English market when this book went to press.

A spicy red Yugoslav or Bulgarian wine may accompany Gloucester well.

LYMESWOLD
BLUE AND WHITE

The English Milk Marketing Board's blue Lymeswold cheese was a provocative marketing experience when it was introduced in 1982. It was Britain's first modern, Milk Marketing Board cheese, the result of wide theoretical and scientific research backed by considerable funds; and it was also her first rich, spreadable cheese with blue, induced-mould streaks.

Several continental Brie-style blue cheeses, mostly double cream cheeses, were being sold on the English market when it was decided to enter the field. The makers of Blue Lymeswold therefore profited by the experience of tasting others and finding out what the British public thought of them. As a result, they gave Lymeswold the mildest possible Brie-style flavour with only a hint of a 'blue' taste; and they gave it a lower fat content than almost any other 'blue Brie' – only the oldest, the French Brie de Melun Bleu has less fat, just 45 per cent compared with Lymeswold's 48 per cent.

Blue Lymeswold is entirely creamery-made. It is available in 1.2 kg/2 pound 10 ounce wheels on delicatessen counters or in half-wheels; but most of the cheese the ordinary consumer sees reaches him in 150 g/5 ounce wedge-shaped, pre-packed portions from the chiller cabinet. In its youth, it is a pale, cream-coloured cheese encased in a white velvety rind; its light, buttery flavour is enlivened by only a slight cheesy tang. As it ages the paste softens as in any surface-ripened cheese, and the flavour becomes much more marked.

When you buy a wedge, the cut surfaces should be bright and moist, but not runny. At home, the cheese should be allowed to continue to ripen naturally; follow the advice given in the ripening guide printed on each packet, remembering that the cheese must be brought to room temperature, if refrigerated, at least an hour before it is eaten. Check, too, the 'Best Before . . .' date on the package. From three to two weeks before this date, the cheese will still be mild, delicately flavoured and firm to cut. 'For a riper, richer flavour with a creamy texture, it should be near the "Best Before . . ." date'. (*Prodfact* British Food Information Service, 1988).

Getting Lymeswold established was not all plain sailing. But the faith of its sponsor, the Milk Marketing Board of England and Wales, was justified by sales, and in 1986 White Lymeswold also came on the cheese scene. It is made from full milk enriched with fresh dairy cream, and a special starter is used to give the cheese an especially smooth creamy texture. It has a gently supple, white floury coat which is edible unless the cheese becomes overripe. But normally a 150 g/5.3 ounce portion does not last long enough for that to happen.

Serve Lymeswold (blue or white) with cream crackers or digestive biscuits, and with fruits such as fresh peaches, black grapes or raspberries. Ginger in syrup is also good with it, provided you do not want to drink wine. If you do, choose a full-bodied but dry white wine, or a rosé with character. A fruity Hungarian Riesling or Tavel Rosé would drink as well as anything.

CURWORTHY

Modern Curworthy was a post-war arrival on the English cheese scene, but it seems likely to stay on cheesemongers' lists and in consumers' minds for a long time. Partly, perhaps, because of its looks! It cuts cleanly, its creamy paste contrasting pleasantly with the black wax rind which seems to be more commonly displayed than the plain-rinded version. It attracts attention, encouraging one to try it.

The shape of the cheese, and the appearance of its paste, encourage one further. Curworthy is made in various sizes and weights of tubby truckles, but even the biggest cheeses are not really tall, so a modest 125 g/¼ pound slice is a reasonable size, not paper-thin. The paste is even-coloured all over, near-glossy when young, dryer and flakier when mature.

Another point of interest is that the cheese is based on a seventeenth-century local Devon recipe. This argues that it

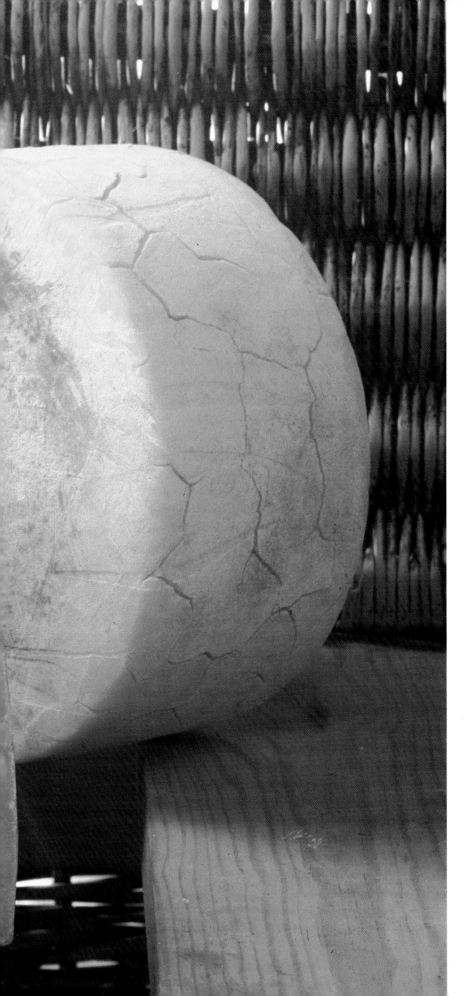

CAERPHILLY SALAD

Serves 4 to 6

iceberg lettuce	1	1
cucumber	7.5 cm/3 inch piece	3 inch piece
medium-sized tomatoes	4	4
spring onions	6 to 8	6 to 8
Caerphilly cheese with rind removed	175 g/6 ounces	1 cup
green bell pepper	$\frac{1}{2}$	$\frac{1}{2}$
red bell pepper	$\frac{1}{2}$	$\frac{1}{2}$
Dressing		
natural (unflavoured) yoghurt	150 g/5 ounces	$\frac{2}{3}$ cup
single (light) cream	2 tablespoons	2 tablespoons
lemon juice	1 tablespoon	1 tablespoon
salt	$\frac{1}{4}$ teaspoon	$\frac{1}{4}$ teaspoon
black pepper	$\frac{1}{4}$ teaspoon	$\frac{1}{4}$ teaspoon
cayenne pepper	pinch	dash
paprika pepper	pinch	dash
mayonnaise	1 tablespoon	1 tablespoon

To make the salad, rinse and dry lettuce (if very large, use only $\frac{1}{2}$ head). Shred the lettuce. Slice the cucumber into thin rounds. Quarter the tomatoes. Prepare and slice or chop the onions, both bulbs and leaves. Dice the cheese. De-seed and chop the peppers. Combine all the ingredients in a salad bowl.

To make the dressing, pour the yoghurt into a bowl. Beat in the cream, lemon juice, seasonings and mayonnaise. Taste and add extra seasoning if you wish. Pour into a chilled sauce boat. Serve with the salad.

Note: 6 to 8 drained, canned peach slices cut into small pieces make a good addition to the salad.

was probably once made of sheep's milk because the farm where it is made is just north of the highest point on Dartmoor.

Curworthy is now, however, made wholly from full-fat unpasteurised cow's milk, pressed and matured for four to six weeks for a mild 450 g/1 pound cheese, 10 to 12 weeks for a 2.3 kg/5 pound one, both cured in natural underground cellars. The result is a mild but not bland cheese with a creamy, buttery taste.

A deeper full flavour is supplied by the 4.5 kg/10 pound cheeses matured for five to six months. When fully mature they may be sold as Devon Oke.

Another version of the cheese is called Belstone, which is made without animal rennet but using pasteurised milk; it is matured for fifteen weeks. Belstone and Curworthy are both made in the 2.3 kg/5 pound rounds, but only Curworthy is made in the smaller and larger sizes as well.

Eat this good-tempered cheese for a picnic-style lunch with split toasted rolls, apples and rough cider; or for a more sophisticated choice, mix cubes of cheese and lemon-dipped apple as a salad to go with cold pheasant or other game meat. Try a red Graves wine or a modest one from the Bourg district.

CORNISH YARG

The Duchy of Cornwall is, by its landscape and, still more, its folk history, closely bound to its own traditions. Many of these, like its people, are of Celtic origin, and are shared in some degree by Welsh folk. It was understandable, then, that Welsh-bred Alan and Jennie Gray, who settled in Cornwall and studied traditional Cornish recipes in literature, experimented and finally teamed up with Duchy farming tenants Michael and Margaret Horrell to produce and market a range of Cornish cheeses.

Stated like that it sounds easy, but it took, in all, three years of negotiations with official bodies and of capital investment in a purpose-built cheese-room and equipment to get to production point in 1983; for instance, the Grays' almost century-old vat and presses were solid and beautiful but not suitable for the scale of cheese-making planned. The two present herds of pedigree Holstein and Friesian cows had luckily already been built up.

The result is that Cornish Yarg, and its sister soft cheeses Cornish Pepper and Cornish Herb and Garlic, combine the best features of old traditional cheese-making with those of modern hygienic production and distribution – which effectively means that Yarg is one of our most popular cheeses of recent years, because it is consistently good and reasonably widely available.

A prototype of Yarg was made in the early fifteenth century, when wealthy Englishmen and their ladies ate rich Brie-style cheeses, often flavoured with herbs and drained on nettles.

Yarg itself is a wheel of lightly pressed, full cream cow's milk cheese, about 25 cm/10 inches in diameter and 7.5 cm/3 inches high, weighing about 3.2 kg/7 pounds. A 900 g/2 pound 'truckle' is also made. The making begins when the milk is put into the vats after being pasteurised and raised to blood heat. Starter is added at once, and about an hour later vegetable rennet substitute; after another hour or so, firm curds have formed, the mass is cut by hand, and the whey is drained off for the cows to drink. The semi-drained curd is then stirred gently, re-cut and turned by hand as required until it is drained dry enough for milling and filling into moulds, usually in the early afternoon. The cheeses are pressed until the following morning when they are unmoulded and immersed in brine for six hours. Lastly they are transferred to the maturing room. Frozen nettle leaves (collected from the local terrain by youngsters as in the far distant past) are applied to the surface, and the cheeses are racked on shelves in a controlled temperate, humid atmosphere, and left to ripen – or almost so, because the three week ripening process demands daily turning by hand while the mould (*Penicillium candidum*) is developing; this takes three to four days to give the cheeses their white downy rind and special consistency.

With its 30 per cent fat content and 40 per cent moisture, Yarg lies between a semi-hard and semi-soft cheese. Its mould-ripening produces a creamy layer on the surface with a moist, crumbly interior close to the texture of Caerphilly. It may be ripened to taste, but there is a tendency for most people to prefer it younger than its makers would like; it has a clear fresh taste before its mature flavour develops.

The nettles, by the way, are edible, even if your dinner-party guests pick them out daintily.

Yarg is, without doubt, one of the leaders of the new generation of British farmhouse cheeses, notably one which has managed to meet the needs of large-scale retailing without sacrificing quality. It has won prizes, for instance, at the Nantwich International Cheese Show, and it features regularly in government-sponsored food displays, on television and in radio programmes. It has even been the subject of a national newspaper cartoon in mid-1988. Fame indeed!

BRITISH ISLES AND EIRE
WALES

CAERPHILLY

Caerphilly is the most junior of the British regional cheeses, having only been born in the early 1800's. An unusual feature of its infancy was where it was made – in dozens of small farmhouses clustered about the Welsh market town of Caerphilly just north of Cardiff. In other words, it was a cottage industry product, sold by the farmer's wives to factors who supplied the South Wales mining communities.

It also became very rapidly a Welsh-language cheese with its own folklore. It could only be made, it was said, from the milk of Hereford cattle, and only those fed on pastures west of the Usk, the 'river full of fish'. It was called Caws Cymru until the name of Caerphilly took over, probably because the market was held there. Even our modern Caerphilly has old Welsh predecessors too. It is floated in brine in the course of its making, in essentially the same way as the medieval Welsh laws of Hywel Dda record. Cheese-making also remained part of every Welsh farm girl's training much longer than it did for English girls, which may explain the cottage making, and the emergence of Caerphilly from the 'poor thin' farmhouse cheeses which Welsh cookery expert Bobby Freeman describes in her book *First Catch your Peacock*.

The Caerphilly we know is a semi-hard cow's milk cheese made from pasteurised scalded milk. The drained curds are cut, salted, moulded into muslin-covered wheels, then pressed for about thirty minutes before their brine bath. During the following four days, according to John Arlott, they are turned daily, and dusted with rice flour and whitening to make them ready for sale after only two weeks' curing. This is where modern Caerphilly parts company with its past, at least to some extent. It is whiter, softer and sharper in flavour than the fully developed nineteenth century cheeses sold at about six months old.

Some of the cheeses were always sold young, and the modern short curing time may go back to this. It may have come about because, quite early in its life, demand for the cheese outran supply. For a while, the need was met by Somerset farmers who crossed the Bristol Channel to make Caerphilly in Wales; the method of making was akin to that of Cheddar-making which they knew. However, the Welsh dairies could not supply enough milk to meet the Welsh miners' demand for cheese (which they ate cut into wedges like cakes) and so the making of Caerphilly was taken back to Somerset where it profited the farmers well. Caerphilly was much more economical to make than Cheddar, and its sales turnover was faster.

The briefly matured cheese was not a long keeper, and so, in spite of protests from the miners, production was forbidden from 1942 to 1954. However, when it was resumed, the cheese was, by and large, as popular as ever, and it is still so now. It is also still made in Somerset and in other English counties – but not in Wales!

Caerphilly is now made in blocks as well as in 4 kg/8 to 9 pound rounds. (The blocks can vary very considerably.) Pre-packed portions are also available in supermarkets, although they have a tougher consistency than cheese cut to order from the round. This cheese has almost no scent. It is close-textured, virtually without holes in the paste, and slightly acid on the palate. This is one reason why Welsh miners are still said to prefer it to all other cheeses; its other merits are its moisture content (it does not dry out) and its distinctly salty flavour. (Lancashire has the same merits for Lancashire miners.)

Not being a miner, I myself prefer Caerphilly with green salad vegetables rather than as a block on its own in a packed meal. Cheddar is frankly better for the classic Welsh cheese dish called Caws Pobie or Welsh Rarebit, but Caerphilly comes into its own with fresh fruit in summer, a mélange of dried fruits in winter. Whenever you buy it, though, eat it quickly; it will not keep for more than two weeks even if foil-wrapped and refrigerated. Drink with it a Portuguese Vinho Verde, or a young light claret with a respectable background.

PENCARREG

There have emerged during the 1980s a number of well-made cow's and goat's milk cheeses from the pastures of Welsh hillsides, some from farms, and some from small dairies which combine the milk of organically fed animals with vegetarian rennet and low sodium or sea salt. There are signs that these are consolidating their organisation, for instance by sharing distribution facilities, and it augurs well for the future. One can already note certain 'stayers' among the cheeses of individual producers.

One cheese easy to assess because it is made by at least two producers is Pencarreg. This is a full-fat, soft, unpressed white-mould cheese, made from Channel Island and Ayrshire pasteurised whole cow's milk, curdled without animal rennet. As may be imagined, it is always rich, having a fat content of about 58 per cent. Its beautifully pristine, snowy rind promises luxury, and the paste confirms it. Being surface-ripened, it is sometimes (like many such cheeses) dispatched from home slightly underripe, and if not yet fully ripened when it is eaten, its consistency may be moist and slightly chalky; but as its ripeness develops, so does its character. Its clean, mild flavour deepens and it develops a bouquet fit for gourmets as well as a creamy, supple consistency.

Pencarreg is available year-round in 1.6 to 1.8 kg/3½ to 4 pound rounds or pre-packed 150 g/5 ounce portions. It won first prize in its class at the Royal Welsh Show in 1987. There is also a savoury version with garlic, but do not let the choice divert you from trying the unflavoured version first.

Do not store this cheese if you can help it. If it must be kept when already ripe, fold it in foil and refrigerate it, but watch it carefully. Eat it as soon as you can, on bread or wholegrain crackers, and drink with it a Beaujolais or Portuguese Dao.

LANARK SLAW — **Vegetables**

Serves 6 to 8

hard white cabbage, about 1.8 kg/4 pounds whole	$\frac{1}{2}$	$\frac{1}{2}$
parsley sprigs (leaves only)	4	4
crisp apples	225 g/8 ounces	$\frac{1}{2}$ pound
small carrots	100 g/4 ounces	$\frac{1}{4}$ pound
fresh thyme leaves or dried thyme	$\frac{1}{2}$ teaspoon	$\frac{1}{2}$ teaspoon
salt and black pepper to taste		
pinch of curry powder		
Lanark Blue cheese with rind removed	225 g/8 ounces	$\frac{1}{2}$ pound
commercial sour cream	65 ml/$\frac{1}{8}$ pint	$\frac{1}{3}$ cup
mayonnaise	65 ml/$\frac{1}{8}$ pint	$\frac{1}{3}$ cup

Shred the cabbage very finely. Soak it in cold water for 2 hours or longer, changing the water 3 or 4 times. Drain, and dry it well in a salad shaker or basket.

Finely chop (mince) the parsley leaves. Peel and core the apples, and top and tail the carrots. Grate, not too finely, the apples and carrots. Combine the parsley, apples and carrots with the cabbage. Add thyme leaves, seasoning and curry powder. Mix well.

Cut the cheese into 1 cm/$\frac{1}{2}$ inch cubes and fold them into the salad. Combine the sour cream and mayonnaise in a jug, and pour it over. Toss to mix shortly before serving.

CASHEL CREAM SOUP

Serves 4

large square slices of toast with crusts removed	2	2
garlic clove	$\frac{1}{2}$	$\frac{1}{2}$
Cashel Blue cheese scraped free of rind	175 g/6 ounces	$\frac{3}{4}$ cup
warm milk	575 ml/1 pint	$2\frac{1}{2}$ cups
large egg yolks	2	2
double (heavy) cream	150 ml/$\frac{1}{4}$ pint	$\frac{2}{3}$ cup
chopped (minced) parsley	1 tablespoon	1 tablespoon

Rub the toast with the cut side of the garlic clove. Cut each slice into 4 small squares. Put 2 squares in each of 4 warmed soup bowls. Keep warm.

Chop the cheese roughly. Put it into an electric blender with the milk. Process until smooth. Transfer to a saucepan, and stir over medium heat until steaming. Draw the pan to the side of the stove. In a small bowl, beat the egg yolks into the cream, then add about 225 ml/8 fl oz (1 cup) of the cheese soup. Return the whole mixture to the pan, and stir over very low heat without boiling until well heated through. Pour the soup into the bowls, and sprinkle the surface with parsley.

Freezing The soup should not be frozen after the egg and cream liaison is added. Rather than waste freezer space, freeze the cheese alone, and thaw it when you want to make the soup.

BRITISH ISLES AND EIRE
SCOTLAND

LANARK BLUE

This modest cylinder is the first British 'blue' sheep's cheese for centuries. Commonsense says it cannot be the 'first ever'; medieval French monks at the great Yorkshire abbeys cannot have been ignorant of Roquefort and how to make it; and that kind of knowledge crossed boundaries easily in the Middle Ages, carried by pilgrims, friars, peddlers, and itinerant sheep-shearers, even while the Celtic north fought the Saxon South.

Lanark Blue has been overtly based on Roquefort by sheep-farmer Humphrey Errington and expert consultant Janet Galloway of the West of Scotland Agricultural College in Ayr, both of them steeped in Roquefort lore; plus, with good fortune, the skills of an experienced cheese-maker, Ian McLheary, who joined the enterprise early on. The result is a semi-hard, uncooked, unpressed cheese made from whole unpasteurised sheep's milk. A whole cheese is 28 cm/7 inches in diameter, and about 10 cm/4 inches high, and the weight of the half moons usually marketed is 1.5 kg/3¼ pounds.

The cheese's flavour derives first from the herbs and clover of the southern upland pasture, near the watershed of the Clyde and Tweed rivers, where the two Errington sheep flocks graze; there are 250 ewes in each, one lambing in spring, the other (uniquely) in autumn for winter milk. Much of the credit for developing both the flavour and texture of the cheeses made from their milk must certainly go to the first shepherdess and cheese-maker, Mary Lang, who was trained by Janet Galloway. As a result, she created in Lanarkshire a cheese most certainly smoother than Roquefort and perhaps a whit less salty, but otherwise with a distinctly similar mould flavour.

It should have. *Penicillium roqueforti* is sprinkled into the morning and evening mixed milk in liquid form at the beginning of the making process. So too, is the starter culture powder. The curd is set, broken, drained, then ladled into hoops, and settled by further draining and turning. It is dipped in brine twice, being transferred to a fresh hoop each time and is then dry-salted. Three months maturation at a controlled temperature and humidity follow, with daily turning, and a final scraping before the cheeses are packed for sale.

There is, of course, a lot more behind the making of about thirty cheeses a day than this. Humphrey Errington has

invested £100,000 in modern buildings, comprising a milking parlour, cheese room, salting, ripening and washing rooms, a laboratory, chill room, packaging and dispatch areas. Equipment has been installed too, from vats to storage racks.

There has also been a large and wise investment in cultural and historical knowledge, drawing on, and revitalising at the same time, the role of Scotland's sheep products in song and story, and their place in her economy from the end of the seventeenth century. There is still much to find out, and many fragments need expanding. One would like to know more about the cheeses paid as rents to the Duchess of Hamilton in the 1690s, and the sheep's cheeses Doctor Johnson wrote about in the Hebrides in 1773. But Mr Errington has reminded us of Sir Walter Scott's presentation of the Scottish farming scene and Meg Dod's description of making – and eating – Scottish cheese 'as good as Stilton'.

His modern cheese developed between 1981 and 1985 has therefore got excellent antecedents – and it lives up to them. Jane Grigson, for instance, has praised it as destined, in her view, to become a classic, especially for its long-term eating quality. That being so, it clearly deserves a long-kept, preferably classic wine, if possible from Bordeaux – a Pauillac or St-Estephe if you can afford one, or a Pomerol.

CABOC

Caboc has a splendid, if largely unwritten, past. It is said to have originated in the Western Highlands of Scotland in the fifteenth century, when it was the Chieftain's cheese – plausible enough since rich, soft cheeses were reserved to nobility in those days, and called 'white meats'. The Chieftain in question was the Macdonald of the Isles, and his daughter Mariota de Ile passed the recipe on, in due course, to her own daughter. This recipe (still kept secret) has been handed down from mother to daughter ever since, the present maker being the well-known Mrs Suzanne Stone of Tain who works with a team of eight other local women. Their cheeses – Caboc is not the only one – are sold under the seal of Highland Fine Cheeses Ltd.

As 'white meats' go, Caboc is certainly rich, probably the richest of all British cheeses and the only double-cream one. It is lightly fermented, to give it a slightly buttery (and even richer), delicately cured flavour before it is moulded into a narrow tube shape about 3 cm/1¼ inches in diameter and 4½ inches long. The completed cheeses are rolled in toasted, pinhead oatmeal and packaged in gift-style tartan card boxes.

Besides these small, luxurious morsels, weighing about 100 g/3½ ounces, Caboc is sold for cutting in 908 g/2 pound blocks.

Large and small, Caboc was unknown outside Scotland until *Paxton and Whitfield*'s proprietor was introduced to it in 1960, and realised its sale potential south of the border. His assessment was right, for the cheese is now widely popular. In spite of this (which means that the turnover is rapid and cheeses do not stay in a shop long), it is very important – even more than when buying other soft cheeses – to check the 'sell by' date on the carton before buying one of the small cheeses for home use.

Caboc bought at its peak will keep well for a fortnight in its original carton; it may then last another week with luck, if cut with a clean knife. However, it will pick up any extraneous flavour, thus losing, to some extent, its own delicate taste.

It is, none-the-less, a superb combination cheese. Mixed or sprinkled with a little liqueur (Drambuie or liqueur malt whisky) it is a dessert in itself. It can be piped as a filling for fresh stone fruits or as a base for fresh raspberries. If the coating is left on, the slightly rough oatmeal gives an interesting and worthwhile new texture. Serve chilled rosé wine with it. For after-dinner or perhaps summer lunch-time use, serve it with watercress or chicory and dry brown toast. In this case a fresh red wine, such as Beaujolais, may be best.

ORKNEY, PLAIN AND SMOKED

The Isles of Orkney, off the north east coast of Scotland, have rich sea-girt pastures, once the home of barely tamed cattle, goats and sheep and the crofters who bred them for wool, meat, milk and probably cheese. The stony terrain, its isolation and lack of resources confined the inhabitants – whether old Picts, Scots invaders, or ninth-century Norse pirates by origin – to agriculture or fishing as a settled livelihood until modern times. In the 1930s, peasant crofters' homes had hardly changed since the Middle Ages, to judge by local museum photographs. In the 1960s, agriculture was still the only listed occupation, and 87.4 per cent of the people were island-born and probably mostly farm-bred.

The people's earning pattern may not have changed, but their farming, especially their dairying, practice has changed very much indeed. For a start, the Shorthorn cattle which, by the nineteenth century, had become the main dairying breed, have given way to Friesians. Much more important for cheese-lovers, however, have been three major cheese-making developments which have changed all hard Scottish cheeses and their making radically – Orkney which has the oldest name of them all, among the rest.

Before the 1680s when Barbara Gilmour created Dunlop, the first hard full fat cheese, most if not all Scottish cheeses seem to have been soft like Crowdie (page 124), many of them being made from skimmed milk. In the islands, skim-milk cheeses were certainly a commonplace product of the smaller crofts both before and after the method of making hard cheeses had been learned. The actual making method, especially of hard cheeses, was however pretty hit-or-miss until the major Dunlop makers, concerned about slipping standards, called in the noted Somerset Cheddar-maker, Joseph Harding to standardise the making of their cheese. His ideas spread, and so did those of Canadian Cheddar experts employed in the 1870s to make more improvements.

By the 1930s, their techniques were being used on the majority of Scottish farms, even those not making Cheddar itself.

With the war, inevitably, production on farms ceased. Today, the predominant cheese made in Scotland (all of it in creameries) is Scottish Cheddar. But there is a little Dunlop being made again at the Torrylin Creamery on the Isle of Arran by the Scottish Milk Marketing Board; and rather more hard, full-fat Orkney, plain and smoked is made at the Claymore Creamery, Kirkwall, Mainland, in the Orkneys, by the North of Scotland Milk Marketing Board.

This modern Orkney cheese, as its label suggests, is a full-fat hard cow's milk cheese made in 450 g/1 pound discs 12.8 cm/5 inches in diameter and 3.5 cm/1½ inches thick. There is a white and red version. At first glance, the annatto-tinted variety looks suspiciously like a small-sized round Scottish Cheddar but a closer look demonstrates that, like its white brother, it is different in texture and cutting quality. A taste confirms its individuality. Either version is obviously one of the Cheddar group of cheeses, and the West of Scotland Agricultural College responsible for grading describes both as 'modifications of a Dunlop-type cheese', but they have the distinctive flavour of their sea-girdled grassland, and are smoother in texture and cleaner to cut than Cheddar.

The smoked cheese, of course, tastes of smoke, or rather of the resins which give the smoked cheeses a particular, identifiable tang, whether hickory or applewood provides the smouldering fire.

All the cheeses, white, red and smoked, are vacuum-packed in polythene, and will keep for half a year in a refrigerator if still fully packaged. They even freeze reasonably well. Closely wrapped in foil, any of them should keep for two to three weeks after cutting. Remember to bring any cheese to room temperature an hour – preferably more – before serving.

Plain white or red Orkney goes best with a red wine of medium strength and maturity, and with oatmeal bread or clapbread. Smoked Orkney should be eaten on brown toast, and it can take a more robust red wine.

BRITISH ISLES AND EIRE
EIRE

CASHEL BLUE

Ireland's only raw milk, farm-made blue cheese, Cashel Blue gets much of its quality from the milk of the farm's dairy herd of Friesian cattle. The fact that it is carefully hand-made also

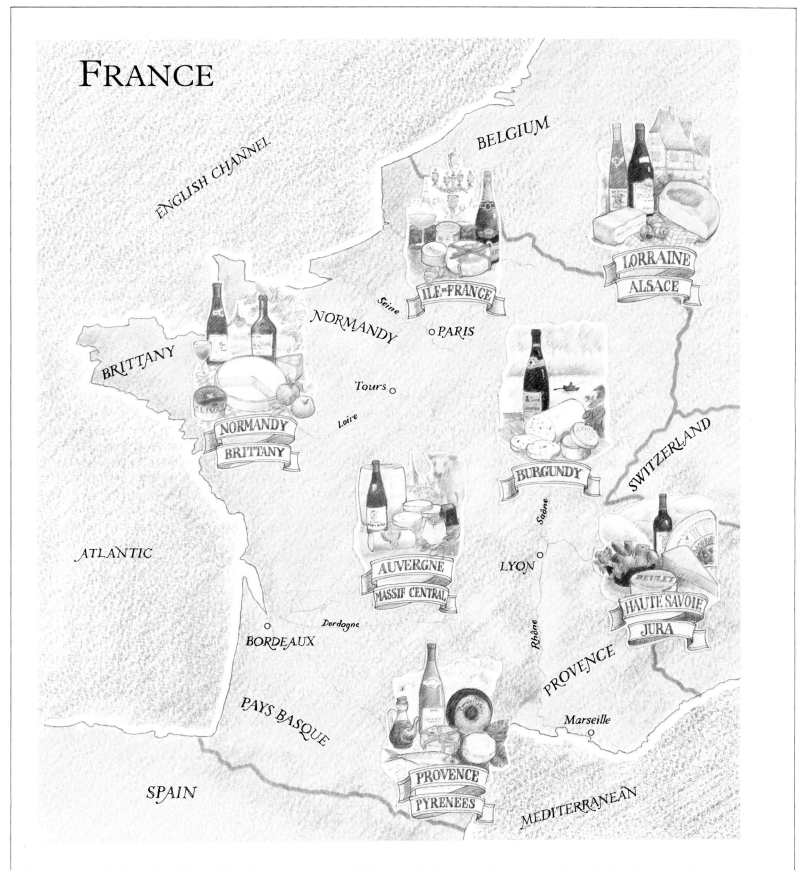

FRANCE

ENGLISH CHANNEL

BELGIUM

Seine

ILE DE FRANCE

LORRAINE

ALSACE

NORMANDY

○ PARIS

BRITTANY

Tours ○

Loire

NORMANDY

BRITTANY

BURGUNDY

Saône

SWITZERLAND

ATLANTIC

AUVERGNE

MASSIF CENTRAL

LYON ○

HAUTE SAVOIE

JURA

Dordogne

BORDEAUX ○

Rhône

PROVENCE

PAYS BASQUE

PROVENCE

PYRENEES

Marseille ○

SPAIN

MEDITERRANEAN

contributes. It is a whole milk cheese usually made from unpasteurised evening and morning milk with excess butter-fat removed and with a deliberately low salt content. The moisture content of the completed, semi-soft, richly moist cheese is 50 per cent.

The cheese is named after the local historic town of Cashel with its ancient ruin (The Rock of Cashel) featured on the cheese wrapper. Louis Grubb, its first maker with his wife Jane, developed the cheese from his knowledge of local technology, adapting the continental system of making blue cheeses to their own homeland's climate and pasture. The cheese's softness and its pink surface flor are accidents for which he makes no apology.

The newly-made cheeses are matured on the farm until the blue mould (from *Penicillium roqueforti*) is well developed. They are then washed in brine, dried and wrapped in gold-coloured aluminium foil, and transferred to a cold store where they mature further at 4°C/39.2°F. They are dispatched from the farm between three and six weeks old, when they can be eaten by the young and hungry; but they are softer, creamier and more appealing if matured for between two and four months at the same cold temperature. They must, of course, like all good cheeses, be brought to room temperature before being sold or served.

The cheeses are packed two 'to a case. Their normal diameter is 15 cm/6 inches, and their height is 10 cm/4 inches, making them like small round grindstones. The normal weight of each whole cheese is around 1.5 kg or 3 pounds. However, for the faint-hearted blue cheese eater, half round sections of the cheese are also sold, weighing about 350 g/¾ pound.

Eat Cashel Blue with Irish potato scones or soda bread. Add a few saladings to nibble 'on the side', and for drink choose a good French village red wine fairly light in flavour, or – admirable – Irish whiskey.

MILLEENS

This award-winning soft cheese is made from unpasteurized whole cow's milk on a mountain-side farm in southern Ireland. Nearby sea breezes may have contributed to the makers' idea of producing a washed-rind cheese although they do not claim it. It is made in two sizes, a round 23 cm/9 inches in diameter and a smaller cheese 10 cm/4 inches across. The larger cheese weighs about 1.5 kg/3 pounds and the smaller one 225 g/8 ounces. Their fat content is about 45 per cent.

The cheese, although barely ten years old, was the first Irish cheese of modern times, and can justly be said to have founded an infant but thriving industry. It did so almost by accident. Its makers, frustrated by the closure of their local old-style, grocery-cheese store, started making cheese to use up the milk of a single one-horned cow which they acquired with a farm. Hardly a professional or even a deliberate beginning! However, an initial success and thereafter a great deal of theoretical

and scientific study and application, led quite rapidly to the development of the consistently excellent prize-winning cheese of today.

Its awards include the Championship medal for the best farmhouse cheese at the Royal Dublin Show in 1986, the Housewife's Choice trophy at the Nantwich International Cheese Show in 1987 and first prize at the London International Cheese Show in 1988, beating Germany and France which came second and third.

The making of Milleens is now a strictly scientific process. Throughout, the temperature and acidity of the curd, and later the cheese, is carefully monitored. So is milk quality. Starters are carefully chosen for their influence on flavour and quality as well as for their power to repel undesirable alien bacteria.

The cheese is ripened on the farm for up to twenty-one days, and is dispatched in carefully designed wooden boxes, made and stencilled on the farm. Advice to retailers on how to complete the ripening of the cheese is supplied with it. Ideally it should be washed in a saline solution and turned daily until it suits the customers' requirements.

Advice to the consumer follows a standard pattern. The cheese has only a short shelf life. If it must wait, it should be refrigerated, but be allowed to recover at room temperature for at least an hour before use. It is excellent with salads or hot vegetables, and better still as a table cheese, with russet apples and partnered by a Beaune. If you prefer a white wine, try an English wine such as Frogmore or Michaelmas House marketed by Heywood Wines in London.

FRANCE
NORMANDY/BRITTANY/HAINAUT

CAMEMBERT FERMIER

'Camem-bert. Isn't that a kind of bree?'

Ludicrous as this may sound to older gourmets, French Camembert cannot honestly be said to be beyond doubt the world's best-known soft cheese any more. Pre-packaged portions of Brie are just as common, at least on British supermarket shelves, and a wheel of snowy whole Brie makes better drama on any 'deli' counter. I would not care to count up, either, the references to 'Philly' in cooks' manuals or its sales across the world.

This is not to denigrate Camembert, certainly not a beautiful farm-made Camembert (Camembert fermier). It is still a superb cheese, to be cherished the more because it is not quite so often found on a European cheeseboard as formerly, and because it has been copied with more or less success on farms and in factories in almost all countries with a dairying industry. The name Camembert, like that of Cheddar, has circled the globe. But the cheese itself, the true aroma and flavour of Camembert, most certainly has not.

This Camembert forms with Livarot and Pont l'Évêque, the great trio of cheeses of the Vallée d'Auge in the Department of Orne whose origins probably lie in the discussions of dairymaids a thousand years ago or more. John Arlott has pointed out that William the Conqueror enjoyed Augelot cheeses from the lush pastures fed by the Auge river, but we have no way of knowing what they were really like; we only know that they were almost certainly rich, creamy, soft cheeses which *may* have been surface-ripened and drained on nettles or other herbs. We know, too, that like almost all cheeses with a long past, they have changed, not once but often, in the course of their history. Camembert, for instance, once had (so it is said) a reddish rind, and later a blueish one from unwanted mould spores.

One of the changes brought about in Camembert (already a renowned cheese) was the doing of Mme Marie Harel, née Fontaine, a skilled cheese-maker. Around 1791 she seems to have discovered how to induce regularly the bacterial mould she wanted in her cheese. She left her daughter, Mme Marie Paynel her method, who with her husband sold the cheeses in the market town of Vimoutiers not far from the village of Camembert (where Marie Harel never lived). The well-behaved, Harel-style cheeses became very popular. So M and Mme Paynel and their children encouraged the growth of a legend that Mme Harel had invented Camembert. (It was a pity because her actual achievement was quite enough to make her name in an age when no one knew anything about bacteria or how to control them in a dairy.)

Local popularity might still have been Camembert's only lot, but for a cheesemonger of Vimoutiers called Ridel, 100 years later, who made, patented and used a chipwood box as light as shavings in which he sold his Camemberts. Hitherto they had been packed in straw, but now they could travel far beyond Paris safely, even overseas. It was his doing, more than anything else, which turned Camembert into a famous globe-trotter.

This, plus the contribution of one M Roger who, in 1910, introduced the white flor mould *Penicillium candidum* which is the one used today.

This modern farm Camembert is a round cheese which must not be less than 10 cm/4 inches in diameter, about 3 cm/$1\frac{1}{4}$ inches thick, and with a fat content of not less than 45 per cent. It should weigh 250 g/9 ounces and contain 2 litres/$3\frac{1}{2}$ pints of unpasteurised, unskimmed cow's milk per cheese.

Farm-made cheese is cut by hand, drained and salted, then sprinkled with the *Penicillium* mould and poured, usually semi-mechanically, into tall perforated forms in which it settles and drains (with frequent turning) until the true Camembert shape is achieved (about twenty-four hours). The new cheeses are then transferred to the curing rooms. In high humidity but at a low temperature of about 15°C/59°F, they are cured until the white flor mould appears. Some (probably a good many) are then sent out for sale, their remaining ripening being achieved en route and in the store to which they go.

The cheeses at their best have a soft white downy rind touched with red streaks, and a smooth, supple, pale-to-dark-cream paste. Their fragrance has a certain tang, that reminds most people of mushrooms – but what mushrooms! Grown, one might say, in the ditches of Heaven.

You would expect this lovely little old cheese to be protected by a strict *Appellation d'origine contrôlée*. It is nothing of the kind, due to its rather muddled past, and because it did not achieve wide distribution until M Ridel developed his wooden boxes and made wholesaling possible. Its only protector is the *Syndicat des Fabricants du véritable Camembert de Normandie*, a group of some 120 more important Camembert makers. Having been formed too late to prevent widespread pirating of the name of Camembert inside and outside France, it at least demands that the name of the place where any so-called Camembert is made appears on the box and on the wrapper of the cheese.

Talking of names, that of Marie Harel has been an unexpected export, bringing an even more unexpected profit to the people of Vimoutiers. In far away New York, USA at the end of the last century, a Manhattan delicatessen owner sold an imported pungent Schlosskäse cheese to his immigrant customers, but also wanted a local, new substitute cheese which would be cheaper. After three years, his Swiss partner in a small cheese factory, created such a new, soft and smelly cheese and the 'deli' owner in his pleasure christened it after a famous New York singing club to which he belonged. The new cheese, Liederkranz, 'took off'! It rapidly became a well-known, much-liked, American 'original', and went into permanent production in Ohio. After fifty years, the Liederkranz workers had come to feel so closely identified with some of Europe's ripened cheeses that they raised the money for a statue of Marie Harel to be erected in Vimoutiers where her cheeses had first been publicly sold. It brought numerous tourists to Vimoutiers to buy many souvenirs besides cheese.

If you buy a 'veritable' Camembert fermier in Vimoutiers or anywhere else, press it gently for softness. If it is soft, it is ripe and should be refrigerated if you do not want to eat it right away. Eat it within a week, though, testing it daily. A firm cheese should be left in its box, just in a cool place, to continue ripening. After you have cut it, wrap it in foil, refrigerate it and eat it as soon as you can. Don't let it get overripe; it will smell of ammonia, and taste like a new-made midden.

You will not find a suitable wine to drink with your

CROQUETTES DE CAMEMBERT **Light dish**

Serves 4

plain (all-purpose) flour	50 g/2 ounces	$\frac{1}{2}$ cup
ground rice	50 g/2 ounces	$\frac{1}{3}$ cup
milk	175 ml/6 fl oz	$\frac{3}{4}$ cup
single (light) cream	1 tablespoon	1 tablespoon
softened butter	150 g/5 ounces	$\frac{2}{3}$ cup
Camembert fermier cheese	450 g/1 pound	1 pound
salt, cayenne pepper and ground nutmeg to flavour		

Combine in the top of a double boiler, the flour, rice, milk, cream and butter. Scrape the rind off the Camembert, and blend the cheese in. Season, taking care to preserve the subtle flavour of the cheese by using cayenne and nutmeg sparingly. Place over simmering water. Heat, stirring constantly, and making sure that the mixture does not boil until it is very thick. Spread it on a tray or baking sheet to cool. When it is quite cold, mould it into croquette or cork shapes. Dip in beaten egg, then roll in bread crumbs – better still, fine cream cracker crumbs. Leave to stand for 20 minutes. Fry in deep, very hot oil just until the coating is crisp. Serve immediately.

Do not freeze.

Back: Large Munster; *front*: Munster and Carré de l'Est

OPPOSITE: *Back*: St Paulin; *centre left*: Pont l'Evêque; *centre right*: Camembert fermier; *front*: Livarot

CIGARILLOS **Snack**

Makes 8 snacks

Carré de l'Est cheese in one rectangular piece	75 g/3 ounces	3 ounce piece
large thin square slices of dryish brown bread	8	8
oregano	$\frac{1}{4}$ teaspoon	$\frac{1}{4}$ teaspoon
eggs, beaten	2	2
melted butter for brushing		

Cut the cheese into four equal-sized slices or strips about 7.5 × 2.5 cm/3 × 1 inches in size. Cut off the rind, then cut each strip in half lengthways, making 8 'fingers' of cheese. Cut the crusts off the bread slices. Mix the oregano into the beaten egg. Dip each cheese finger in egg. Lay it on a slice of bread. Roll up the bread like a miniature Swiss roll (jelly roll), with the cheese finger in the centre. Dip the bread rolls in the remaining egg. Place them, cut side down, on a buttered baking sheet. Brush them with melted butter. Bake at 180°C/350°F/Gas 4 for 10 minutes or until the egg coating has 'set', then raise the heat to 220°C/425°F/Gas 7 for a few moments to brown the cigarillos. Serve warm as brunch or barbecue snacks.

Do not freeze these snacks before or after baking.

Camembert in Normandy. Neither Normandy's cider nor its apple brandy, Calvados, is quite the thing. Wine experts have suggested a Château Haut-Brion. Yes, certainly, if you can afford it. But keep in mind too a slightly less costly Côtes de Beaune Villages, or a similar light, elegant and spicy wine.

PONT L'ÉVÊQUE

Pont l'Évêque is one of the renowned triumvirate of fine glorious soft cheeses of the Pays d'Auge in Normandy. Camembert and Livarot are its confrères. Its name might suggest that it is a monastic cheese in origin, but like Livarot, it is christened, in fact, after its local market town in the Lisieux district. However, it is certainly a medieval cheese, if not a monastic one; and it is said to have been christened only in about 1600, because before then it was called Angelot, which was the name of a medieval gold coin. (England had a comparable coin called an angelet worth about three shillings and fourpence in English coinage in 1480.)

Pont l'Évêque has, in fact, been made (at least until 1973) almost entirely on Normandy farms and sold in the market-place rather than the supermarket. It is a cow's milk product made in small 10 cm/4 inch squares, 2.5 cm/1 inch thick which weigh about 350 g/12 ounces each. It has a very smooth, washed or brushed golden rind, a tender supple consistency and a fat content of 50 per cent. Its smell, when fully ripened after about six weeks, is distinctly savoury, its taste tangy to match.

This is poor praise because it is in fact a very beautiful cheese. Rather listen to what the critical epicure Edward Bunyard wrote about it in 1937:

'. . . a cheese quite by itself, and in my view the best of the small French cheeses. Less ammoniacal than Brie or Camembert, it has a nutty flavour which is ideal for clarets and Sauternes. A luncheon cheese. Calvados is its home; it is never seen in quantity, as Camembert (is), but in autumn and winter, it should be enquired for . . .'

It should indeed! And Bunyard is perhaps being slightly unfair only in relegating it to a luncheon cheese. Today, when our palates are more tender (or more attuned to bland supermarket flavours if you like) it is an excellent after-dinner cheese. It is not perhaps a cheese for heroes; but it is certainly one which angels will enjoy, if they eat it soon after it comes from its six-week sojourn in the curing cellar (or refrigerate it, carefully wrapped, until they can get to it). Once beyond its ripening point, it sinks, smells and pours out of its skin like liquid lava.

Most people will enjoy a claret with it and a fairly full-bodied one. Christian Plume suggests as alternatives a Fleurie, good Beaujolais or successful Bourgueil, besides several grander wines.

PORT DU SALUT, PORT SALUT AND SAINT PAULIN

Not far from the small town of Laval in Brittany, is a parish called Entrammes where a Trappist monastery now stands. The original buildings were put up in 1233 to house a priory of monks of St Génévieve, and no doubt they made cheeses throughout the centuries to feed themselves, as all rural communities in dairying areas do. Then, in the French Revolution, they were driven out, like all their brothers. Many went into exile.

Among them was a small group of monks from the very strict monastery at La Trappe in Normandy. Before the Revolution, the Trappists had been almost unknown outside France, but in 1790 their novice-master fled with twenty of them to Val-Sainte in the dairying area of Fribourg in Switzerland. There they made their strict Rule even stricter – and yet it proved so popular that postulants flocked to them.

These Trappists found cheese-making a near-ideal occupation for their rigorous and almost silent way of life. Their 'Rule' demanded that they spend seven hours a day in prayer and three and a half hours at work, and the various processes of cheese-making could be slotted in between church services as many other crafts could not. Also, their spare diet needed a concentrated protein food because they then ate no fish and hardly any eggs.

They returned in 1815 to the empty abbey at Entrammes with a dozen dairy cows and a cheese recipe learned from their Swiss hosts. They re-christened the abbey *Notre Dame de Port du Salut* (Haven of Safety) and set to work to make cheese, called Port du Salut, first for their own use and then for sale.

Soon the demand for the new cheese outran supply. The brothers increased the size of their herd, enlarged their dairy, and then started buying in milk from local farmers. In 1873, a Paris merchant, M Mauget was entrusted with selling the cheeses, to 'bring in a modest profit' as one brother put it. They were an instant triumph. When M Mauget put up a notice that the cheeses had arrived, the batch was sold within the hour.

Popularity arouses pirates. By 1878, the name of the abbey cheese was being used to sell other cheeses similar to it but not the same. The name was registered to protect it from infringement but without success. In 1909, the monks entered into an agreement with a commercial manufacturer to use their authentic recipe and the cheese names Port du Salut and Port Salut, and withdrew from large-scale manufacture themselves. But they went on making the cheese for their own and for local use, often under the name Entrammes until 1988; and other Trappist communities have attached their own monastery label to their own cheeses. So there are now a number of Port-Salut-type cheeses sold under different names.

One such name used by commercial manufacturers in France and elsewhere who do not wish to steal the name of Port du Salut is Saint Paulin. It is now the accepted generic name for cheeses of the Port du Salut type.

Port Salut, today, is a 2 kg/4½ pound wheel about 20 cm/8 inches in diameter and 7 cm/2¾ inches thick, with a natural annatto-tinted rind and 45 to 50 per cent fat content. (There is a miniature size, weighing only 150 g/6 ounces.) The cheese is made with pasteurised whole milk, and is lightly pressed, giving a smooth, semi-hard paste which varies in colour and flavour with the cheese's age. A mild young Port Salut may be the colour of rich cream and quite bland, whereas a well-aged one can be amber-coloured with a fruity, deep flavour.

It is imitated today, perhaps more than ever. In a number of countries, Port Salut and Saint Paulin alike are names used for more or less close taste-alikes. However, both reputable factory cheese-makers and monks still use the recipe taken to France from Val-Sainte long ago. In Brittany Trappist monks make cheeses such as Briquebec, Citeaux, Echournac and Tamié in what has come to be called Trappist style. In Belgium, too, similar cheeses are made, while in Canada, not far from Montreal, Trappist brothers made Canada's best-known speciality cheese Oka, a Port Salut derivative, for over seventy years with much profit.

Port Salut and its derivatives all over the world are good-tempered about what they are served with. Bread or toast can be used as a carrier; a light rye is good, or a mixed-grain, whole-grain loaf. You could drink a light red wine, or, perhaps a *still*, dry cider. Braver souls can try applejack brandy or Genever.

LIVAROT

The wide sweep of dairy land called the 'Road of Great Cheeses' which adorns Normandy is rich in towns and villages with names that read like a cheesemonger's catalogue. Moreover, the cheeses are not only among the finest of the French, but include some of the oldest. They go back, so it is said, to the medieval Angelot (golden) cheeses; and among the most ancient, and the most notable, is the increasingly rare *Appellation contrôlée* cheese, Livarot.

Livarot's native home is the market town of the same name and its surrounding valley of Viette, a mere nine kilometres from Vimoutiers, famous for its association with Camembert (page 48). It is a soft, cow's milk cheese with a red-smear washed rind. In shape, it is like a small cake, about 12.5 cm/5 inches in diameter, 5 cm/2 inches thick, and weighing about 350 g/12 ounces, with a fat content of 40 to 45 per cent. Locally, a slightly smaller version is called Petit Lisieux.

In its prime, Livarot looks and feels smooth and firm, in no way sunken or squashy, with a glossy, dark tan or chestnut surface.

But these facts tell you very little about Livarot. You can imagine it better by knowing that it was probably an ancient monks' cheese, and the old monks, deprived of so many other flavours in the foods forbidden to them, liked their cheeses strong. So they made their cheeses from unpasteurised, skimmed evening milk mixed with the full cream milk of the next morning. When set, the curd was roughly chopped, drained to some extent, set in wooden moulds called clichés, and salted. At this stage, the cheeses were called Livarots Blancs, and they could be eaten as they were or matured.

Much the same method has been used until today by the farmers who have followed the monks. Now, the demand for Livarot is such that it is increasingly a factory cheese. But the remaining farmers in its home area, the Pays d'Auge, still send their cheeses to the local *affineur* who, in Normandy, is called a *caviste*. This finisher or refiner has as his main equipment a series of curing 'cellars' and store-rooms in which the temperature and humidity are scrupulously controlled. But he relies most of all on his skill, his eye and palate.

He rubs the cheeses with coarse salt. Over the next two to three months he turns and salts them often, and moves them from one humid curing room to the next; betweenwhiles, he observes them through glass panels in the curing room wall. To keep the temperature stable, no draughts are allowed in the curing room, no hint of outside air. The smell, as the cheese nears ripeness, has been variously described:

'... overpowering; like the odour of slowly rotting apples, combined with ammonia, a whiff of rich Camembert, and a slight suggestion of seaside ozone.'   T A Layton.
'... town drains running into the sea.'   Ibid.
'... the feet of God.'   Leon-Paul Farque.

The taste is also savoured with varied comments:

'... a full rounded taste ... at its best in autumn and winter.'   J A Arlott.
'... haut en couleur, en odeur et en saveur ...' Christian Plume.
'... the flavour ... is mild and fresh ...'   Nancy Eekhof-Stork.
'... assertive ... the curing cellars are not ventilated, and the aromas thus contained help give the cheese its strong piquant flavour.'   Evan Jones.

Conflicting as these views are, there is one thing on which all commentators agree. Livarot is among the very best of the world's cheeses – is perhaps *the* best, even if its compatriots Camembert and Pont l'Évêque (also of the Pays d'Auge) run it close.

This lovely cheese (when it is handled properly) is said, even with a hint of seriousness, to wear a sash of rank to mark its eminence among the Norman cheeses. A normal-sized Livarot does, indeed, wear a 'belt' of five thin strips of sedge or paper around its middle – but I'm afraid for the same mundane reason that a middle-aged woman wears a corset – to stop it sagging (in its three-month maturing period, it

MONASTERY LEEKS — Vegetable dish

Serves 4 to 6

Munster cheese with rind removed	100 g/4 ounces	½ cup
white wine (preferably Alsatian)	1 to 2 tablespoons	1 to 2 tablespoons
egg yolk	1	1
double (heavy) cream	2 tablespoons	2 tablespoons
small leeks	700 g/1½ pounds	1½ pounds
salt		
butter	25 g/1 ounce	2 tablespoons
plain (all-purpose) flour	25 g/1 ounce	¼ cup
milk	220 ml/scant ½ pint	1 cup and 2 tablespoons

Cut the cheese paste in half. Chill one half. Mash the other half with the wine, egg yolk and cream until blended. Set aside.

Wash the leeks and remove any coarse green leaves. Cut white stems and tender green leaves into 2.5 cm/1 inch pieces. Simmer in lightly salted water for 7 to 10 minutes until tender.

Meanwhile, melt the butter, stir in the flour, and cook, stirring, for 2 minutes. Gradually blend in the milk and stir until the mixture comes to a boil and thickens. Remove the pan from the heat, and stir in the cheese mixture.

Shred the chilled cheese on the coarse holes of a grater.

Drain the leeks when cooked. Turn them into a warmed serving dish. Pour the Munster sauce over them. Sprinkle with the shredded cheese. Place in the oven at 160°C/325°F/Gas 3 for 8 to 10 minutes until it is melted. Serve with a dish such as crumbed veal escalopes or grilled chicken, or as a separate vegetable course after a garnished meat dish, in the French style.

SWEET BRIE CHEESECAKE — Dessert

Serves 8 to 10

Base		
plain (all-purpose) flour	100 g/4 ounces	1 cup
caster (fine white) sugar	50 g/2 ounces	¼ cup
softened butter	100 g/4 ounces	½ cup
Filling		
Philadelphia soft cheese (unflavoured)	450 g/1 pound	1 pound
Brie cheese	200 g/7 ounces	⅞ cup
plain (all-purpose) flour	1 tablespoon	1 tablespoon
caster (fine white) sugar	75 g/3 ounces	⅓ cup
egg yolks	4	4
double (heavy) cream	125 ml/4 fl oz	½ cup
vanilla	1 teaspoon	1 teaspoon
egg whites	4	4
salt	¼ teaspoon	¼ teaspoon

Bring the cheeses to room temperature while making the case. For the case, grease separately the sides and base of a 23 cm/9 inch springform cake tin (pan) about 7.5 cm/3 inches high. Mix the flour and sugar. Blend in the butter to make a smooth soft dough. Spread half evenly over the base of the tin. Bake at 200°C/400°F/Gas 6 for 8 minutes or until firm and beginning to brown. Cool. Fit the sides on the base of the tin. Spread the remaining dough over about 5 cm/2 inches of the sides to make a shell. Chill.

For the filling, remove the rind from the Brie. Beat the cheeses together until very smooth and creamy. Beat in the flour and sugar. Then beat in the egg yolks, one at a time, the cream and vanilla. Beat the egg whites and salt until the whites hold firm peaks. Fold them into the cheese mixture. Pour the mixture gently into the prepared shell.

Bake the cheesecake at 180°C/350°F/Gas 4 for 45 minutes or until the cheesecake is just firm in the centre. Do not open the oven door more than a crack to inspect it. Shut the door gently, turn off the oven and leave the cheesecake to cool for at least 1 hour. (If possible cool it completely in the oven, to prevent it cracking.) When the cheesecake is fully cooled, remove it carefully from the tin. Chill it for at least 2 hours before cutting it. Serve it with a bowl of fresh raspberries or other soft fruits.

Freezing All cheesecakes freeze well for up to 1 month. Thaw slowly in the refrigerator.

BRIE DE MEAUX
PAXTON & WHITFIELD LTD

45%
FAT IN DRY MATTER

MUST BE WEIGHED AT TIME OF SALE

BOURSAULT

Chaource
Lincet
30

Coulommiers
BRIQUE EN BRIE
MATIÈRE GRASSE

develops a tendency to dip on top and in the middle too). Local people, however, still affectionately call Livarot 'the Colonel' because of the stripes on its red 'jacket'.

This red-smear jacket is a lick of colouring given it after its final wash, before it is sent out for sale. It should then be *à point*, supple but resilient to touch. Since it has ripened purely from the surface moulds, not from any injection, any white chalky line through the centre can only mean that it still contains residual whey insufficiently drained out earlier. This hardly ever occurs. Once you have cut the rind off, as you must, the paste should be creamy all through with baby 'eyes' and a delicious taste, positive yet subtle and satisfying. It will go a long way; keep it (uncut) for five or six days if you like, and once cut, wrap it closely and keep it for a few days longer.

You can sip the local liqueur with it, which is Calvados. But when you want wine, buy a big beauty. With a creamy Livarot just spread on bread, broach your Hermitage, Côte Rôtie, Corton or a good Côtes du Rhône.

MAROILLES

Maroilles or Marolles is one of the few great cheeses known to be more than a thousand years old. What's more its character shows signs of not having changed much during that time; it seems to typify the ancient, simple and smelly cheeses made by monks in the abbeys and their farms of the Frankish, and later the early French, Church.

Just over a thousand years ago, the bishop of the nearby town of Cambrai stimulated the monks of the great abbey of Maroilles, which was in his diocese, to create a cheese. There were several reasons why he may have done so – possibly he wanted a regular supply of one which he liked for his own table. The biddable monks did their best to please him, we assume. They produced a cheese. At the time and for long after, the country folk around its home called it Craquegnon, later still (and today) it became called *Vieux Paunt* (Old Stinker), because of its strong smell. Even André Simon who respected strong cheeses said its smell was 'assertive, sometimes quite aggressive'. The great gastronome Maurice Curnonsky said, 'Its thunderous savour resounds like the voice of the saxophone in the symphony of cheeses.' (He meant that it tasted strong too.)

The abbey of Maroilles had been built near Avesnes in the area of Thiérache in north eastern France in the seventh century, under the Merovingian kings. At that time, in a period of secular chaos, the Church provided a stable, secure society and a job in return for obedience from its professed members and its tenant farmers. It was the custom then and later for those abbeys with large lands to rent them out in return for military and other services and for produce, including cheeses.

This happened at Maroilles. In 1174, the then abbot decreed that the inhabitants of the four villages nearest to the abbey should make cheese of the milk their beasts yielded on St John's Eve (June 23rd) and deliver it to their parish priest on St Remi's Day (October 1st) for the Abbey. This suggests that they probably all made much the same kind of cheese which ripened at the same time, most likely the one developed and taught them by the monks, and this is borne out by the fact that several only slightly different forms of the parent cheese, Maroilles, exist, with different names.

This ancient Benedictine cheese is now made from cow's milk; it is unskimmed, unpressed, fermented at a low temperature and washed with brine regularly while it cures. With a fat content of 50 per cent, its semi-hard, blonde paste is enclosed in an orange-brown smear rind, shiny and supple to touch. Its shape is a square, 13 cm/5 inches across; it is 6 cm/2½ inches thick, and weighs 800 g/1¾ pounds.

The cheese is made in an area restricted by an Appellation Order to the countryside of French Hainaut in the ancient province of Picardy, and in the area around Avesnes. On one side lies the north-eastern edge of Champagne, on the other the Belgian frontier. The cheese is still quite often made in farm dairies, usually from the milk of Pie Noir cows. It is renneted and left to coagulate for four hours before being drained in boxes with pierced bottoms, and thereafter set in square moulds and regularly turned. Once firm, the cheeses are salted, and cured in humid cellars for up to four months with regular brine-washing.

It all sounds simple enough, conventional – a standard way to make cheese. And so it is. But to appreciate the character of this cheese, you must take into account the northern soil, the cattle and pasture, the abbey and farm cellars – perhaps originally impregnated with vine-bred moulds, or built of stone from distant Caen – and certainly the slow ripening the climate allows.

And the result?

A cheese so fine that, in the late 1620s, King Louis XIV allowed an unripened white Maroilles with herbs to be named after the Dauphin who had 'fallen for' it. (It is still so called.)

A cheese – I believe the only cheese ever – to have had celebratory pontifical mass said for it. On May 28, 1961, the Most Reverend Father Abbot Dom Jean Gaillard celebrated mass for its 1000th anniversary, and Father Maurice Lelong in his sermon said of it: 'Vigorous and aromatic, there is nothing quite like this marvel, Maroilles, glory of French Hainaut . . . which the medieval inhabitants claimed they held "of God and the sun".'

Complimentary, of course! But then even among cheeses, a 1000th birthday is a rare event and one for congratulation!

Maroilles is not overwhelmingly strong to eat; the smooth paste, slivered on split white rolls or light toast is wonderful. Eat it as soon as it is ripe, ie when it feels soft (or refrigerate it fast). Don't, whatever you do, waste it by letting it hang about. Drink a big wine with it, perhaps a Chateauneuf-du-Pape or Nuits-St-Georges – or a good Corbières would deal kindly with it.

FRANCE
ILE DE FRANCE

THE FRENCH BRIE CHEESES
Brie de Meaux/Brie de Melun/Brie de Coulommiers

Brie must surely, these days, come near to rivalling Cheddar in its geographical distribution if not yet in the quantity sold. Of all the soft cheeses which have achieved hitherto undreamed-of popularity since the 1950s, Brie is the most widely travelled and renowned.

It could hardly be otherwise because the 'jewel of the Ile de France', as Frenchmen call it, has been known beyond the borders of France for centuries. Every cheese lover knows the accepted story of how it became famed in the international *beau monde*. After the French Emperor Napoleon's final defeat, the statesmen of Europe met at Vienna to reshape its map. Among the wealthy and brilliant aristocrats, the French representative, M de Talleyrand (Charles Maurice de Talleyrand-Perigord), had little status and less say at first. But he was the most astute of diplomats. He wormed his way on to the top Council, and set to work to get every advantage he could for France, however small, out of the complicated squabbles of her conquerers. At one of the innumerable dinners shared by the most exalted statesmen, it is said that the discussion turned to the merits or otherwise of various national cheeses. Talleyrand suggested a competition between them – and at the end produced Brie as his contribution for France. It was immediately, and it is alleged unanimously, pronounced the king of cheeses.

If this is true, Talleyrand was on pretty safe ground in boasting the merits of Brie because it had already been famed for at least 600 years; it had even been exported to England before 1400 – Richard II's cooks had created a sweet, spiced Brie flan for him then.

There can be very few cheese lovers around the globe, now, who have not tasted Brie in some form. Most consumers recognise the wide snowy disc of cheese on a delicatessen counter, and some (although not too many get the chance these days) recognise the rusty streaks and bumpy surface of a traditionally-made cheese. But not many know the names and sizes of the six different French Bries listed in Pierre Androuet's *Cheese Guide*, or could recognise without a label a foreign Brie: English Brie, American Brie, Australian or New Zealand Brie, let alone all the European mainland Bries.

Traditional French Brie comes from quite a small area east of Paris, and the three main types take their names from their nearest market towns. The finest is generally agreed to be the Brie de Meaux, and the farm-made Brie de Meaux fermier, using raw milk, is esteemed more than the pasteurised-milk Brie de Meaux laitier from commercial plants. Several authorities go so far as to call it the finest cheese.

It is also, as a bonus, the largest of the Bries, commonly being 36 to 40 cm/14 to 16 inches in diameter, although only 2.5 cm/1 inch thick. It weighs when ripe about 2 kg/4 pounds 6 ounces and has a 45 per cent fat content. Under its red-flecked, straw-pocked rind, the paste is butter-coloured, yielding but not fluid, with a full scent of matured milk and its own unique flavour. This is due, it is said, to the large size of the cheese surface on which the mould-forming bacilli can get to work.

Brie de Meaux does not get quite all the plaudits. There is the smaller but interesting Brie de Melun which can be bought in its own area in three different forms: as Brie de Melun frais which is almost unripened, just slightly salted (27 cm/10½ inches diameter), as Brie de Melun bleu, which is not 'blued' at all but is just the fresh cheese sprinkled with powdered charcoal; and as Brie de Melun affiné, which is a long-matured and therefore slightly shrunken Brie de Melun (24 cm/9½ inches in diameter), with a more grainy texture than Brie de Meaux. Brie de Melun frais is very white, and smells and tastes of gently-set curds. Brie de Melun affiné is a fiercer cheese altogether, with a reddish rind, a strong smell of fermentation, and a fruity flavour. This is because no *Penicillium candidum* is added to it, so it matures only naturally and slowly and takes two and a half months to ripen fully.

The third in this trio of fine Bries is the Brie de Coulommiers sometimes made in a 25 cm/10 inch disc 2.5 cm/1 inch thick, but more often just called Coulommiers and made in a small size, only 13 cm/5 inches across. It is like a baby Brie de Meaux with a supple paste, a pleasant, mushroomy scent and flavour. It is a good traveller, being less fragile than the wide wheels.

There are also a number of other modestly-sized Bries made in the area, such as Brie de Montereau (an 18 cm/7 inch disc) which is matured for six weeks so has pretty pronounced vitality.

The method of making Brie de Meaux fermier sets the pattern for the rest. Carefully ripened whole evening milk is mixed with fresh morning milk, is mellowed, renneted and lightly salted. The curd is then spooned in six successive layers into the wide, shallow hoops standing on straw mats, the whey is skilfully taken out, and the cheeses are allowed to drain, being turned over regularly onto fresh mats. After a week of this treatment, the *Penicillium candidum* which creates the white flor is sprinkled on the cheese surfaces, and the cheeses are left to firm and ripen (in the case of Brie de Meaux, for a month).

VEAL FRICASSÉE   **Main dish**

Serves 4

veal fillet (round roast)	450 g/1 pound	1 pound
small onion, thinly sliced	1	1
sprig of parsley	1	1
squeezed lemon (whole fruit)	$\frac{1}{4}$	$\frac{1}{4}$
boiling water	275 ml/$\frac{1}{2}$ pint	1$\frac{1}{4}$ cups
salt and pepper to taste		
Tomme de Savoie cheese	100 g/4 ounces	$\frac{2}{3}$ cup
milk	150 ml/$\frac{1}{4}$ pint	$\frac{2}{3}$ cup
butter	25 g/1 ounce	2 tablespoons
plain (all-purpose) flour	25 g/1 ounce	4 tablespoons

Cut the veal into 5 cm/2 inch cubes. Put the meat cubes, onion, parsley sprig and piece of squeezed lemon in a casserole. Pour the boiling water over them, and add a little seasoning. Cover tightly. Bake at 160°C/325°F/Gas 3 for 2 hours.

While cooking the meat, take any rind off the cheese. Cut the paste into very small dice. Set 2 tablespoons of the dice aside.

Remove the cooked veal and onion to a buttered shallow serving dish. Combine with the cheese dice. Keep warm in a low oven under buttered paper. Strain the cooking liquid in the casserole into a jug; discard the parsley and lemon. Mix 150 ml/$\frac{1}{4}$ pint ($\frac{2}{3}$ cup) of the cooking liquid with the milk.

Heat the butter in a small pan, add the flour and stir well to blend them. Still stirring, slowly trickle in the milk mixture. Bring slowly to a boil, stirring constantly; the sauce will be thick. Stir in the reserved 2 tablespoons of cheese dice. Allow them to melt. Season the sauce if required, and pour it over the veal. Serve at once.

The dish is not suitable for freezing.

It sounds simple but takes much skill, knowledge and vigilance by both the cheese-maker and the affineur who ripens his cheeses. It is all too easy, the pundits say, to make a bad Brie; and we have all seen wedges with a chalky unripened line through the middle which has no hope of maturing before the outer layers smell of ammonia and go bad. A Brie once cut will not ripen any further, it will only 'go off', and quite quickly at that.

The enormous modern popularity of Brie means that fewer and fewer of the cheeses are being made in the small dairies or on the farms, and more and more in large commercial plants from pasteurised milk. To prevent these mass-produced Bries 'going off', they are often stabilised during making; while they taste pleasant enough, they do not ripen naturally and so never develop the full flavour of which they are capable.

At what point of ripeness you eat your Brie is a matter of choice. Do not let any self-styled expert tell you it must be runny before it is eaten; it must not. If you wait to eat it then, teetering on the edge of bitterness, you have only yourself to blame if it goes 'over the top' before you get to it. The Coulommiers called *Fromage à la pie* is always eaten practically fresh. On the other hand, Brie de Melun, being slow to mature is distinctly 'niffy' and strong-flavoured by the time it is ripened all through. As for a great and glorious Brie de Meaux, it is usually thought to be 'à point' when the whole paste is butter-coloured and glossy, smooth – that is *onctueuse* – on the palate, noticeably aromatic but definitely not smelly.

John Arlott reckons that this Brie, at this moment, deserves to be eaten alone with a knife and fork, accompanied by the best claret you can find – and which you almost certainly cannot afford. He is quite right. But, being practical, any respectable Saint Emilion or Graves-Saint Emilion which you like and trust will do.

Note You will find paragraphs on Blue Bries, French Brie au Bleu, and Bries with Flavourings in the Glossary.

BOURSAULT

Boursault is emphatically not to be confused with *Boursin* although both are small rich cheeses made with a variety of added flavourings or coatings such as crushed peppers. Comparisons are odious, but to my mind Boursault has a unique freshness and subtlety which no other cheese of its type can match. Its alternative name, Lucullus, will explain its character at once to anyone aquainted with the classics.

It is a baby soft cheese made from pasteurised, enriched cow's milk in parts of Normandy and the Ile de France. The little cylinder is only 7.5 cm/3 inches in diameter and 5 cm/2 inches high. It weighs about 200 g/7 oz, which is – and this is the Lucullan touch – 75 per cent butterfat. Some of it is derived from the rich milk of the area around Brie which is used to make the cheese, and some is the pure rich fresh cream of Normandy which is added. Not surprisingly, the cheese feels soft rather than resilient or flaky, and feels even softer

when it has matured. This only takes three weeks to a month, in cool humid cellars at the modern hygienic plant where it is manufactured. During that time it develops what Pierre Androuet calls a downy, pinkish rind with a marked aroma of fermentation, a texture like cream, and a really quite mild flavour considering its impact on the nose.

Go by the flavour when buying it and by the manufacturers' statement on the bottom of the package. This gives a packing date, followed by the pronouncement that the cheese will still be young for the following ten days, mature after another twenty; and it implies that it will be at its peak for gourmets (if it has been properly cared for) even after a month. But if it has been purchased from a supermarket or neighbourhood store which does not specialise in cheese, this should be treated with caution.

If you do want to buy it from a supermarket or an unknown cheese counter, Boursault is fortunately easy to identify by virtue of its curious, perhaps unique package with a concave top and base and see-through holes at the sides. It is generally a good buy for a cheese-board, catering for those who do not want a strong flavour at the end of a meal – and also good to serve to strangers whose tastes you do not know. It is excellent as a dessert too, served with the rind pared off and grapes or other fruits piled on top of it. In either case, serve a slightly chilled light red wine with a distinct bouquet, as John Arlott recommends.

CARRÉ DE L'EST

This 'square of the East' is a cow's milk cheese, now made from pasteurised milk in commercial dairies in several parts of north-eastern France. It is usually described as a soft cheese, although André Simon called it semi-hard soon after World War II; it may be allowed to mature more fully now, and so softens more. Anyway, it is indisputably a square 9 to 9.5 cm/$3\frac{1}{4}$ to $3\frac{3}{4}$ inches each way, and 2.5 to 3 cm/1 to $1\frac{1}{4}$ inches thick, with a 45 to 50 per cent fat content; its weight varies but is usually about 200 g/7 ounces.

There are two types of Carré de l'Est. The first, Carré de l'Est fleuri, is sprayed with mould spores and grows a downy white coat; it is eaten fairly fresh and bland. The second type, Carré de l'Est lavé, is given a washed rind, develops a reddish coat, and has a more resolute bouquet and flavour.

There are also two schools of thought about the basic character of the cheese apart from these man-made differences. One school maintains that it has the bouquet and flavour of an undeveloped Maroilles, the other – frankly with a rather better case – that it is more like a young, bland Camembert. This school back up their assertion with certain 'evidence'. Some American Camemberts, they say, are in fact made by the method used to make Carré de l'Est, and they imply by this that Carré de l'Est is little different from a square-shaped Camembert.

In fact Carré de l'Est has a quite honest character of its own, if not a markedly aristocratic one. It differs from Camembert in that its curd is chopped before draining, thus accelerating the drainage and making (it is said) a softer cheese. It is certainly soft – *molle* the French call it – and it is lightly salted, but it is neither cooked nor pressed nor milled. After its three-week curing in air-conditioned cellars, its paste under its bloomy rind is a very pale cream colour, and supple. Certainly its flavour has a hint of similarity to Camembert, but it is nowhere near as sophisticated.

In France, and sometimes in England, it is possible to test one's own impressions quite cheaply because the cheese is made in a small size for export. It would be an interesting experiment to try three 'Petits Carrés,' and a Camembert in a blindfold tasting.

You would need a suitable wine, of course. I have seen Bouzy recommended, the still red wine of the Champagne region, home of the cheese. A fine wine, but hard to get. Most of us will have to settle for a more modest red wine, or perhaps a white Alsation Traminer.

LANGRES

Langres looks something like a badly baked cake which has sunk in the middle, or a half-cooked vol-au-vent. But there, emphatically, the resemblance ends. Langres, if you are lucky enough to find it off its home territory, is a scrupulously made product definitely ready to eat. It has a reputation to maintain for that, and does it with care.

Langres is in fact the least well known of the five or six highly aromatic, classic soft cheeses of France. It is a small cow's milk cheese shaped like a church font, that is a truncated cone with a rounded-edged hollow in the centre top; its height is no more than 5 cm/2 inches, its diameter about 10 cm/4 inches and its weight about 300 g/11 ounces. Its rind is light brown or reddish with a strong bouquet.

It is certainly a very old cheese named after its main market-place, the ancient hill-fortress town of Langres, nor-nor-east of Dijon. As folk-tale tells, it was already being made in the time of the Merovingian rulers of northern France, that is between about AD 496 when the king, Clovis, was baptised at Rheims, and the rise to power of Charles Martel who saved Europe from the Saracens at Poitiers in AD 732 and was the grandfather of Charlemagne. It is possible, I suppose, but unlikely because Langres was probably on the direct line of march between the Roman Catholic Franks (soon to be French) and their enemies, the Arian Lombards in the south-east, so the chances of peaceful survival for domestic cattle and farmstead cheese-making were slim.

Whenever the cheese was developed, what does seem likely is that the cattle then, as now, fed on the curving plateau where the Seine rises, from spring through summer. Then, too, the little cheeses with their 'dewpond' centres were probably ripened in pots the shape and size of modern ramekins or were tucked under a layer of ashes to keep the temperature constant, before being marketed wrapped in leaves (which meant that the three-month ripening period had to be finished before the autumn leaves were sere).

Today Langres is still made on farms but more and more rarely; most production now takes place in small dairies or in factories. In all cases, leaves have given way to paper wrappings. However, it has retained its individual personality, and is certainly as respected as its better-known 'confrères', Epoisses, Maroilles, Livarot, Pont l'Évêque, and Munster.

This makes it obvious that Langres is not a bland cheese. The forceful bouquet of its brine-washed rind can be off-putting, especially if it is allowed to get an ammonia-like tang (keep it cool). A strong smell does not mean an overpowering cheese, however. The taste of Langres is full, spicy and distinctly rich, to be 'sipped' from a knife point or the tip of a spoon if you lack confidence at first. You will soon want more.

The hollow in the centre is believed to have been used for residual salt water between the cheese's washings – or for a little brandy, marc or kirsch to fortify the consumer.

It is usually wiser, however, to enjoy your classic Langres with a good Burgundy wine, such as the Beaune Villages which John Arlott recommended to the *Paxton and Whitfield* Cheese Club. Have two bottles to hand because once you have cut the cheese, it will not keep for more than three days. It must, by the way, stand at room temperature for two to three hours at least before you eat it.

CHAOURCE

It is impossible to write about the cheeses of the Ile de France or Champagne without repeating oneself. One all too soon runs out of adjectives to describe the galaxy of similar yet individual small cow's milk cheeses of these parts. Champagne is as blessed in her pastures as in her vineyards, and her cheeses are as beautiful and as saleable as her famous wine.

This is not surprising in the case of Chaource because, although until the early 1970s it was only made on farms and in small dairies, its production was based on the chief market town of the area from which it takes its name. Its background was one of commercially-minded farmers' enterprises. Furthermore it had been so for centuries because the town of Chaource had been encircled throughout the high Middle Ages by the great international Champagne Fairs at Troyes, Provins, Bar-sur-Aube and Lagny, which for nine months of the year attracted salesmen, merchants, bankers, court officials and commission agents from all over Europe and parts of Asia. Their influence must have lasted.

At all events, the cheese which was only made in small quantities for local consumption until the early 1970s has increasingly been recognised as a sophisticated 'winner'.

It is a neat, proud little cheese 11.5 to 12.5 cm/$4\frac{1}{2}$ to 5 inches in diameter and 6.5 cm/$2\frac{1}{2}$ inches high, like a section of a round pillar. It has a thin, bloomy white rind and a glorious paste

Left: Reblochon; *right*: Gruyère de Beaufort

POTATO-CARROT CASSEROLE   **Vegetable dish**

Serves 4

potatoes for boiling	700 g/1½ pounds	1½ pounds
salt for flavouring		
oil for frying	2 tablespoons	2 tablespoons
finely chopped (minced) onion	75 g/3 ounces	½ cup
small can of peeled tomatoes	227 g/8 ounce can	8 ounce can
dried basil	½ teaspoon	½ teaspoon
salt to taste		
grinding of white pepper		
butter for brushing		
melted butter for sprinkling		
medium-sized carrots, grated	2	2
Reblochon cheese with rind removed	1	1
dry toast crumbs to cover		

Boil the potatoes in their skins until just tender. When cool enough to handle, peel them and cut them into 2 cm/½ inch slices. Season them with salt. Set aside.

While boiling the potatoes, make the sauce. Heat the oil in a saucepan. Add the onion and fry until it softens. Add the tomatoes, basil and a little seasoning. Mix well, reduce the heat to very low, and cover the pan. Simmer for about 20 minutes until the tomatoes are a thick pulp. Take the pan off the heat.

Brush the inside of a 1 litre/1¾ pint (4½cup) casserole with butter. Place ⅓ of the potato slices in the bottom. Sprinkle with a little melted butter. Spread with half the grated carrot. Slice the cheese and spread half of it over the carrot, then spoon half the sauce over the top. Repeat the layers, finishing with the last ⅓ of the potato slices. Cover them with crumbs, and sprinkle well with melted butter. Cover the casserole and bake at 190°C/375°F/ Gas 5 for 30 minutes. Uncover and bake 10 minutes longer. Serve hot from the casserole. Good with smoked haddock or strongly flavoured small game.

Freezing The dish can be frozen after baking. Thaw until softened, then reheat in a low oven.

with a texture just – but only just – creamier than a crumbly dry curd. Its flavour depends on its fat content – 50 per cent – and on how long it has been cured for. It is sometimes sold semi-cured, for two to three weeks only, when its flavour although pleasant is quite youthful; or it may have been fully cured for one to two months before sale and have exchanged its babyhood 'milky' flavour for a more generous one which has a hint of pears or even of a filled ripe fruit-basket in its roundness. Only refrigerate this cheese if you must, and while it is still uncut and wrapped. Once you have cut it, find a cool place for it, and eat it within a day.

Chaource is one of the fine classic cheeses of France and richly deserves the protection given it by French law in 1970, that any Chaource made in France must carry the stamps of the *Syndicat de Defense du Chaource* and of its *Appellation d'Origine*.

FRANCE
EASTERN FRANCE
Alsace/Haute Savoie/ Jura/Burgundy

MUNSTER AND PETIT MUNSTER

The Munster cheese I am writing about here is *French*. There is a German version called Münster with an umlaut over the u. There are, besides, at least half a dozen versions of Munster (or Muenster, or Mynster) made in different countries, of which the American one has diverged so far from the original that it is almost a different cheese. But the name of French Munster (without umlaut) which is the 'national' cheese of Alsace is confined by a legal *Appellation d'Origine*, if it is farm-made, to cheeses from the milk of Alsatian cattle in the area, made according to the traditional methods and standards of Alsace.

This Munster fermier is a cow's milk, semi-soft cheese with a washed rind the colour of red autumn leaves. It is made from milk gained from the short grass of the Vosges mountain slopes in summer and autumn. In shape it is a flat round varying in size from 13 to 20 cm/5 to 8 inches across and 2.5 to 5 cm/1 to 2 inches thick, and its fat content is 45 to 50 per cent. The smaller cheeses are cured for five weeks in humid cellars, larger cheeses for two or even three months.

There are two schools of thought as to how the cheese originated. The name Munster, like the English word *minster*, is said by one group to be derived from the latin word *monasterium*, because a community of Irish Benedictine monks built an abbey in the Vosges mountains near Colmar, in the seventh century. They had to be self-sufficient, and among other things, make their own cheese. The modern farm-made cheese is said to be produced in accordance with the traditional methods of those old monks.

The second school of thought attributes the cheeses' origin – and its present high reputation – to centuries of farmhouse cheese-making in the same mountain valley. The summer and autumn grazing is reputed the best, producing superb ripened cheeses from November until May. Some have cumin seed added in the making; perhaps because in the twelfth and thirteenth centuries, the area was close to the great land trade route from the Mediterranean bringing eastern goods to northern Europe.

Even today, small farm-made Petit Munsters can be seen drying outside farm doors before being stored in the cellars alongside mature cheeses which donate their flor to the newcomers.

The popularity of farm Munster has ensured that factory and dairy production is now quite widespread throughout the Vosges area. Most of the cheeses are Munsters but there are some sizeable, commercially-made cheeses, first produced on the Lorraine side of the mountains which have been christened Géromés. These cheeses are very like Munsters, but are not identical.

Commercially-made cheeses are born of pasteurised milk and a lactic acid starter, the milk then being warmed before rennet is added. The curd lies in its whey for up to two hours before draining, moulding, turning and (after four days) salting takes place. The final stage is curing – although on its home ground, Munster is eaten less than fully aged.

Although this half-fresh cheese is popular, a mature Munster, especially one made on the farm, is a more splendid cheese, with a supple but not runny paste, an urgent aroma demanding closer inspection, and a ripe tangy flavour.

Eat it with a glass of good Alsatian Gewurztraminer. Alternatively, try it in the dish called Munster Plate (the local ploughman's) which consists of a good slice of fully ripe creamy Munster with raw onion, caraway seeds, crusty new bread and a mighty mug of beer.

TOMME DE SAVOIE

Nine of the twenty-four French *tommes* (semi-hard, pressed cheeses) come from Savoy, two of which are goat's milk cheeses and the rest are from cow's milk. Only the oldest and the best know of them, however, is named Tomme de Savoie; the others have local birthplace names or descriptive ones.

This 'one and only' Tomme de Savoie has always been made from whole cow's milk. It comes mainly from the area of Les Beauges in Haute Savoie, and from valley pastures in the Tarantaise and Mauriennes mountain ranges. In some ways, it has had to compete for attention with neighbours, also made from cow's milk. The great French Gruyères, for instance (page 68)! They are also tommes and of imperial proportions. However, the more modest Tomme de Savoie has held its own in the popularity polls, partly perhaps because of its modesty and lack of pretension.

It is a 20 cm/8 inch low cylinder of pressed, uncooked full cream cow's milk cheese, 6.5 to 12.5 cm/2½ to 5 inches high. It weighs 1.8 kg/4 pounds to 3 kg/6 pounds 10 ounces, depending on its height and has a fat content of 20 to 40 per cent, depending on its making.

It was originally made on farms or in the mountain chalet cheese-houses called fruitières, but the making has now largely been taken over by commercial dairies. The essentials of the traditional method have been retained, in the way that the curd is cut into pea-sized bits, is drained, turned over, pressed and salted. At this point, the naturally grey, already dry rind may be brushed with brandy; and the cheese is then matured slowly, in humid natural caves at 12° to 14°C/53° to 57°F for a month. During this time the humidity encourages the formation of the grey rind. Another month in a warmer curing place brings out red and yellow spots on it, not the sign of any fell damage but the outward and visible sign of a tasty flavour in the supple, pale gold paste with its few 'eyes'.

If you have a client to impress who does not know much about cheese, serve a whole (if possible) Tomme de Savoie. Its grey, seemingly aged appearance will impress him, its friendly flavour will not frighten him, the price will frighten you much less than many other cheeses, and the cheese's excellent keeping quality, wrapped and refrigerated, will give you at least a week to finish up the leftovers.

Add as a drinking companion to the cheese, a local white Seyssel wine, or a light red wine from the Languedoc, say a Minervois; or on a summer's day with a bread-and-cheese picnic, well-chilled Chambéry with a squish of soda.

REBLOCHON

It is quite easy *not* to take this delightful peasant cheese seriously because of the folktale and customs attached to it. That would be a pity because a moment's amusement adds to one's eating pleasure, rather than detracting from it. The story concerning the origin of the cheese's name (and the cheese itself) exists in several versions. The most plausible one suggests that its name comes from *reblocher*, a Savoy patois word meaning roughly 'to milk a second time'. This may mean simply that it is in truth made from rich, raw milk of the 'second time round'; or it may mean that peasant cowmen milked once for their masters and again for themselves; or – third alternative – that they did not milk the cows dry on the days when the lord's steward came to inspect the yield so that the withheld milk and similar amounts daily could be turned into cheese for the herdsmen's own use. All of these were probably true at one time or another, and explain the name which strictly appears to mean the milk dripping from the cow's teats after milking.

Associated with this trio of tales is the idea that the cheese is very ancient, but was kept secret for a very long time because of its illicit origin. The only trouble about this story is that there is an old ritual which contradicts it. As John Arlott tells it, the cheese-makers and their families used to walk down the mountains through the night with loads of cheese on their heads to reach the market-place of their local town at dawn. There, he says, in a long-established ceremony, the peasants of the district still pray that their chalets may be blessed, and make an offering or sacrifice of Reblochons called the *fromage de devotion*.

Well, whether poacher's perks or symbolic sacrifice, Reblochon is an attractive dumpy little mountain cow's milk cheese of the old monastery type. The milk, still warm from the udder, is renneted and left to curdle for half an hour at 36°C/96.8°F. The curd is cut, then drained, cooled awhile, and put into muslin-lined moulds. It is warmed to the same temperature as before, and is pressed lightly for twelve hours before being removed from the moulds and salted. It is turned daily while drying for a week, is washed, and thereafter is cured for four to five weeks at a temperature of 13°C/55.5°F before being offered for sale (or to *le bon Dieu*).

The cheese is best which comes from the high mountain pastures on the Aravis plateau of the Haute Savoie in summer and autumn. It used to be made high above the little town of Grand-Bornand, but now much of it comes from farms, chalets (fruitières) and commercial dairies round the resort of Thones (where the cheeses are mostly cured). Its washed, skin-coloured rind covers a stubby disc of cheese which looks like a large English muffin; it is 15 cm/5 inches in diameter and 2.5 cm/1 inch thick, weighs 450 g/1 pound and has 50 per cent fat. A top-class Reblochon has a soft rich paste, cream-coloured and tasting quite forcibly of 'mountain flowers chewed in tranquility'. Once cut, it should be eaten quickly – which usually presents no problems at all.

Eat it on brown bread, or for luxury, with melon, paw-paw or kiwi fruit. Drink with it a quite robust white wine – Alsatian Gewurztraminer or a white Burgundy from nearer home.

MORBIER

Morbier is a gentle cheese with a serene character. Compared with its fellow-provincials, the Gruyères, this French-Comté cheese is quite small; a pressed, uncooked disc of cow's milk cheese, 30 to 40 cm/12 to 16 inches if made on farms from raw milk, 23 to 25 cm/9 to 10 inches if it is a pasteurised-milk creamery cheese. It weighs 6 to 8 kg/13¼ to 18 pounds in the farm version, 4 to 5 kg/9 to 11 pounds in the creamery one.

The centre of its production is a village of the same name in the district of Sainte-Claude, renowned for briar pipes. But the cheese has a more important connection with smoke because it has a horizontal line of ash right through its centre, narrow but distinctly black, originally the work of mountain herdsmen who were the first makers of the cheese; they made

Left: Pipo Crem'; *back right*: Epoisses; *front*: Rigotte

PIPO 'STRAWS' (Pailles au Bleu)   **Snack**

Makes 50 to 60 'straws'

plain (all-purpose) flour	150 g/5 ounces	1¼ cups
salt	pinch	dash
paprika pepper	¼ teaspoon	¼ teaspoon
unsalted butter	25 g/1 ounce	2 tablespoons
lard	25 g/1 ounce	2 tablespoons
cold water to mix		
Pipo Crem' softened	50 g/2 ounces	⅓ cup

Sift the flour, salt and paprika into a bowl. Cut or rub in the butter and lard, until the mixture is like fine crumbs. Mix to a firm dough with cold water. Roll it out on a floured surface into a rectangle 3 mm/⅛ inch thick. Sprinkle the softened cheese evenly in small dabs over half the dough, leaving 5 mm/¼ inch uncovered round the edge. Fold the uncovered dough over the cheese, matching the pastry edges. Press the edges to seal. Roll out thinly so that the cheese shows faintly through the pastry. The sheet of pastry should be about 225 mm/9 inches wide. Cut the sheet into 3 strips. Then slice each strip into thin fingers 75 mm/3 inches long and 5 to 7 mm/¼ to ⅓ inch wide. Place on a lightly greased and floured baking sheet. Bake at 200°C/400°F/Gas 6 for about 10 minutes. Cool on the sheet. Eat with clear soup or, instead of potatoes, with a creamy fish dish.

it in the chalets in the foothills of the Jura where they tended their Franche-Comté cattle.

It is said that they made it for their own use during the autumn and winter. Having curdled the warm morning milk, they left it to drain, protecting it from marauders (mice and rats) by sprinkling the surface with a layer of ash from the bottom of the pan the milk had been warmed in. The curdled evening milk was then spooned on top of this in its turn, and the curd was left overnight to drain again before being pressed, I understand, in a linen-lined hoop.

The early spring cheeses made during the winter are still reputed the best of the raw-milk cheeses. But most of the cheeses now come from modern dairies in Champagne to the north-west, and the best are said to come from early autumn pastures. They are given an initial pressing without their ash layer. Each is then sliced in half, sprinkled by hand with soot or charcoal dust, and reassembled; the cheese is wrapped in linen and is then pressed for twenty to twenty-four hours, during which time it is warmed to harden its crust.

This, though, is not quite the end of the processing because the cheeses are taken home to their district of origin to be matured for a minimum of two months at 12 to 14°C/53 to 57°F until the holes in the paste develop, thereafter at only 6 to 8°C/42 to 46°F for their slow maturing. They are turned and brushed with brine daily for the first month, then weekly.

The result is a lovely cheese, but not assertive. It has a dry, honey-coloured or greyish rind and a pale ivory paste with a gentle lactic aroma. It feels firm yet supple and it cuts smoothly. Yet its taste is firmer than its mild fragrance suggests, and has its discernable cendré taste in the centre as well. It is excellent as a lunch-time cheese, especially for packed meals because you can eat a sustaining amount of it without it palling – just as its local makers do (and have always done). They eat it for breakfast too, to keep them going throughout the day.

It should properly be eaten with a local Jura wine. Experts in its own home recommend a Chardonnay Côtes de Jura. The red wine is made from the unusual Poulsard and Trousseau grapes.

THE FRENCH GRUYÈRE CHEESES

In the Middle Ages, the border between France and Switzerland was hardly noticeable. Whether you lived in French Haute Savoie or Franche-Comté or in one of the neighbouring Swiss cantons, you battled with the same land of steep mountains and deep river valleys, snow-bound in winter and beset by gales. You spoke the same language when you met, but that might not be often; the narrow mountain tracks were rough, and most farms were isolated. You grew and raised the same foodstuffs, and you made the same basic cheese, with some regional differences.

This cheese, which took its name from the Swiss Gruyère valley not far from Neufchâtel, was developed as a firm, condensed, long-maturing product which could be stored until the farmers who made it could get over the mountains to market. Each cheese used a large quantity of milk; so to make cheese production practical, neighbouring farmers in each small area collected their milk until they could combine it, and then made large communal cheeses, in chalets which they called *fruitières*. The cheeses were their 'fruits'.

The origin of the name, so Pierre Androuet says, is that way back in the past the mountain village produce or 'fruit' was subject to a tax collected by *agents gruyers*.

The two main French 'fruits' derived from the basic Gruyère cheese are Comté, or if you prefer Gruyère de Comté, and Beaufort. For some reason, perhaps because it was officially christened as Gruyère de Comté in July 1952, Comté, is generally treated first, as the senior of the two, when they are discussed together, as they tend to be. (There is also, one should note, an immensely popular French Emmental which is sometimes regarded as a French Gruyère; but it was only imported in the nineteenth century when German-Swiss cheese-makers came into Haute Savoie and Franche-Comté as immigrants, so it has no real common background with the older Gruyère-based cheeses.)

Comté, very obviously, is a Franche-Comté cheese, but is more specifically one made in the region of the Doubs, Jura, Haute-Saône and various communes in the Departments of Ain, Haute-Marne, Vosges and Côte-d'Or. It is made from the milk of Montbeliard and Pie-Rouge cattle. The ripened, skimmed evening milk is mixed with raw morning milk and processed without scalding, which slows the draining and maturation. The cheese ends up with a 45 per cent fat content and with a slightly yielding feel, if you can find a solid piece to press between the large irregular holes sometimes as big as cherries. Its colour is a pale ivory-yellow, and its taste is much fruitier and saltier than you expect on sniffing it.

The cheeses are large thick wheels 65 cm/25½ inches across and just over 10 cm/4 inches thick, weighing 32 kg/77 pounds, so there is not enough space in the fruitières to ripen them while still producing new cheeses. The Comtés blancs (unripened) cheeses are therefore taken to the cellars of affineurs where they are cured for two months at 16°C/60°F, and thereafter at 6 to 8°C/41 to 46°F for the rest of their cool ripening time. In these cellars they develop a tasty rind mould which the affineur encourages by wiping or sprinkling the rinds with a brine-soaked cloth. The rinds therefore remain slightly moist and crumbly as well as patchy with mould. (The warm, curing room temperature helps the holes to develop.)

The farmers, cheese-makers and affineurs have together formed the *Syndicat du Véritable Gruyère de Comté* which has set up strict regulations governing the cheese-making to protect its standards. Its label is a guarantee of quality.

In contrast to Comté, Beaufort (or Gruyère de Beaufort)

has virtually no holes at all. It is made from unusually rich milk yielded by cows pastured high in the alps of Savoy and Dauphiné on the amazingly lush seasonal herbage. It is made in the chalets, or fruitières, of Beaufortin, Maurienne and Haute Tarentaise by farmers using the whole fresh rich milk, and methods passed down from generation to generation, possibly since Gallic cheeses were made here in Roman times.

Their product is a pressed cooked cheese with a fat content of 50 per cent, shaped into a flattened cylinder 61 cm/24 inches in diameter and 11 to 13 cm/4½ to 5 inches high, weighing 40 to 60 kg/88 to 132 pounds. These monarchs are ripened in the co-operative *Cave de Gruyère de Beaufort* for about six months, at a low temperature of 10 to 12°C/50 to 54°F. During the first two months of their curing time, they are salted and brushed every other day, later every third day, to produce their dry, slightly rough natural rind.

Their size and shape are imposing enough, but it is their quality which makes them special. In the nineteenth century, the grand gourmet Brillat-Savarin called Beaufort 'the prince of Gruyères', and modern connoisseurs cannot better that description. The paste cuts smoothly with only a few horizontal cracks. It is supple, resilient, fragrant with a matching fruity, salty flavour. No wonder French gourmets more or less absorb the relatively small supply.

Both Comté and Beaufort are splendid daily table cheeses, although they have achieved their widest popularity for their legion of uses in cooking. Any classically-trained chef has been taught to use one or the other as a standard ingredient in every type of cookery, for the swift, supple melting quality they offer. This has been so for as long as cheese has been used in cooking and there have been chefs to use it.

To drink with the table cheeses? Experts suggest as the ideal the rare *vin jaune* of the area, the golden-yellow wine of the Savagnin grape matured in oak casks for at least six years and having the flavour of walnuts and – yes! Gruyère. But you and I will have to settle for something more modest such as the sharp, pale, local Arbois Rosé or a simple, silky local red wine.

EPOISSES

Cheeses made in vineyard areas where the pasture picks up the scents and herbs which live with vines seem to have a special personality, whether wine is used in their curing or not. Epoisses is such a cheese, named after its home village in Burgundy near Dijon, and made both there and around Auxois to the east.

It is a soft, cow's milk cheese, traditionally made from the whole unpasteurised milk of a breed of cattle called the Pie-Rouge de l'Est (although partly skimmed milk is sometimes used now, and the cattle breed has changed). Its shape is that of a small cake, 10 cm/4 inches across and 5 to 6.5 cm/2 to 2½ inches thick, weighing between 250 and 300 g/9 and 11 ounces. Its washed rind is smooth, almost glossy and is coloured, cloudily, between gold and russet.

It is an old and classic cheese, and has been described for over 200 years as one of the great French cheeses – in the opinion of some gourmets such as Brillat-Savarin the greatest, or 'king of cheeses'. It is made from well-chilled evening milk mixed with fresh, warm morning milk and renneted in the past with herb-flavoured rennet. Traditionally, its initial ripening should take place on rye straw, after the milling and salting, but it is likely to be done on plastic mats these days. While the cheese is still soft, it is moistened with *marc de bourgogne*, the spirit made from grape 'must' or wine lees. It is then cured for three months in humid cellars and is soaked again, either in marc or in marc and lightly salted water. A month later it is ready for sale, its rusty-red rind proclaiming that it is *Affiné au Marc de Bourgogne* (ripened in Burgundy spirit) or is *Confit au vin blanc* (preserved with white Burgundy wine).

Its rind also offers an initial experience of the penetrating, spirituous smell of the cheese – a smell one might dub to be in the gothic style. The texture is deceptive when you cut the cheese, rather like that of a very good Madeira cake. As soon as you taste it, however, its noble, tangy fruity flavour comes through, and the richness of its 45 to 50 per cent butterfat.

Once strictly only a seasonal cheese, best eaten between November and May, Epoisses is now made and eaten all year round – although even commercial production does not keep pace with demand and it is not easy to find outside France. If you do find it, no matter where, pay it the compliment its character deserves and drink with it a red or white Burgundy rather better than you can afford. You will not regret it.

FRANCE
MASSIF CENTRAL/AUVERGNE

CANTAL

The Roman authors, Varro (117–27 BC) and Pliny the Elder (AD 23–79) both commented on the cheeses exported from Gaul to Rome. One in particular mentioned by Pliny (Book XI) seems to have been very like Cantal, although the mahogany-brown Salers cattle whose rich milk now makes the cheese were certainly not around then. Perhaps 500 years later when St Gregory of Tours praised the cheese of the mountain region called Cantal, cattle similar to modern breeds, if smaller, were herded there in summer.

One thing at least we can be sure of: as regional cheeses go, the highly esteemed, semi-hard, pressed Cantal made on the farm is very old.

SALADE D'OEUFS A L'AUVERGNATE **Starter**

Serves 6

cooked small new potatoes	450 g/1 pound	1 pound
Bleu d'Auvergne cheese with rind removed	185 g/6½ ounces	1 cup, heaped
cold hard-boiled eggs	4	4
salt and freshly ground white pepper to taste		
commercial soured cream	150 ml/¼ pint	⅔ cup
lemon juice	2 teaspoons	2 teaspoons

Slice the potatoes lengthways. Place them in a level layer over the base of a 1.4 litre/2½ pint (3¾ pint) decorative shallow salad dish. Slice thinly 100 g/4 ounces of the cheese and spread it over the potatoes. Slice the eggs lengthways, and place them in one layer on top. Season well. Rub the remaining cheese through a sieve into the soured cream, and mix with a spoon until smooth; if necessary, sieve again. Blend in the lemon juice. Spread the cheese cream over the salad, cover and chill.

Do not freeze this dish.

What does seem odd is that the French, having made this excellent, pressed cheese did not repeat the experiment more extensively: Cantal remains one of the few, select, semi-hard French cheeses. Select indeed, for its identity has been protected since 1957 by an *Appellation d'Origine* which limits its production to the department of Cantal and certain communes in the regions of Puy-de-Dome, l'Aveyron, Corrèze, and Haute-Loire!

Cantal fermier, or perhaps one should say *montagnard*, is made by the cowmen on the flowery summer mountain slopes, from the raw, rich milk of their Salers and Aubrac cattle. It is uncooked (but pressed twice), and has a natural rind, brushed and washed with weak brine while curing, when it is made in the traditional way. Traditionally, too, it is made in the form of a drum (a *fourme*) 35 to 45 cm/14 to 18 inches in diameter, 35 to 40 cm/14 to 26 inches high, weighing 35 to 45 kg/77 to 99 pounds, and with a fat content of 45 per cent; very large cheeses indeed considering that they are only matured for three to six months in the humid mountain caves. Possibly the limited space in the *burons* (the mountain chalets where the herdsmen make the cheese) originally dictated their size when lush quantities of rich summer milk were available and must be processed fast. The herdsmen made, and still make, smaller cheeses called Cantalons or Cantalets from the surplus milk, or in autumn when the bulk supply is small but the milk is at its richest.

These smaller cheeses which may only be 15 cm/6 inches across by 25 cm/10 inches high and weigh only 4 kg/9 pounds reflect the herdsmen's pride in their beasts and their milk, their determination to waste none of it. This pride is reflected too in the alternative names they give the big cheeses: Fourme de Cantal is one, Salers or Fourme de Salers is another. These stress the fact that the name Cantal was once more or less synonymous with a *fourme* – the drum shape originally invented by local men. Cantal is still France's only large, tall cylinder cheese.

Other proud titles are Cantal Haute-Montagne, which may only be borne by a Cantal fermier made from the milk of a single herd at an altitude of at least 850 metres/2,800 feet; and Cantal Laguiole (pronounced *lay olé*) a name given only to cheeses made in that little Aveyron town, with milk from the Aubrac pasturage.

The making of Cantal fermier begins when the cows are milked on the pasture. An hour after the whole, raw or slightly ripened milk is renneted, the curd is finely cut, then drained and lightly pressed to drain it more. It is then left to ripen for twenty-four hours – a vital step in the making – before it is broken up, salted, kneaded, put into hoops and pressed again, this time for forty-eight hours, being turned two or three times. Lastly, it is unmoulded, dried off, and taken to the caves or curing cellars, where it ripens for two to three or even sometimes six months – no longer! Very occasionally it may 'blue' but it is more likely to dry out if left too long.

The rind of this enormous drum-shaped cheese (by French standards) is smooth, and changes from yellowish to near-russet and then to grey stippled with gold. The paste resulting from its pressing and low-temperature curing is compact, with a strongish scent of the dairy when first cut, and a nutty flavour distinctly reminiscent of the herb-rich pasture. It is definitely a seasonal cheese, best bought in late summer or autumn at the end of its curing period.

A fine Cantal fermier is not often exported – a Cantal Haute-Montagne almost never – and so, inevitably, a lot of this sought-after cheese is made in creameries in the valleys. The milk is pasteurised, and cheese-making goes on year-round, with a rapid turnover since this 'laitier' cheese is only matured for two months. Compared with the 'fermier' cheese therefore, the scent is definitely 'milky', and the flavour bland under the thin whitish rind. It is still, however, a good everyday cheese. It is also excellent for cooking, akin to the partly cured fermier cheese used by the local cooks in France. Rather cook with it than store it for any length of time, by the way. Any Cantal dries out quite quickly unless wrapped with care and kept cool.

Drink with Cantal a good, fresh wine – a young Bourgueil or Chinon would be fine.

SAINT NECTAIRE

An ancient and a lovely cheese, Saint Nectaire is, to judge by its style, almost certainly of monastic origin. We know that it has been made in the Puy de Dome area of Auvergne since the Middle Ages, and it has all the hallmarks of having been made, then and since, for lords, abbots, princes and above all, for discerning gourmets.

Its name certainly has an aristocratic origin. An eighteenth-century Maréchal of Saint Nectaire (the largest town in the producing area) served it to King Louis XIV, perhaps Europe's greatest royal trencherman, who approved it and put it on the map.

The cheese thus raised from obscurity by royal (rather than saintly) favour is a flattish wheel 20 cm/8 inches in diameter and from 4 to 7.5 cm/1½ to 3 inches thick, weighing about 1.4 kg/3 pounds. It is pressed and uncooked, made from whole cow's milk, which gives it a fat content of 45 per cent. It has a brine-washed, bouquet-coloured rind; and its resilient paste is supple and smooth, pocked occasionally by small holes, aromatic and with a tangy inimitable flavour.

Now made both by farms as in the past and by modern dairies, it comes from milk yielded in the high Mont Dore pastures by the renowned long-horned red Salers and the Ferrandaise cows, called by André Simon the aristocrats of the milkers. On the farms, the flattish discs of cheese are made twice daily, while the milk (used raw) is still warm from the morning and evening meals. The curd is worked by hand, using a curd-breaker, is cut into squares and drained under pressure and by hand-squeezing. It is also moulded and turned by hand, and during the processing is washed in hot water and dry-salted. After being pressed for twenty-four hours, it is dried out at a temperature of 18°C/64.4°F for a few days until a batch of cheeses is assembled. Every week or two during the summer and autumn, the farmer takes or sends his cheeses in packs of six or a dozen to market, for sale to an *affineur* or 'finisher' who will ripen them.

If he is a local man, the affineur will keep the cheeses for at least eight weeks on mats of rye straw, in deep rocky cellars, probably in the old houses of the town of Clermont-Ferrand or a near-by hamlet. There he will nurture them, watching the temperature and humidity of the curing rooms, and washing his charges with brine frequently to make them develop their colourful dry rinds with the greyish-white ground, patched with russet, beige and yellow.

Whether they are made on the farms or in a commercial dairy, the names of the Saint Nectaire cheeses have a degree of legal protection. Within France, only cheeses made in the Mont Dore district between the mountains of Cantal and the district of Sancy qualify to use the name, and to be labelled with it. They have been granted an *Appellation d'Origine* similar to an *Appellation Contrôlée* in the case of a wine. Such an Appellation normally defines the essential features of a product as well as where it must come from to qualify for the (price-enhancing) status, and Saint Nectaire is no exception. Cheeses made on farms from raw milk have an oval green label, bearing the registered number of the farm or maker. Cheeses made in dairies bear a square label indicating, as a rule, that pasteurized milk has been used.

Similar cheeses to Saint Nectaire, but usually of a different quality, are made in the area around the narrow limits of the cheese's 'territory', called Savaron, Murol and Vachard.

Whether the people of the 'territory' praise the name of Saint Nectaire, we do not know, but they certainly should, for the cheese brings both prosperity and a staple for their autumn and winter diet. Moreover, not only is it a splendid cheese to eat as it stands, it is also good for cooking – especially perhaps when another day will see it 'go over the top', as may sometimes happen to a raw-milk cheese which has been cut and not finished up. When this happens, it can be baked on bread or toast slices, or used in a potato dish of the region. Local folks also use it in the traditional so-called soup made quickly after midnight mass on Christmas Eve, by mixing slices of Saint Nectaire into a broth of water, stale bread and salt, with perhaps a few spoonfuls of whipped cream.

Good drinking with this rich, subtly luxurious cheese would be a Chenas or Fleurie, or a decent Côtes du Rhône.

BLEU D'AUVERGNE

The dishes of Auvergne, being based on cabbage and potatoes, are not generally exciting, but the names of fine, strongly-flavoured cheeses resound in the *burons* – the stone huts in which the shepherds or cowherds live in summer, in the mountains. Cantal, Chevrotin d'Ambert, La Rigotte, Saint Nectaire, Gaperon and, of course, Bleu d'Auvergne are names which every cheese-lover knows.

Bleu d'Auvergne is only just over a hundred years old, but it is firmly established. It was born out of the decision of the mountain cheese-makers of Cantal, Aurillac and Vic-sur-Cere to attempt a cow's milk version of the famous, ancient sheep's milk blue cheese, Roquefort. It is not like Roquefort; but it is nonetheless a very good blue cheese which can take its place alongside its older sister cheese, Bleu de Laqueuille, which was the pioneer cheese of its type.

The soft blue Auvergne cheese is made of top-quality milk from the dark chestnut Salers cows. The raw summer and autumn milk of the mountain pastures is adjudged best, but pasteurised milk can be used if necessary. Cooled evening milk is warmed and added to the next morning's fresh milk, and the method followed is the same thereafter as that for Roquefort. The blue mould is formed by sprinkling the white curds with *Penicillium glaucum* as soon as they are put into hoops. They are then drained, being turned often, for three to four days before being transferred to the salting rooms where they are dry salted by hand and pricked with needles to create paths for the mould spores in the curd. The rinds are washed, and as soon as mould is 'spotted', the cheeses are foil-wrapped to finish maturing in damp cellars for about three months. Gone are the days when it was matured for twice that long in the *burons* or farm curing cellars; it is now largely a creamery cheese.

The resulting cheese is a low cylinder 19 cm/$7\frac{1}{2}$ inches in diameter and 10 cm/$3\frac{3}{4}$ inches high. It weighs 2 to 2.5 kg/$4\frac{1}{4}$ to $5\frac{1}{2}$ pounds and has a fat content of 45 to 50 per cent. The paste is fairly firm with well-scattered blue veins, but has a slightly greasy consistency to the eye, as it also has on the palate. The taste is none-the-less pleasantly sharp and clean when the cheese is freshly cut.

As to the keeping quality of a piece you buy cut from the round, it should keep for a week close-wrapped in foil in the refrigerator. However, buy, if possible, a reasonably thick wedge, and give it at least an hour at room temperature before serving it. Cover it with a very slightly damped cloth during this time (it will save you and your guests eating the first part of your meal enveloped in the scent of blue cheese).

There are, I believe, cheese experts who drink a sweet white wine with this type of blue cheese. I can understand their taste, but do not share it. I would pick a Crozes Hermitage, or well-developed Cahors – anyway, a red wine with body and a strong but not forceful personality.

GAPERON/GAPRON

Gaperon (or Gapron) looks like a toy igloo, or more realistically like the product of primitive hand-craft, that is, of curd moulded between the palms and slapped down on shelves to harden, flattening the base. Although this picture is not quite a

St Christopher's Flan   **Dessert**

Serves 4 to 6

Prepared short crust pastry, thawed if frozen	175 g/6 ounces	6 ounces
Filling		
Chevre 'log' (275 g/10 ounce)	1	1
Philadelphia soft cheese (plain)	50 g/2 ounces	$\frac{1}{4}$ cup
caster (superfine) sugar	50 g/2 ounces	$\frac{1}{4}$ cup (scant)
small eggs	2	2
brandy	1 tablespoon	1 tablespoon
ground nutmeg for sprinkling		

Roll out the pastry and use it to line a shallow 200 mm/7 inch flan ring standing on a baking tray. 'Rest' it for 20 to 30 minutes. Bake it 'blind' at 200°C/400°F/Gas 6 for about 12 minutes until just firm.

To make the filling, pare or scrape any surface rind off the chevre cheese. Break it up with a fork. In a food processor, or using an electric beater and a bowl, beat together both cheeses, the sugar and the eggs. Beat in the brandy. Spoon the mixture into the flan case. Bake the flan at 190°C/375°F/Gas 5 for 20 to 30 minutes until just set in the centre. Sprinkle with nutmeg before serving.

Do not freeze this flan.

Note: the beaten filling mixture makes a delicious chilled dessert for 2 to 3 people, without being baked. Serve it with crisp light almond biscuits.

fair one, there are elements of truth in it. The cheese has always been a semi-skimmed milk or buttermilk product like many primitive early cheeses, and it is sold tied with yellow ribbons in the same way as cheeses and other foods were once offered as peasant wedding gifts or harvest symbols.

It has been made on farms in the uplands and plains of the Haute Auvergne for nearly two hundred years, although now the lush plainland pasture has largely been taken over by small dairy factories which use both the good milk and the fresh garlic from the fields. The traditional methods are still used. Semi-skimmed milk or buttermilk or a mixture is acidified with garlic. When the curds have formed, they are mixed with crushed fresh garlic in perforated bowl-shaped moulds, are seasoned by hand, pressed, and drained through coarse-weave cloth. While 'setting' they are moistened from time to time with buttermilk. Then they are unmoulded, and are matured on shelves, sometimes on rye straw, for one to two months.

The result is a small, dome-shaped cheese 9 cm/$3\frac{1}{4}$ inches across the base, and 6 to 8 cm/$2\frac{1}{2}$ to $3\frac{1}{4}$ inches high, with a whitish natural rind which should not yet be sticky or grey. An over-aged Gaperon looks – and also smells – fearsome. But the paste of a pleasantly well dried cheese six to eight weeks old smells quite mild, although it already has a strong dry taste, partly of fermented, skimmed curd, partly of garlic. Many people prefer it younger, at only three to four weeks old, when it is still quite moist and fresh.

Gaperon is not a cheese to which pundits pay much attention. Some cheese writers have ignored it entirely, perhaps because in the past it was often sold too late and tasted harsh, or perhaps because it is, for genteel palates, an acquired taste. It is one which slimmers will do well to acquire because it provides maximum flavour for its low fat content of 35 per cent. Vegetarians may welcome it too.

Folklorists and food historians may also find it interesting because even modern technology has not tampered with it overmuch. Here you can taste cheese very similar to the ones which ploughman and dairymaid ate themselves in the seventeenth, and very likely in the fourteenth century – or even earlier because buttermilk was one of the Saxon shepherd's 'perks' when he made butter and cheese for his lord's table. The cheese's name suggests this possibility because *gap*, *gape*, is an old local word for buttermilk.

The identifying ribbons remind one of a pleasant popular folk-tale concerning the cheese. In the past, it is said, the farmers used to cure their Gaperons by hanging them from the kitchen rafters by the window. The number of cheeses was supposed to indicate the farmer's wealth and give an idea of the dowry he would offer with his daughter. What the story does *not* tell is whether some of the cheeses were kept for a second milking season to increase the offer if the maiden remained unwed.

One does not know of course whether the farmer celebrated the selection of the lucky suitor by sharing his cheeses at a festive meal with his new son-in-law-to-be. If so, they may well have drunk buttermilk with it (not the cultured, thick kind we know), or a local wine. But to my mind, a lively Spanish red will drink well with it – assuming that you are eating it when it's no more than eight weeks old, and have kept it well wrapped in foil in a cool place. Any mouldy rind should have been cut off, not because it betokens decay, but because it will cross-flavour everything else in the fridge or larder.

GOAT'S MILK CHEESES
Ste Maure, Chabichou, Crottin de Chavignol, etc

In times long past, sheep and goats were milked as much as cattle throughout Europe and the Middle East. In mountainous and stony areas, and wherever pasture is poor or the land is dry, they still are. All round the Mediterranean, in Greece, the southern Balkans, parts of Italy, Spain and southern France, sheep's, goat's and sometimes buffalo's milk cheeses are made in abundance. Goat's milk cheeses of many varieties are made in particular, simply because any rural family which can afford it keeps a goat, and makes soft, often pickled, cheeses.

Further north, for instance roughly following the course of the River Loire, in the uplands of the Massif Central, the same pattern of domestic goat-keeping occurs.

By tradition and practice, therefore, goat's cheeses are generally small-sized; cheeses which can be hung in a muslin bag to drain or cured on shelves in a farmhouse cellar. They also stay soft even if pressed, compared with sheep's and especially cow's milk cheeses, because the chemical composition of the milk is different; goat's milk has smaller, more mobile fat globules. Being small and lightweight, goat cheeses are easier to make and handle than larger, heavier and harder cheeses, and are easier to transport. They have proliferated and so, in France especially, there are a great many different goat's cheeses which may have similar names or characteristics. (France, in fact, as Evan Jones has pointed out in *The Book of Cheese* now makes two-thirds of the world's goat cheeses.)

For this reason, it has seemed sensible to consider these French goat cheeses as a group, and to cluster a few typical ones in this section as examples.

The name of Sainte-Maure is sometimes thought of almost synonymously with goat's milk cheese in France. It is a soft log with a straw running lengthways through it to prevent it breaking, and with a natural bloomy rind. It was originally made only on the Sainte-Maure plateau in and around the town of that name in Touraine, but it is now also made in Anjou, Charentes and Poitou. Because its name is not protected by an Appellation d'Origine, many imitations are also made elsewhere which ought to be called just *chèvre* (the French word for goat) or *chèvre pur* (made with goat's milk alone).

Sainte-Maure fermier is, as its name implies, farm-made, 15 cm/6 inches long and 3.5 cm/1½ inches in diameter. It is made from fresh whole milk. When made and salted, the cheeses are sprayed with *Penicillium candidum* if they are to be eaten 'fresh', that is after maturing for four weeks or just long enough to develop a white downy surface. They then taste pleasantly mild. If a stronger flavour is wanted, they are sprayed with *Penicillium glaucum* and are kept for two months, when they will have a greyish rind and a distinctly 'goaty' flavour. They have a 45 per cent fat content and a typical, very white paste.

Sainte-Maure laitier is the dairy-made version; it is the same size and shape as the 'fermier' cheese and is matured in the same ways, but it is usually packaged in a brand-name wrapper. There is also a Sainte-Maure cendré rolled in wood ash. The town of Sainte-Maure is a main centre of goat cheese-making, processing 30,000 hectolitres of goat's milk a year. You can buy there any type of goat's milk cheese, from the mildest to the most 'goaty', and any shape – not only 'logs', but the equally classic truncated pyramids and cones, little drums and 'buttons'. However, well-known goat's milk cheeses are made elsewhere too, notably south of Touraine, in Poitou. Of these Chabichou is the most celebrated, and the oldest.

Chabichou is just one of a number of similar names (such as Cabichou, Chabi, Cabecou) which all mean 'little goat' in the old Poitou dialect and may even go back to the eighth-century Saracen invaders' word for goat, *chebli*. It is certainly a medieval cheese. Until quite recent times it was a farmhouse cheese only, but now it is widely made in dairies as well. It is usually sold as a truncated (topless) cone weighing about 100 g/3½ ounces. It is about 6 cm/2½ inches across the base, 5 cm/2 inches across the top and 6 cm/2½ inches high. It is made from lightly pressed curds, drained through muslin into a sandstone or wooden colander, then salted and dried on straw or leaves for two to four weeks, before (sometimes) being stored in wicker baskets called 'coffins' (a medieval word for a raised pie crust). The farmhouse version has a greyish rind flecked with red but the dairy type is a soft powdery white. Both types have 45 per cent fat, and have the 'solid snow' look typical of goat's cheese when cut; and both, too, have a quite strong smell and flavour, unmistakably of goat. Once only a seasonal summer and autumn cheese, the laitier version is now made year-round from frozen milk.

From nearer the source of the Loire comes another small, fairly typical goat's milk cheese called Crottin de Chavignol. Chavignol is a village of the Sancerre vineyard, and its little cheese was originally made as a snack or dessert for the grape harvesters. It is a small, flattened ball of cheese only 4 cm/1½ inches in diameter, 3 cm/1¼ inches thick and weighing 70 g/

about 2½ ounces. It is dried in maturing and its rind darkens to reddish brown or dark grey giving point to the farmer's slang name of *crottin* ie horse dung. Its flavour and texture also deepen and harden, so that although it is 'officially' a soft cheese and has a 45 per cent fat content, it may when mature be quite fierce to taste and brittle to bite on.

Crottin de Chavignol is an Appellation contrôlée cheese, which means that only a traditional farmhouse-made, dried cheese from the village of Chavignol or nearby can legally bear the name. Unfortunately, because demand in recent years has outstripped supply, genuine Crottins have become hard to find, and inferior quality or imitation ones are all too commonly foisted on unwary purchasers.

A real Crottin can be eaten mild, at two weeks old, 'drunken' after some weeks' soaking in white wine, or when fully mature at three months. When farmhouse-made, ripened and dried in a cool cellar, it is strong but not harsh, easy to eat at a sitting and well worth it. Never let it hang about, in the refrigerator or afterwards.

Goat's cheeses like the ones mentioned here take quite kindly in their younger days to local white wines (as they are meant to do); a Sancerre or Pouilly Fumé, for instance. Alternatively, a Chinon or Bourgueil red wine from Touraine can be very pleasant. Pamela Vandyke Price has called these wines fragrant, supple and capable of true finesse; luckily they are also capable of standing up squarely to a forceful Sainte-Maure or Crottin.

These are just three of a whole crowd of goat cheeses which will give you much pleasure once you have acquired the taste for them (if you have not done so already). For a few others, see Banon (page 116), Chevret, Chevrotin (page 121), Le Chevrot (page 132) and Rigotte (page 136).

ROQUEFORT

It is difficult to write about Roquefort because it seems that everything has already been said, every note of praise has been sung. It has been called the world's greatest cheese, or at least the greatest sheep's cheese – or its finest blue cheese if you are a blue cheese addict.

The bare facts about this paragon of cheeses are that it is a semi-hard 'blued' cylinder of whole, unpasteurised sheep's milk, 18 cm/7 inches in diameter and 10 cm/4 inches high. It weighs 2.7 kg/5½ pounds and its quite high fat content (considering the bare terrain which it traditionally comes from) is between 50 and 60 per cent. Its name comes from the village of Roquefort-sur-Soulzon, stuck like a transfer to the sheer side of a collapsed mountain in the area called Aveyron.

Roquefort is certainly the world's oldest *named* blue cheese of international repute. It must be just about as old as Christianity because it was already well known when Pliny the Elder wrote about it in his encyclopedic *Naturalis Historia*, perhaps in AD 70 when he was in France. Yet although its reputation had reached Italy then, we have no record that the

VOYAGERS' SALAD

Serves 4

cut garlic clove	$\frac{1}{2}$	$\frac{1}{2}$
prepared small carrots	225 g/8 ounces	$\frac{1}{2}$ pound
celery sticks with leaves	100 g/4 ounces	$\frac{1}{4}$ pound
Doux de Montagne without rind	50 g/2 ounces	$\frac{1}{4}$ cup
fresh thyme leaves	2 teaspoons	2 teaspoons
grinding of black pepper		
finely chopped walnuts	$1\frac{1}{2}$ tablespoons	$1\frac{1}{2}$ tablespoons
French dressing	1 tablespoon	1 tablespoon
salt to taste if needed		

This good-tempered 'portable' salad is basically just the *carottes rapees* offered in delicatessen all over France. Pilgrims, merchants and other travellers have carried such salads in their packs for centuries.

Rub the cut clove of garlic round the inside of a salad bowl or other container. Grate the carrots and celery into a bowl; use a 4 mm grating disc if doing it in a food processor. Shred the cheese on the coarse holes of a hand grater. Mix these ingredients with a fork. Then mix in the remaining ingredients in the order given.

Good as a side salad with curries, ham and other spiced pork meats or with salt beef.

Does not like being frozen.

cheese itself did so in ancient or in medieval times. It was an excellent traveller; it was carried almost the length of France at least twice a year between AD 800 and 814 from Aveyron to the Emperor Charlemagne's palace at Aix-La-Chapelle. But until much later there probably was not enough of it to export. The pasture on the *causses* – the French name for the arid scrubland of its area – is still so poor that only a remarkably hardy breed of sheep can survive on it. In days when only local milk was used, Roquefort was a rarity as well as a delight.

A foodstuff fostered by monarchs is itself a rare phenomenon. Roquefort was so fostered by royal charter when, in April 1411, Charles VI gave the villagers of Roquefort-sur-Soulzon a monopoly to ripen their cheeses in the caves which pitted the mountain of Combalou as they had done 'since time immemorial'. Six later kings renewed the charter, and then a law of July 1925 specified that the cheese was to be made only of pure, whole sheep's milk, and must be ripened strictly according to local usage in the natural caves under Combalou (which amounted to an award of an Appellation contrôlée). Finally in 1951, Roquefort was one of only four cheeses given complete international protection by the Stresa Convention. The crucial feature of that protection is that a cheese can only be labelled and named Roquefort if it is ripened in the Combalou caves.

However, no one has said anything about the milk!

The current milk supply from the local Lucaune flocks makes nowhere near enough cheese to meet the demand from the mass and the gourmet market. So the flocks have been increased and have spread over the surrounding similar terrain, and further away still to the Basses-Pyrénées and the Gironde. Another milk source has also been found in Corsica where the sheep, pasture and climate are similar to the French. The rules which govern the cheese-making have been bent slightly to allow a training school to be set up so that local shepherds can be taught the 'Roquefort Method'. They have been bent still more, so that today the flocks are inoculated, and milked mechanically, and then the cheeses are made locally under conditions of strict hygiene by mechanised methods. Every aspect of the operation is streamlined to produce a perfect finished product.

It is an almost incredible exercise in modernisation without loss of quality, demonstrating in every detail a respect for the living material that the cheese-makers are handling.

But still the cheeses themselves, whether from the Pyrénées, from Corsica or from the foot of the mountain, all come ten to twelve days after their making, to be ripened in the caves called *cabines* under Combalou.

The milking is done morning and evening during the lambing season. The morning and evening milk are mixed and curdled with lamb's rennet at 32.5°C/90°F; the curd is broken, and inseminated with the blueing agent, *Penicillium roqueforti*, before being heavily salted, hooped and drained, and sent off to Combalou for cleaning up, pricking and curing.

What is the magic of Combalou that makes Roquefort a unique tasting experience? Sheep's milk is more 'flavoured' than cow's, and contains more fat, casein, milk sugar and mineral salts; but there are other 'blued' sheep's milk cheeses which do not have the same effect on the taste-buds as Roquefort. So the secret lies somewhere in the caves.

It lies, in fact, very largely in the nature of the caves. Millennia ago, water seeping down through the friable limestone of Combalou may have washed away some of the mountain's foundations and it collapsed into a fissured heap of broken blocks, lying tilted over a huge, deeply subterranean lake. The fissures (called *fleurines*) in the fractured rock are paths for downward and horizontal air currents at a more or less constant, very cool temperature, and a very high degree of humidity from the lake water. This unique combination of damp and flowing air lets the massed rows of cheeses, rank upon rank, cure very slowly while letting the *penicillium* take its full flavour hold on the snowy, sheep-white paste.

Half the cheese is cured in the eleven storeys or levels of the oldest curing 'cellar' inside the mountain, the *Cave de la Rue*. Eight thousand tons a year out of the total of sixteen thousand! It is an enormously impressive experience to join one of the many daily tours to perambulate the caves (all the fourteen accredited producers run them). Even first-class photographs cannot bring home to one what the massed cheeses look like, still less what they taste like 'on the spot' after they have completed their four to six months' *affinage*.

Remember, if you buy Roquefort from the cylinder or in a pre-packaged wedge, that it hates the real cold. Do not put it anywhere colder than the vegetable drawer of the refrigerator, and even there keep it in a box with a moisture-proof lid. Take it out at least three-quarters of an hour before you will use it. Serve it with any wine except a sweet one – even a dry champagne if you like, although a noble red is the preferred choice of most gourmets: Clos Vougeot, Pape Clement, Chambertin. There is no more to be said.

FRANCE
THE SOUTH – PYRÉNÉES AND PROVENCE

PYRÉNÉES

Strictly speaking, Pyrénées is a word which means nothing. It is neither the name of a particular cheese, nor a general term for all cheeses of the French side of the Franco-Spanish mountain border. However it does, rather vaguely, stand for two different groups of these mountain cheeses – or for an individual cheese belonging to one of them if you don't know its local name. So it is a convenient name to use here, to discuss three or four cheeses of the area, none of them very notable, but all pleasantly edible and useful for the traveller to know about.

The first small group of cheeses consists of traditional sheep's milk cheeses made while the flocks are on summer pasture. A typical one is Laruns, a large pressed, semi-cooked round 'loaf' with a straw-yellow rind and a tender, mildly nutty flavour at two months old. Like the other classic Pyrenean ewe's milk cheeses, Ardi-Gasna and Esbareich, it is seldom found outside its own mountain areas.

Cheeses of the second group are, however, sometimes on sale in UK and US delicatessen. They are creamery-made, cow's milk cheeses with a firm, springy, pale yellow paste containing small 'teardrop' holes, and with a flavour which is usually quite tangy. Often, too, the cheeses have a black wax (allegedly edible) or hard brown (definitely inedible) rind.

An intriguing feature of these cheeses is that, although their personalities are seldom aristocratically distinguished or even markedly different, their names give them a certain cachet. Take, for instance, Roey de Quercy; *Roey* is Old French for king or 'the first' (Quercy is the name of the province where the cheese is made – and where, by the way, the robust Cahors wines come from). Or consider Prince de Claverolles, a modern and similar cheese. What about Primat des Gaulles, the 'Primate of the People', and (like the Roey) a *tomme noir*. Then, to pick one more out of the hat, there is the less aristocratic but more winsome Doux de Montagne – Sweetness of the Mountain – which only belies its claim to gentleness by having a bronze, armour-plate of rind.

These are all cow's milk cheeses now, although once, no doubt, made from ewe's and goat's milk; and they are the most formal, easily sold cheeses of the border country. There are other, smaller, farm cheeses made and sold for local eating, such as Bethmale and Castillon; but these tommes are the ones to buy for keepability, packed meals and sensible snacks.

Roey de Quercy is fairly typical. You may find it sold under its own name, but it is more likely to have lost it with the first wedge cut and to be labelled simply with its brand name or as Pyrénées. When whole, it is a solid grindstone shape, 23 cm/9 inches in diameter and 11 cm/4½ inches high. It weighs about 4.5 kg/10 pounds and has a fat content of 45 per cent. Its resilient, heated, semi-hard paste is lightly pocked with tiny holes, but it cuts smoothly, and has a distinct sharpness under its buttery fluency. It is ripened for fifteen days, then finishes maturing in its black wax jacket on its way to the sales counter. It keeps excellently, whole or in a wedge or slab, if well wrapped and refrigerated; you may be able to keep it for as much as three weeks.

Doux de Montagne, by contrast, is shaped like a large bun or a cottage loaf without its top-knot. Its bronzed rind, reminding one of sun-tanned beach bodies, is slightly wrinkled on top. Like the Roey, it is a semi-hard cheese, but its slightly flaky paste is definitely firmer. It weighs 3.3 kg/7 pounds, and its 50 per cent butterfat gets 'through' to your palate only after you have experienced its slightly fruity first taste. Ripened in traditional style, it, too, keeps well in its airtight jacket.

Either of these cheeses or their cousins will give you pleasant if not exciting eating through the day. They are not really after-dinner cheeses. Cider or perry, or perhaps a Spanish or Portuguese white wine could be a practical choice depending on where you are and what you are eating (besides cheese, of course!).

SWITZERLAND

EMMENTAL SWITZERLAND

Every dairying country in Europe makes and cherishes some fine cheeses; but only in Switzerland does cheese provide the two best-known and most loved national dishes. In 1955, André Simon wrote that the Swiss then made and exported more cheese per head of population than all other peoples, and it would be hard to gainsay that today. The only difference, one would guess, is that now more people all round the globe have taken to copying what they call 'Swiss'.

They mean Emmental.

This is primarily because Emmental is the most dramatic Swiss cheese to look at. It is a huge flattish wheel of tan-coloured cheese, 81 to 86 cm/32 to 34 inches in diameter and 23 cm/9 inches thick at its edges. (It rises slightly in the centre, and its sides bulge slightly too.) Its weight, if you could ever lift it, is 80 to 99 kg/176 to 220 pounds. Its hard, smooth brushed rind is stamped all over with the word Switzerland in red if you meet it off its home ground. On the inside, its resilient, smooth, ivory-yellow paste with its 45–47 per cent fat content is pitted with irregularly scattered holes, ranging in size from a cherry-stone to a walnut or even larger. It is made from raw or pasteurised cow's milk and because each huge cheese uses 1000 litres/220 gallons or more, every step of the processing is very strictly controlled to prevent errors.

This care begins with the flowery pasture and sturdy cows attractively pictured in so much Swiss so-called folk art. It continues through the renneting, curdling and setting of the curd, its cutting and draining, and then its heating ('cooking') to firm and condense the curd. The solid curd is then drained in a big cheese-cloth, and lowered into a mould. The young cheese is drained again under pressure and is turned often for several hours before being dry and wet salted.

MOUNTAIN LAMB CASSEROLE   **Main dish**

Serves 4 to 6

lamb fillet without bone	450 to 700 g/1 to 1½ pounds	1 to 1½ pounds
flour for dusting	50 g/2 ounces	½ cup
salt and pepper to taste		
finely chopped (minced) onions	2	2
potatoes, about 150 g/5 ounces each	2	2
large red bell pepper	1	1
large courgette (zucchini)	1	1
medium-sized tomatoes	2	2
olive oil	1½ tablespoons	1½ tablespoons
haricot (navy) beans, cooked or canned	125 g/4½ ounces (one 213 g/7½ ounce can, drained)	¾ cup
black pepper to taste		
rosé wine	75 ml/3 fl oz	⅓ cup
Banon cheese, mashed with a fork	100 g/4 ounces	¼ pound
commercial sour cream	150 ml/¼ pint	⅔ cup
dried oregano for sprinkling		

Cut the meat into 5 cm/2 inch pieces. Season the flour with salt and pepper. Toss the meat with the flour in a paper bag, to coat the pieces. Also season the minced onions. Peel the potatoes, and de-seed the pepper; then slice the potatoes, pepper, courgette, and tomatoes thinly. Heat the oil in a casserole which will stand direct heat. Sauté the meat until lightly browned all over. Remove the meat with a slotted spoon; then sauté the onions in the remaining fat until soft and golden. Add the potatoes to the onions, and sauté for 2 minutes. Then add the meat pieces and the cooked beans. Season well. Cover with the pepper and courgette slices, then top with the tomato slices. Pour in the wine. Let it bubble up for 1 minute, then remove the casserole from the heat.

Blend the mashed cheese with the sour cream until smooth. Spread the mixture over the dish, and sprinkle with oregano. Cover the casserole and bake at 190°C/375°F/Gas 5 for 40 minutes or until the meat is tender when pierced with a skewer. Serve hot.

Freezing Cool, then fast-freeze before baking. Thaw in refrigerator for 6 hours, then bake as above for 50 minutes to 1 hour.

The last stage is curing in a warm cellar where gas bubbles are encouraged to form in the paste, to create the characteristic holes. The warmth also encourages the slow development of the mild but fruity aroma and flavour over a period of six to ten months – after which the glorious cheese will keep (if uncut) for a further period of at least a year in a cool place.

The holes, although they give Emmental an obvious identity (together with the red-stamped rind) are not an unmixed blessing for the cheese. A minor hazard is that elderly and fumbling-fingered consumers find the 'holey' cheese hard to cut and to grate. Much, *much* more serious though is that the holes make faking all too easy. Many in-different or rubbery cheeses are passed off as Emmental or, more likely, as 'Swiss'. Indeed 'Swiss' has become almost a label for any cheese with holes in it – even if the nearest it has got to a Swiss mountain is a fusing tower in a cheese factory.

This is a great shame because it has taken the meticulous Swiss dairymen centuries to perfect the grand hard cheeses, first in their original home, the valley of the Emme in central Switzerland, and then increasingly in other parts of the country as its fame spread.

At first the cheeses, made in the mountains, were quite small and hardly holey at all, but from the sixteenth century larger and larger cheeses were made until they attained their present cartwheel size. There is a pleasant tale that because the cost of highways was met by tolls collected along the way, cheese-makers or factors might have to pay a considerable sum before they got a cartload of cheeses to market; but the tolls were payable on the number of cheeses carried, not their weight, and so the shrewd, experienced fellows developed larger and larger cheeses to reduce their overheads. The larger a cheese was, the longer it took to cure, and the larger the holes which might develop in it. Also, and this was important for exported cheeses, the longer it would keep after curing. It was also hard enough to travel without getting damaged.

Because the Emmental cheeses had these virtues, travel by highway led to transport by barge, and in time to travel by rail and by ship – and its world-wide fame was assured.

Together with Swiss Gruyère, Emmental achieved nineteenth century fame as a cooking cheese – and rightly, both in Europe and, notably, in the United States. Take any American cook-book and count how many recipes in it use 'Swiss' cheese – and at first it really *was* Swiss cheese. Tourism added to the repertoire, as more and more travellers came to know the pleasures of a genuine Swiss fondue – which can only be properly made and enjoyed with genuine Swiss Emmental and Gruyère as its main ingredients.

With a Swiss fondue, drink a glass of the Swiss white wine with which the fondue was made (or for non-drinkers black tea is suitable). With Emmental as a table cheese, and even as a cheese sauce over mildly flavoured foods, a good, dry white wine is also best, as crisp and shining as you can get it, even perhaps with a hint of a sparkle.

GRUYÈRE SWITZERLAND

First made in the dairying canton of Fribourg, Gruyère is the grand old lady of Swiss cheeses, and one of Europe's greatest. It goes back at least to the early twelfth century when the first Count of Gruyère, to help maintain the Abbey of Rougemont which he had founded, levied a church tax to be paid partly in cheese from the region. Probably the cheese has changed somewhat since then, but not as markedly as its great companion cheese, Emmental; and almost certainly it was always renowned for the same qualities which make it great today. It is a wonderful cooking cheese and a splendid traveller; long-keeping, satisfying and good for every use, at any time. The Swiss call it 'the cheese which never gets tired'.

It is made from the whole milk of the black and white Fribourg cattle, cooked and pressed into a 61 cm/2 foot wheel about 10 cm/4 inches thick; the wheel weighs 30 to 40 kg/66 to 88 pounds, about half that of Emmental. Other differences occur in the cooling and curing.

The making of Gruyère begins in much the same way as Emmental: after the milk has been heated to 34°C/93°F and has had starter and rennet added, the curd is cut, drained and reduced to pea-sized fragments. It is then heated to 57°C/135°F before being moulded, followed by a slow cooling period and pressing during which the gas bubbles formed by rapid fermentation during heating more or less disappear. Finally the cheeses are cured in relatively cool, humid rooms which discourage gas fermentation even more. The rind is kept moist, giving the cheese a tanned appearance. As for the paste, it develops in the first five months, a gentle flavour and aroma, and a soft cutting quality – and it is sometimes sold at this stage. But for its true great strength without harshness, it requires the full ten to twelve months' maturing after which it is indeed probably the world's finest 'cooked' cheese and the most loved by both genders and all ages.

It is so much beloved that it has been imitated world-wide although true Swiss Gruyère is unique in the subtle flavour it dispenses and in the quality of its paste in cooking. It can never be mistaken, even for Emmental, because of its harder consistency, its generally higher fat content of about 48 per cent, and its easier grating and cutting quality due to its texture and few small holes. And it can never be mistaken for imitation Gruyère either, even if you buy a rindless piece which provides no proof of whether it is the genuine article.

True Swiss Gruyère came into its own in the sixteenth century as a great table cheese. We know that it was exported then to France and Italy by road and by water. Now, it is best eaten as it probably was in those days, cut in thin slivers from a wedge or piece, and piled on crusty wholegrain or mixed grain bread. A glass of crisp white or light red wine go with it equally well.

In the nineteenth century, it also became renowned as the known world's greatest cooking cheese. From the time of the English Prince Regent and throughout the Victorian age,

Swiss and French chefs who had become much-travelled émigrés in the French Revolution, served the crowned heads of Europe (one was Queen Victoria's Swiss chef Gabriel Tschumi). They also created the lavish decorative cuisines of the new high-class restaurants and the Englishmen's clubs. In those cuisines, the only possible cheese for soufflés and sauces and the after-dinner savouries of the English table was Swiss Gruyère. Any high-class Victorian cook-book, say by Soyer, Francatelli, Mrs de Salis or Mrs Marshall, reveals the fact.

Among its elaborate dishes, the nineteenth century saw the arrival of the simple Swiss fondue on the tables of the international *haute monde* after Brillat-Savarin praised it in 1824. It is indeed a delightful dish but it *must*, because of the hazards of melting cheese in quantity, be made only with the best ingredients, that is with genuine Swiss Emmental and Gruyère.

Cheese fondue (as originally created) is the best known of the two national cheese dishes of Switzerland. The other is raclette, originally very much a thing of shreds and patches, a peasant's dish and none the worse for that. It is perhaps the best addition you can have to a winter Guy Fawkes party-bubbling melted cheese over baby boiled potatoes.

The diversity of dishes made with true Swiss Gruyère defeats any attempt to recommend a particular wine or wines to accompany them. White wines of character and quality are generally called for, but light reds or rosés also have their place with, for instance, veal. The rest of the menu must dictate. Swiss Gruyère as a table cheese is easier to match with a good companion wine. A Swiss Fendant from the canton of Valais is excellent with it. But if that is not possible, try to get a dry English white wine with some flavour of fruit, such as a Hambleden or Frogmore, or even a Portuguese white if you can find one with some character.

SBRINZ SWITZERLAND

Compared with Emmental and Gruyère which are so well known and openly referred to as 'Swiss', Sbrinz has managed to remain almost anonymous in the English-speaking world; yet it has as strong a personality as either of the other two cow's milk 'cooked' cheeses, if not stronger. It is surprising in a way that it has not become called the Swiss Parmesan, because it shares several characteristics with the Italian cheese: notably for grating as a topping or a sauce flavouring.

It is less surprising to hear that Sbrinz was being exported regularly to Italy by mule-train in the fifteenth century through the St Gothard Pass – perhaps much earlier because it is alleged that the *Caseus helveticus* praised by Roman writers was the forerunner of Sbrinz. But whether it was, in fact, so must remain conjecture.

However, we do know that Sbrinz has been made, since very early times, in the high central cantons of Switzerland called Uri, Unterwalden and Schwyz (where centuries later the first murmurings of European republicanism were heard).

We know, too, that the making method of this mountain-pasture cheese is much like that of Gruyère up to a point – a significant point which makes Sbrinz very special among Swiss cheeses.

Like Emmental and Gruyère, Sbrinz curd is cut into very fine fragments, then heated before being moulded and pressed. It is heated to an even higher temperature than Gruyère, however; and it is pressed into slightly thicker, weightier wheels, with the same 61 cm/2 foot diameter, but a thickness of 13 cm/5½ inches, and weighing 36.2 kg/80 pounds to 59 kg/132 pounds (40 per cent fat).

What is more remarkable, in fact almost unique in cheese-making, is that Sbrinz may be cured for up to three years. If it had not become a time-honoured process long ago and demonstrated the rare properties it gives the cheese, it would never have been attempted, so uneconomic would it seem.

The process begins after the wheels of cheese have been pressed, turned and brined. The young Sbrinz is then given a sauna in a 'sweating room' with a temperature of 20°C/68°F, where it sweats out fat and water, both being regularly wiped off. It is also well brushed and oiled. After four months, it is set on end in a rack, where air can move round it freely, and is left to its long maturing. At the end, it is in effect a grana cheese, as dense as a well-aged Parmesan.

Not every Sbrinz is given the full curing time, but they are always left for long enough to let the flavour develop fully in the dense, firm yellow paste. A piece of a great wheel may then be broken up and eaten as a table cheese; crumbled, on freshly buttered bread, or sliced very thinly with a slicer. It is then so tender that it seems to melt in the mouth; and in some parts of Switzerland one can buy the thin slices in delicatessen under the name of Hobelkäse. It may also be used for cooking, as its long maturing makes it cook smoothly without going ropey.

The inspection and sale of Sbrinz cheeses is as strictly controlled as that of Emmental and Gruyère. It pays off because a good deal of the exported Sbrinz goes to Italy.

If you get the chance to buy Sbrinz in a cuttable piece, as it is sold in Switzerland, treat it with the respect it deserves, like Gruyère or Parmesan. Depending on how you use it, accompany it with a high-quality red or white Italian wine.

ITALY

PARMESAN

Italy is second only to France as a cheese producer, and her cheese-making industry is probably older. Her main cheese-

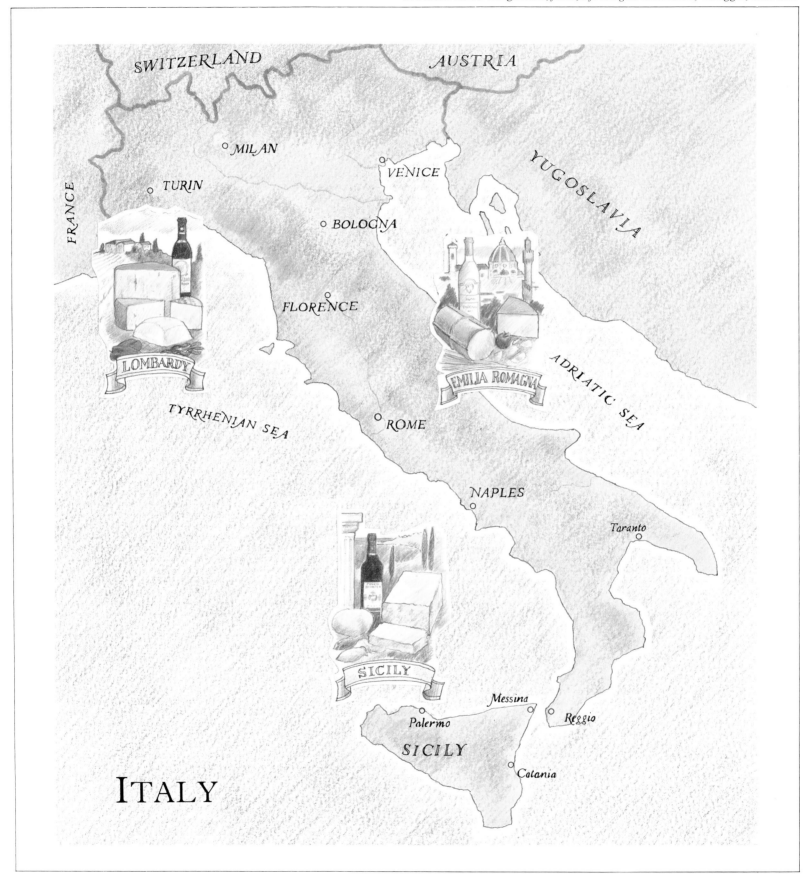

SWITZERLAND

AUSTRIA

YUGOSLAVIA

FRANCE

○ MILAN

○ TURIN

VENICE

○ BOLOGNA

LOMBARDY

FLORENCE

EMILIA ROMAGNA

ADRIATIC SEA

TYRRHENIAN SEA

○ ROME

NAPLES
○

Taranto
○

SICILY

Messina
○

Palermo
○

Reggio
○

SICILY

Catania
○

ITALY

making centre is in the north, in the lush Lombard plain where cattle thrive. Further south, down the long spur which forms most of the mainland, mountains and scrub prevail over pasture so that sheep, goats and buffalo are the main milch animals. However, Italians have not gone in for making a lot of small, soft, cow's and goat's milk cheeses as the French have done south of Normandy. The Italian climate and the people's needs have demanded that they make fewer and more 'hard-wearing' types of cheese on the whole.

This is quite largely because, except for great landowners, must rural Italians are poor. Really poor. A few olives and a little grated cheese over a dish of pasta is a main meal for many of them. Grated Parmesan goes a long way.

Parmesan is easily the best known Italian cheese name, although strictly speaking, it is only an English and French informal name. Under Italian law, and by an agreement at the Stresa Convention in 1951, *Parmigiano Reggiano* is the official name for all hard grating (grana) cheeses made in the districts of Parma, Bologna, Mantua, Podena, and Reggio, south of the Po river. (*Grana Reggiano* is an alternative name for these cheeses.) However, Parmesan has become an accepted name for both the cheeses called Parmigiano Reggiano (first made around Parma) and Grana Padano (made north of the Po, around Padua) if they do not reach the standard required for them to be sold 'in the piece' as table cheeses or for grating at home. Just about all Italian grana cheese sold ready-grated in the English-speaking world is labelled Parmesan – the cheese from Parma.

The quality of both cheeses is rigidly controlled by the *Consorzio del Formaggio Parmigiano Reggiano* or the *Consorzio per la Tutela del Grana Padano*.

The cheeses are sometimes hard to distinguish because there are only a few small differences between them (including the small-scale similar cheeses such as Grana Lodigiano (from Lodi) and Grana Lombardi (from around Milan)). For instance, they are all classed as grana cheeses because they all have a grainy – and rock-hard – texture when old. However, one significant difference is that Parmigiano Reggiano takes longer to mature than Grana Padano. It stays tender longer, and it is the grana cheese most widely eaten in Italy and elsewhere as a table cheese, while it is still quite young.

Grana cheeses are said to be of very ancient origin, having been made in the Po valley well before the Roman republic became an empire. However, the firm documented existence of Parmesan goes back only to thirteenth century Parma. It must have become a widely popular cheese soon after, because, by 1351, it was already the stuff of legend in Boccaccio's description of the Place of Good Cheer in the *Decameron*, where it was used, grated, over macaroni and noodles.

The modern cheese is made by small cheese factories between mid-April and mid-November. Skimmed evening and fresh morning milk are combined, and after curdling, the curd is carefully cut and vigorously stirred while being steam-heated to about 55°C/131°F for thirty minutes. This condenses the curd which is then allowed to cool in the released whey for a short while before being pressed and then turned and salted at intervals for twenty to twenty-five days. The cheese then takes at least a year to mature, when it becomes *giovane* (young table) cheese; after one and a half to two years it is *vecchio* (old); the best, called *stravecchio* (very old) take over two, usually three years or more, and even older cheeses are designated as *tipico*.

The mature cheeses are great golden millstones, 33 to 45 cm/13 to 18 inches in diameter, 18 to 24 cm/7 to 9½ inches high, with a 32 per cent fat content. The rind is brushed often during curing and after a year is given a coating of oil or of fine dark earth mixed with oil. The cheeses without this blackish coat are printed with the logo Parmigiano Reggiano on their convex sides. Inside the 'jacket' (which is usually steel-hard) a cheese's 'body' (hardly a paste!) is delicately grainy, yellow, hard (yet it melts on the tongue), spicy but not sharp, rich in spite of its low fat content.

The older cheeses are, of course, most often used for grating; and once you have grated your own, you will never (if you have any respect for your palate) buy ready-grated Parmesan in a carton again. If you have the chance to find a younger table cheese, you are in good fortune. It makes excellent cocktail cubes with whatever short drinks you are serving; or put it on a cheeseboard (I suggest with one mild blue and one Stracchino-style cheese such as Robiola, which is not too creamy). Drink with it a full red wine, possibly a Sicilian Corvo or a robust Australian Coonawarra claret.

GORGONZOLA

There was a locality, now in the north-eastern suburbs of Milan, where herds of cattle used to stop for rest and water on their annual migration south from Alpine summer pastures. Sometime in the distant past, a thousand years ago or more, the people of the surrounding area began making cheese from the milk of the weary, lowing cows; a moist, thinly flavoured cheese because the poor trackside herbage had offered only meagre nourishment. They called it *stracchino* ('tired' in the Lombard tongue) *di Gorgonzola* – later, just Gorgonzola – and they carried their cheeses to natural caves in the valleys of Valsassina and Val Brembana to mature in cool, draughty air for as much as a year.

They did not know at first that they had created, by their special method of making it, one of the world's half-dozen greatest cheeses. Perhaps not until French troops, returning home from Naples between 1799 and 1801, carried back parcels of the pale-veined aromatic cheese.

Even then, Gorgonzola remained a regional product made by small cheese-makers until, later in the nineteenth century, cellars for maturing the cheeses were built, and curing houses in the larger cities of the region took over the ripening process.

This very special cheese, made with whole cow's milk, gained its reputation by being handled in an unusual way. The raw evening milk was curdled, cooled and drained, then the following morning was lapped in still-warm, drained morning milk curds in moulds. These moulds were placed in a chill cave for three to four days; and the cheeses were then salted and cured with the addition of suitable mould cultures, and rested in their chilly home until a characteristic red mould developed on the surface. Even then, three to four months' maturing were thought necessary to bring the cheeses to perfection.

Today, creamery production and speed are essential because demand for the beautiful cheeses outruns supply. *Penicillium gorgonzola* and an acidifying agent are added to fresh pasteurised milk, and the chopped curd is kept in warm, humid conditions for about three weeks, until mould appears. Then it is taken to the curing cellars, cool and airy, to complete three months' maturing in all.

The vital statistics of the cheese are worth noting. It is usually a cylinder with slightly rounded edges, 25 to 30 cm/10 to 12 inches in diameter, 16 to 20 cm/6 to 8 inches high. Its cream-coloured, rich-tasting paste is semi-hard, with a 48 per cent plus fat content, and it is veined with greenish-blue mould. The natural rind, scraped and washed from time to time while it cures, is slightly wrinkled, tan in colour with russet streaks. Its aroma is noticeable (keep it out of the dining-room during dinner). Its flavour, however, is milder than that of its great fellow-blues, as well as moister and more buttery. It is beautiful.

It fully deserves its status as one of the four fully protected named cheeses; the name may not be used by any other maker in Europe.

You can now get Gorgonzola all year round, although it is said still to be best during winter. If you are travelling in Italy try, also, the lighter, white cheese given the separate name of Pannarone, which is seldom exported.

At home, try Gorgonzola with grapes or peaches as a dessert. But, generally, eat it alone just with crusty bread or crackers, and with a generous red wine such as a Barolo or a Côtes du Rhône.

DOLCELATTE

It is unfair to sneer at Dolcelatte as a few purists do, just because it is not Gorgonzola. It is not really even a straight imitation of Gorgonzola as is sometimes claimed, but an adaptation of the famous old cheese to factory conditions and mechanised methods of making; and, like other adaptations (one might mention American Liederkranz, page 132) it has become sufficiently popular under its own name to be assessed as a cheese in its own right.

If you consider it as that, tasting and savouring it with care, you realise that it is not perhaps a great blue cheese, but certainly a charming one suited to many palates; creamy yet

with no aftertaste of fat. While being noticeably more 'blue' than the various 'blue Bries' it still has the near-sweet quality that its name implies – for *dolce latte* means sweet milk.

It is a full-cream, pasteurised cow's milk cheese in a disc shape, usually 28 cm/11 inches in diameter, 8 cm/3¼ inches thick, and with a 50 per cent fat content. It weighs 6 kg/13¼ pounds in the whole round. First made by the firm of Galbani in 1967, its factory origin is not over-noticeable – only the blue-mould colouring is in deep, scored lines in the cream-coloured paste, due to the cheese being pierced to speed up the blueing process; taking only forty-five days to mature.

The rind develops a natural surface mould, but it is seldom seen because the cheese is generally sold in foil-wrapped portions weighing 1.5 kg/3¼ pounds each. If you buy one of these or a smaller portion, leave it wrapped and refrigerate it until you need it; it will keep for about ten days. Give it an hour or two, unwrapped, at room temperature before you eat it; and drink with it a young Valpolicella or similar wine.

BEL PAESE

Even more markedly than Dolcelatte, Bel Paese proves that a modern, commercial cheese can do well, in this case very well because Bel Paese is sold and eaten all round the world. If he had never created another, its inventor, a cheese-maker of Melzo in Lombardy, would have become renowned and wealthy through this one.

It is the foremost of a group of modern soft and similar Italian cheeses dubbed Italico in 1941 under Italian law, but already on sale early in the century. In 1906, a young cheese-maker called Egidio Galbani, who was a keen mountaineer, is said to have gone on a trip through France where he learned to make Port Salut. He liked it – and it triggered in his mind the idea of creating a sound, Italian all-purpose everyman's cheese which would travel – and sell – well. There was room for it because most Italian cheeses which the man-in-the-street could afford were then rather poor stuff, or unstable.

Like most pioneer thinkers, even business men, Galbani must have had some sentimental enthusiasm for his project because he stuck to it for a dozen years or more before he put his new cheese on the market; and I do not believe it was entirely hard-headed marketing focused on juveniles which made him choose the title of a popular nineteenth-century children's geography book as the name of his new cheese, or made him put its author's picture on the label. One can't help feeling that the cynicism of the salesman gave way to the memory of a little boy studying the map of Italy (which also appears on the label) and deciding that one day *he* would climb those mountains. He may have been stimulated too by the fact that Abbot Antonio Stoppani who wrote the book was a friend of his family.

Anyway, Galbani, the mature man, set to work to create a cheese based, it is said, on an old monastic type, but modernised to suit both young and old, rich and poor.

LAYERED GORGONZOLA SOUFFLÉ   **Light dish**

Serves 4 to 6

butter for greasing		
butter for soufflé	50 g/2 ounces	¼ cup
plain (all-purpose) flour	5 tablespoons	5 tablespoons
milk	275 ml/½ pint	1¼ cups
salt and ground black pepper to taste		
Gorgonzola cheese with rind removed, crumbled or mashed	100 g/4 ounces	½ cup
egg yolks	4	4
egg whites	5	5
canned button mushrooms, chopped	75 g/3 ounces	½ cup

Set the oven to heat to 190°C/375°F/Gas 5. Brush a little butter over the inside of a 1 litre/1¾ pint (4½ cup) soufflé dish. Melt the 50 g/2 ounces butter in a medium-sized pan. Add the flour and stir over low heat for 2 minutes. Still stirring constantly, add the milk gradually, and cook for another 2 minutes. The sauce will be very thick and should leave the sides of the pan cleanly; if not, take the pan off the heat and beat briskly. Turn the sauce into a bowl. Beat in a little seasoning and the cheese, making sure that any lumps of cheese are beaten out. Then beat in the egg yolks, one at a time, until fully blended.

In a separate bowl, whisk (beat) the egg whites until they hold firm peaks. Stir one spoonful into the soufflé base mixture, then fold in the rest.

Pour half the mixture gently into the prepared dish. Sprinkle with the mushrooms, then cover gently with the remaining soufflé mixture. With a knife-point, score the surface of the soufflé about 2.5 cm/1 inch from the side of the dish all round to help the centre to rise.

Bake the soufflé for 35 minutes until it is well risen and browned. Serve immediately, protecting the soufflé from draughts on the way to the table.

Do not try to freeze any soufflé mixture.

STRACCIATELLA *Chicken Broth with Egg*

Serves 4

chicken broth made from fresh chicken meat, strained	1.1 litres/2 pints	2½ pints
Egg garnish		
eggs	2	2
fine semolina	1 tablespoon	1 tablespoon
fresh Parmesan cheese, grated	3 tablespoons	3 tablespoons
salt and white pepper to taste		
ground nutmeg	a few grains	a few grains

Cool the broth if freshly made, and skim off any fat. Beat the eggs with a fork until liquid. Then beat in the semolina, grated cheese, seasoning and nutmeg. Still beating, trickle in 5 tablespoons of cooled broth. Heat the rest of the broth until scalding hot, then beat in the egg garnish and continue beating until it is just opaque. Let the soup come to the boil without beating so that the egg-cheese mixture solidifies into strands. Serve it immediately in warmed soup plates.

Freezing You can freeze the broth for up to 3 months. Thaw before use. Only add the egg garnish when reheating.

He succeeded brilliantly; so well that it is now made in Wisconsin in the United States under license, as well as in its native Italy – and in the US the package carries a picture of the Americas instead of Italy.

The cheese is made from pasteurised whole cow's milk, curdled, cut and drained by raking, then moulded, turned, pressed and brine-dipped. After that it gets cured at 4.5°C/40°F for about seven weeks, being washed from time to time to help it develop a mould-free rind.

Those bare everyday processes (in cheese terms) result in a smooth, evenly-coloured, pliable paste, with a milky smell and a mildly nutty, chewable flavour. It is made, normally, in a fairly thick disc shape, in various sizes weighing from 500 g/1 pound upwards; the rind is generally foil-wrapped or covered with coloured cellophane. It probably will not excite you over-much; but neither will it offend you, and it will serve well for a dozen purposes, and for all age-groups from a year old upward.

From one to ten years, milk is the most suitable drink to accompany it; thereafter much depends on the parental attitude to wine, but in later years, treat it with gentle respect for its delicate but real flavour, and drink with it a not-too-dry Italian white wine or a rosé. Remember that it is good with fruit, and useful for toasting or in a quiche; but perhaps best stuffed into cored apples, spiced with nutmeg and baked.

PECORINO

The word *Pecorino* used by itself may simply mean any product – in this context any cheese – made from sheep's milk. But it may also mean a specific, very ancient and interesting grana cheese. This cheese (almost certainly the variety of it known as Pecorino Romano, from its 'home town' area) is the only extant cheese we think we can recognise as having been made in Imperial Rome because we have a recipe. The Spanish-born writer L J M Columella gives it in his work *De Re Rustica*. Like his contemporary and fellow-countryman, the orator Seneca (born 16 BC) he appears to have lived mostly at Rome. Pliny the Elder, (AD 23–79), another near-contemporary, also discourses on one like it.

Until the end of the last century, it is said, Pecorino was a shepherds' or village grana cheese, wherever it was made. Its modernisation started when salt-makers began to process the fresh curds, and set up dairies to do it. These developed into large factories, turning out thousands of the popular, long-lasting cheeses, especially for export. The United States with its large Italian immigrant population was the main market. But today, one or another variety of Pecorino is found in dairy-conscious countries all over the world. In Australia, Canada and the United States cow's milk imitations are made by local factories.

Two varieties of the true sheep's milk modern Pecorino which are particularly important as exports are Pecorino Sardo, from the island of Sardinia, and Pecorino Siciliano from Sicily. (Peppercorns are sometimes added to the curd of the Sicilian cheese to make the spicy Pecorino Pepato.) These two varieties differ slightly from other Pecorinos because they have a higher fat content (45 and 40 per cent respectively) and they are uncooked. They are also matured for a shorter time, for only two weeks to two months as eating cheeses. When aged, Pecorino Siciliano in particular may taste really sharp, even positively bad-tempered.

The variety of modern, sheep's milk Pecorino most widely known and esteemed is still the ancient Pecorino Romano. It is made by both traditional and commercial dairies in spring, autumn and winter when the ewes give milk, although it can be eaten year-round at different stages of maturity, and because the product is so stable. It is a cooked cheese with a minimum fat content of 36 per cent, cured in dry, cool cellars for at least eight months. In shape, it is a cylinder, varying in size and weight a good deal: from 20 to 26 cm/8 to $10\frac{1}{2}$ inches in diameter, and from 13 to 23 cm/$5\frac{1}{2}$ to 9 inches high, with a consequent weight variation of 6 to 12 kg/$13\frac{1}{4}$ to $26\frac{1}{2}$ pounds. The rind is natural, and is brushed with olive oil dregs mixed with ochre instead of the oil-earth mixture used in the past. The paste, as one might expect, is hard and craggy when cut, if fully cured. It may be whitish but is more often yellow. Its smell is slightly 'smokey', and its taste is that of a typical sheep's milk cheese, often sharpened by age.

The same goes for the lesser known Pecorinos which you may come across when travelling. One of the better known, Pecorino Toscano (from Tuscany), which is ripe, delicate and creamy after two weeks, is also sometimes called Pecorino Canestrato; the *canestro* is the draining basket also used for some Pecorino Siciliano cheeses, which then bear the weave-marks of the basket throughout their lives. Other Pecorinos are usually Tuscan ones with their own village names.

Any Pecorino can be eaten as a table cheese when just mature, but is certainly more suited to grating as it gets older. As an after-dinner cheese, team it with a full-bodied Sicilian or an Australian red wine from the Barossa Valley, perhaps a Seppelt Cabernet.

PROVOLONE

Provolone is often linked with Pecorino in export figures, probably because both come from southern Italy, and have been over the years exported in great quantity to the Italian population in the United States.

Once upon a time, too, Provolone and Pecorino were linked by flavour and usage. An old (and therefore hard) sharp-flavoured Provolone, akin in taste to Pecorino and also used for grating, seems to have been commoner than it is today. Smoked Provolone, too, seems harder to find.

It is not really surprising. There is a tendency, it seems, for all popular and therefore exported cheeses to be blander than they used to be. Then, long ago, in its first home, Campagna, Provolone was made partly from buffalo milk which had a different flavour. One is told, too, that for *strong* Provolone, one must find cheese curdled with lamb's or kid's rennet and cured for longer than the minimal one to two months.

Today this seems 'pie in the sky'. The usual Provolone curd is made from whole cow's winter milk (44 per cent fat) curdled with microbial rennet. It is then treated with hot whey, kneaded and pummelled and pulled, to turn it into a *pasta filata* or spun paste cheese (page 133) which, with some industry and a good deal more imagination, can be moulded into quaint shapes such as horses' heads, piglets, saddle-bags, pears, melons and sausages. The commonest shape is the saddle-bag, each cheese looks like a bag of curd, and two cheeses are usually tied together by a cord round the neck of each with a length of bare cord between them.

The hard squeezed cheese curd is matured for a minimum of one to two months, sometimes three; or for three months more (six months in all) if a really strongly flavoured cheese is required. Cheeses aged for a year are not unknown. The minimum time does little more than make the already firmed curd slightly denser, and enhance its delicate lactic scent and mild flavour. It does however give the cheese time to develop its smooth, thin, glossy, mid-yellow rind which contrasts so well with the fine and soft, dense white paste when the cheese is cut open.

There are several other pasta filata cheeses, mostly similar to Provolone. The best known is Cacciocavallo or 'cheese on horseback', because the two bag-like cheeses look so remarkably like saddle-bags. There is Cacetta or Cacietto meaning 'little cheese', and Burrino which has a knob of butter imprisoned in the centre of the curd. Mozzarella is also a plastic curd cheese; and there are several others.

Pasta filata cheeses vary considerably in size; Provolone is no exception. It may be no bigger than 1 kg/2¼ pounds, or it may be a giant sausage nearer 90 kg/200 pounds. The big cheeses are still sometimes smoked as they were in Roman times.

Whatever size and shape of Provolone you choose, whole or in the piece, it is very unlikely to challenge your palate or demand attention for its novelty. Eat it as a table cheese or cook with it, using it for stuffed vegetables, for instance, or in mixed salads. Drink with it a gentlemanly red wine, a chianti perhaps, or a light red wine from Yugoslavia.

MOZZARELLA

Mozzarella at home seems a different cheese from Mozzarella abroad – an interesting surprise for the average foreign traveller who is used to a vacuum-packed block of sliceable – not to say rubbery – milk-food not unlike firm bean curd!

Italian Mozzarella as traditionally prepared in its home areas of Latium and Campania is still sometimes made from the milk of Indian buffaloes, but it is made from cow's milk everywhere else. It is, first and foremost, a hand-made *fresh* cheese; and cheese gourmets to a man (and woman) insist on

its being eaten as soon as it is made – if not straight from the cheese-maker's hands, at least before the same day has passed. In Italian neighbourhood stores, you can find the containers of more-or-less ball-shaped pieces of Mozzarella resting in salted whey or brine, ready for you to choose the size you want. (You can do the same in occasional small Italian-kept delicatessen in the United States.)

You could be pardoned if you were to think that these balls of cheese are just squeezed fresh curd. They look like it when you first cut them, and their scent – even their taste – is so delicate and milky that it seems impossible for them to be a much-handled product. Yet this Mozzarella is one of the most intensively processed soft cheeses during the short period of its making. It is not cured at all. This is because it is a pasta filata, or spun-curd cheese, like Provolone or Cacciocavallo. Its curds are firmed in hot whey, kneaded, pulled into strings, moulded, dipped again, pummelled again . . . and so on until the cheese-maker judges that their consistency is just what he – and his customers – will enjoy most, and he cuts off short lengths to mould into balls and other shapes.

Obviously, there is no set size or weight of a ball of this hand-made Mozzarella; but it is possible to suggest approximately what its consistency and colour should be, whether it comes from buffalo or (as will usually be the case) from cow. It should certainly be a clean, pure white, the faintest edge of yellowing hints that it is past its peak of freshness. Then it should be really quite firm, not porous – slightly yielding when you bite it – and lightly creamy on the tongue. (Its fat content is 40 to 45 per cent.)

The rare buffalo's milk cheese is lovely eating at table; look for the word *bufala* on the price label if there is one. A cow's milk Mozzarella is best used for cooking, like the stabilised, demoisturised foreign copies. Mozzarella, we all know, made its name as a pizza cheese; but it is valuable for any dish where quick melting but no marked flavour is needed: in toasted sandwiches which have spicy other ingredients; in meat and poultry stuffings when it acts as a 'binding' sauce; in any panada or gratin to soften the flavour of another stronger cheese.

If you eat the hand-made cheese fresh at table, alone or with salad, look for a dryish white wine from central Italy. Perhaps the well-known Verdicchio dei Castelli di Jesi.

RICOTTA

Ricotta in Italy is a general name for fresh cheeses made from whey curds; they are sometimes smoked. The whey is the by-product of making other cheeses, from either sheep's milk or cow's milk (depending largely on the area where it is made). The two best known ricottas are Ricotta Romana and Ricotta Piedmontese.

In all the western world's dairying areas whey cheeses have been made since early times by or for poor people, or where thrift in preserving food was vital because of scarcity, as in

RICOTTA TART (RICOTTA PIE) **Dessert**

Makes one 200 mm/8 inch cheese tart (pie)

Pastry

melted butter for greasing		
chilled butter	100 g/4 ounces	½ cup
lard	25 g/1 ounce	2 tablespoons
plain (all-purpose) flour	200 g/7 ounces	1¾ cups
cold water	2 to 3 tablespoons	2 to 3 tablespoons

Filling

Ricotta cheese	225 g/8 ounces	½ pound
butter	50 g/2 ounces	¼ cup
egg	1	1
milk	150 ml/¼ pint	⅔ cup
caster (fine white) sugar	40 g/1½ ounces	3 tablespoons
grated rind of ½ lemon		
raisins	25 g/1 ounce	1½ tablespoons

Brush melted butter over the inside of a fluted 200 mm/8 inch flan ring set on a baking sheet; grease the sheet inside the ring too. Alternatively, use a flan case (pie plate).

Make pastry (pie crust) by cutting or rubbing the chilled butter and lard into the flour until the mixture is like breadcrumbs. Mix to a smooth dough with cold water. Roll the dough on a floured surface, and use it to line the flan ring and sheet or the case. Chill while making the filling.

Mash the cheese with a fork, and melt the butter. Beat the egg in the milk until liquid, add the butter, then beat the milk mixture into the cheese. Beat in the sugar until the mixture is blended and smooth. Alternatively, process all these ingredients in a food processor or blender. Stir in the lemon rind. Pour the mixture into the prepared pastry shell, then sprinkle with the raisins. Bake at 190°C/375°F/Gas 5 for 30 minutes or until the pastry is cooked and the filling is just set. Serve warm or cold.

Not suitable for freezing.

Scandinavia. Poverty has been the prime reason for ricotta being made in Italy. But in more affluent America and elsewhere, the habit has long since been established of making ricotta from whole cow's milk plus whey or just whole milk; and even in the poorer parts of Europe, including Italy, the cheese is now made partly with cow's milk whenever possible. It results in a softer, creamier curd and less astringent flavour than when whey alone is used. It is also more nourishing.

Whey, however, is not lacking in nutrients. It contains albumen (protein), lactose (milk sugar), a certain amount of fat and some vitamins and minerals. There is nothing wrong with it as a food; and there have been times in history when it has been a very snobbish food. The diarist Samuel Pepys, in the seventeenth century, went often with colleagues to a Whey House (similar to a milk bar) off London's Strand.

Whey remained a popular country drink in some places until the nineteenth century. Ricotta, that is moist, crumbly whey or milk-and-whey curds, has become used, however, mostly for cooking, especially for sweet dishes. It is used to make two famous southern Italian desserts, Sicilian *cassata* which is a cake made of chocolate, Ricotta and candied fruit, and *crostata di Ricotta*, a flat pastry shell filled with sweetened Ricotta with grated peel, raisins, candied orange peel, almonds, pine nuts and egg yolks. Among simpler modern desserts is Ricotta sweetened with icing (confectioner's) sugar, flavoured with instant coffee and the Mexican liqueur Kahlua.

As for savoury dishes, Ricotta can be substituted for cottage cheese in any dish. It is used as a spread in sandwiches and pancake fillings, in forcemeats and stuffings, as a sauce for pasta, and in fritters. It is also an essential ingredient of *Gnocchi verdi* (spinach dumplings), certain ravioli, and savoury and sweet pizzas. But I like to dream of it as a mound, perfectly moulded, turned out from an inverted basin, and decorated with fork patterns simulating the weave of a basket. You can cut a wedge like an ice-cream bombe; eating it with strawberries macerated in orange liqueur, without sugar or cream. Make sure that you have enough liqueur – then you won't need anything else to drink.

NETHERLANDS

GOUDA

We know that cheeses were being made in Gaul for export to Rome in the first century AD. There is also evidence that by the fourth century Frankish households were making them in the flat land of salt-marsh and islets to the north as well; perhaps partly at least because it was a common starting and finishing point for travellers going through Europe, whether bent on conquest or on trade. From the indented coast, a fairly easy road ran eastwards to the land called Champagne, and then curved southward until it reached the River Rhône, a perfect waterway to the Mediterranean. A two-way traffic seems to have developed early, and the travellers, whether invaders, traders or, later, pilgrims must always have needed supplies of portable foodstuffs.

The inhabitants must have been well aware that their only natural resources were their rich pastures, cattle and the dairy foods they got from them. They saw that, in order to get grain, beer, meat and timber, they must make enough butter and cheese both to eat and to barter – pressed cheeses which would travel well. These were used almost as currency, for instance to pay feudal taxes and buy protection. In the ninth century they were supplied to Charlemagne's court at Aix-la-Chapelle. The presence of the court meant that ambassadors now joined the flow of travellers passing through the Netherlands.

From the eleventh century, merchants replaced invaders as Europe settled down. The population spread eastward, traffic grew and dairying enterprises in the Netherlands became more skilled and more widespread to serve the travellers. Marketing became sophisticated. For instance, several market towns got a *kaaswaag*, a cheese weighhouse where cow's, sheep's and goat's milk cheeses were inspected for quality as well as weight. Haarlem, 1266, and Leiden, 1303, were just two towns where they were set up, and the civic authorities were as involved as the farmers. The export of cheeses increased greatly too, both to the developing German territories and across the sea to Scandinavia and Britain.

The cheese most often exported then (as it is now) was Gouda. It gets its name from a small market town (once one of Holland's five major trading centres) at the junction of two rivers, the Gouwe and the Hollandse Ijissel, in the centre of the province of South Holland. Cheeses were being shipped out to Britain from there in the thirteenth century, so John Arlott tells us, and merchants sealed their bargains with a handslap as they do today.

The cheeses made then were of course all farmhouse cheeses, and we are told that some cheese-making farms still remain, clustered around the town of Gouda. The weighhouse of 1668 still stands too, and the cheese market is held as in former times, although it now handles many more factory, pasteurised-milk Goudas than farmhouse ones, which are seldom exported. Due to the high standards of making and of quality control, there is probably not much difference between them, except the name Gouda printed on factory cheeses, and all the flavoured cheeses which the factories make.

Gouda is in shape like a thick tyre, with a flat top and bottom and convex sides. The golden cheeses with their paraffined, shiny firm rinds are 25 to 30 cm/10 to 12 inches in diameter and 7.5 cm/3 inches thick with 40 to 48 per cent fat content. The paste may be almost free of holes (in a farmhouse cheese if a solid block of curd has been put into the cheese form or mould) or it may be pitted with small irregular pockets if crumbled curd is used; in mature cheeses, moisture may glisten in the holes. Otherwise, the yellow paste is smooth, resilient to firm with hardly any smell, and with a taste ranging from pleasant but mild to deep and full yet without any sharpness. The quality of flavour depends on the cheese's age, which may be no more than two to three months or as much as twelve months – or even up to two years if a really mature cheese is wanted. Maturing may be accelerated in special drying rooms. These long-matured cheeses are, of course, harder to cut than mild young cheeses and are saltier but splendidly satisfying, inside the black wax or yellow ringed jacket. The weight, however, remains much the same, averaging 4 kg/9 pounds.

Farmhouse and factory cheeses alike are pressed after the curd has been made, reheated, cut, drained and moulded. Then after being pressed, they are stamped with the appropriate identification – Boerenkaas for a farmhouse cheese – and they are re-pressed and given a brine bath. (Under the Stresa Convention, foreign cheeses must be stamped with their place of origin.)

Gouda is a splendid cooking cheese, whatever its age. It is ideal for the traditional Gouda Kaasdoop, a dish of cheese boiled in milk and eaten with boiled potatoes or brown bread. But it is also splendid (especially four to six months old Gouda) as a table cheese, or thickly piled in the common sandwich lunch of Dutch business folk. A really mature old cheese can be grated for a topping. However you use it, though, take care what you drink. Dutch gin (Genever) is one choice, or you could offer a light red Beaujolais or an Alsatian white wine. If you need to, keep your cheese wrapped in foil in the salad drawer of your refrigerator. It should come up smiling for use after as much as ten days.

Some connoisseurs say, probably rightly, that the individuality of farmhouse Gouda cheeses is missing in the factory-made ones. But factory-made Gouda has some surprising merits. One can usually choose, for instance, between young bland Gouda sold unadorned or flavoured with cumin seeds and orange-waxed, shades of the days when the great sailing carracks of the Dutch spice fleet came sailing into harbour. Another choice is a herb-flavoured Gouda (usually green-waxed), and a third choice, pepper-flavoured, has a dark brown wax coat. Gouda with mustard is also very good. But perhaps the best of all – so many gourmets think – of these flavoured cheeses is the rare dry-rinded Gouda with nettles.

EDAM

Edam is the Dutch cheese which foreigners know best. Its red coat on the piles of Edam wedges in any supermarket is instantly recognisable. There are other red-waxed cheeses, but none have the 'hallo there!' quality of Edam. Holland is the world's biggest maker and exporter of cheese, and Edam is now her largest export to the United Kingdom.

One reason is that Edam is renowned as the world's most reliable keeping cheese. Short of being eaten, it is almost indestructible.

There is not really very much difference in the history of Edam and Gouda. Today, all Edam is made with partly-skimmed milk, and it is all factory-made for export. But it was not always so. Until the nineteenth century, Edam was a whole-milk cheese like Gouda, made on farms and pressed in wooden moulds in the same way, and had been so as far back as men could remember. Although in fact, way back in the medieval past, both cheeses had probably only been made as whole-milk cheeses for lords, bishops and kings together with pure rich butter – the milk skimmed of its cream for the butter, made thin Edam and Gouda cheese for the cheese-makers and other peasants.

We know that Edam goes back to medieval times because of the way it is sold. It is named after an old harbour town in the province of North Holland where Friesian Edam cheeses were first exported. But this is not what counts. In the town of Alkmaar, not far away, one of the old medieval guilds (the cheese-bearers) still survives; the porters wear white costumes and different-coloured hats to identify the warehouse to which each belongs, and they take the cheeses to the thirteenth-century weighhouse on curiously scoop-shaped sleds (cheese-berries). The whole performance has a quaint old flavour, and is a major tourist attraction.

A whisper of folklore adds to the interest the market evokes. Dutch dairy farmers in North Holland and Friesland believe, we are told, that their pasture has some special virtue which provides the firm, sliceable, meadow-scented cheeses with the Edam taste. Dutch scientists have confirmed that this is so – but do not divulge what the virtue is which makes the Edam cheeses so popular.

When sold at the market, the golden globes of Edam are not waxed to colour them red; that only happens after they are bought for export, when they are waxed in the warehouse. At first, they are as golden as Goudas, only round. They get their shape from the wooden moulds in which they were first made – an identifying mark because almost no other cheese firms up so early in making and can therefore be shaped into a ball.

The type of old, round wooden mould in which Edam was made has its own story too. It is nicknamed *kaaskop* ie cheese-head, and because it was, in the past, used as headgear during riots, the Dutch came to be known as *kaaskops* in several places in Europe.

The smallest size of Edam is not big enough for a helmet. It

Left: Mascarpone; *right*: Torta (San Gaudenzio)

LASAGNE GAUDENZIO

Main dish

Serves 6

dried lasagne rectangles (from packet)	225 g/8 ounces	½ pound
salt	1 teaspoon	1 teaspoon
thick white sauce	425 ml/¾ pint	2 cups
dried marjoram leaves	¾ teaspoon	¾ teaspoon
eggs	2	2
freshly cooked cauliflower head (use a 25 g/1¼ pound whole cauliflower)	400 g/14 ounces	14 ounces
butter for greasing		
shredded lettuce	40 g/1½ ounces	¾ cup
San Gaudenzio cheese, thinly sliced, chilled	225 g/8 ounces	1 cup
buttered breadcrumbs	2 tablespoons	2 tablespoons

Get a bowl of cold water ready to dip the lasagne rectangles in after boiling them. Heat about 3.4 litres/6 pints (7½ pints) water to a boil in a large pan. Add the salt. Drop in 4 to 5 lasagne rectangles at one time, and boil for 6 minutes only; they should still be firm. Remove them with tongs or two forks, dip them in cold water and lay them side by side on a damp cloth. Boil all the rectangles in this way.

Take any skin off the white sauce if it is cooled. Beat in the marjoram and then the eggs. Break the cauliflower head into small florets. Butter the inside of a 1.1 litre/2 pint (2½ pint) baking dish. Spread ⅓ of the pasta in a flat layer in the bottom. Cover with half the sauce, then half the cauliflower florets and lettuce. Spread about ¼ of the San Gaudenzio over the cauliflower. Repeat the pasta, sauce, vegetable and cheese layers once. Cover with the last ⅓ of the pasta and spread all the remaining cheese in a thick layer over it. Sprinkle the buttered crumbs on top. Bake at 180°C/350°F/Gas 4 for 30 minutes. Serve at once.

Freezing Freeze before baking if you wish. Bake from frozen for 50 to 60 minutes, covered with foil until the last 20 minutes.

Note: Double the quantities and bake two dishes (or 1 large one) for a party.

is called a 'Baby Edam' and weighs about 1 kg/$2\frac{1}{4}$ pounds. The next size up (ordinary Edam) weighs 2 kg/4 pounds, and is 14 cm/$5\frac{1}{2}$ inches tall, 12 cm/$4\frac{1}{2}$ to 5 inches in diameter. Then there is a grand cheese called in the Netherlands *Commissiekaas*, but in France and almost everywhere else *Mimolette*. It is not only grand, it is a glorious dark orange with a brushed rind and a surprisingly soft paste until it ages. It is now made much more in France and Belgium than in the Netherlands and is matured for upwards of six months.

Like Gouda, all these various Edams may be sold young and lightly flavoured, semi-matured but still diffident to taste, or fully matured with a tendency to be assertive.

Like Gouda, too, the cheese may be a compound product with herbs, peppercorns, cumin or nettles to enhance it. A vegetarian-renneted type is also made.

Lastly, both Edam and Gouda are made in a form called *Broodkaas* (Bread Cheese). It is a pressed, semi-hard (40 per cent fat) rectangular loaf for slicing in hotels and the ubiquitous city *Broodjeswinkel* or Sandwich Shop. Broodkaas is a mild cheese, with a somewhat 'dim' flavour although well suited to its purpose. But then, neither young (four-week-old) nor semi-mature (five-week-old) Edam have overly much to say for themselves either; the resilient smooth paste with virtually no holes has virtually no aroma either.

However, a cheese matured for seventeen to twenty-five weeks and with a firm cutting, almost flaky quality begins to show the full flavour Edam can achieve. At seven months, the Dutch themselves call their cheeses 'ultra mature'. An 'old' cheese is a specimen ten months old and a 'vintage cheese' is a year old, no less.

Drink with the milder cheeses a light lager or a medium-dry white wine. The maturer types can 'take' a brown ale or a red wine of character such as Moulin-a-Vent.

LEIDEN OR LEIDSE KAAS

Leiden or Leyden cheese (or Leidse Kaas as it is called at home) is a reputable spiced cheese of some age, although we do not know its exact origins. It certainly started life as a farmhouse cheese, and probably as a peasant cheese since it is made in two grades, either with whole or with partly skimmed milk and buttermilk. Possibly it emerged from an older, unspiced cheese at the time when the Netherlands first took command of the European spice trade between 1595 and 1602. It bears all the marks of rather muddled attempts to flavour it with one spice, then another, then with three at once.

Its respectability is confirmed by the fact that, like Gouda, it is a protected cheese under the Stresa Convention of 1951. Any foreign cheese called Leiden must be labelled with the name of its country of origin, and only genuine Dutch Leiden cheeses may be branded with the two black crossed keys which are part of the coat of arms of the ancient University City of Leiden. (This probably only betokens that the farms on which the cheese was first made were in the duneland near the city

and were therefore so to speak, under its 'wing'.) Leiden today is usually made in factories but a little still comes from the duneland farms around the University.

Factory Leiden is a cow's milk, semi-hard cheese spiced with cumin seed or less often with caraway. The whole milk type which has a fat content of 40 per cent is relatively unimportant, at least to the export market. It is the 20 per cent fat, skim-milk type which – because it preceded by a long time the similar but unspiced modern reduced-fat hard cheeses – made an impact on twentieth-century cheese-eating slimmers, health faddists and the sensible cheese gourmets who appreciate its stimulating taste. Its flavour is full rather than sharp even though it is generally eaten much younger and fresher than the whole-milk type. However, it is certainly not as piquant and tasty as a Leiden cheese made on a farm.

The cheese is not easy to make. The fresh, warm milk is cooled in the cheese-making vat and after twelve or twenty-four hours the cream is skimmed off and made into somewhat odiferous butter. Some of the skimmed milk is then used to curdle the rest, and the leftover buttermilk is added with rennet. The set curd is cut, stirred, drained of its whey, and part of it is kneaded with cumin seed. Once upon a time, a farmer used to wash his feet in whey, then trod the curd as men once trod wine, but this has been abandoned as unhygienic, to the annoyance of some purists. The spiced curd is still, however, as in the past, sandwiched between two layers of unspiced curd, the whole sandwich then being cloth-bound and pressed for twenty-four hours. It is 'undressed' and is pressed again so that the sides bulge, before it is branded with the crossed keys and the farmer's own fat content mark of 30 per cent (it is sometimes even higher). Finally, it is cured for three months in humid, then in dry cellars.

In the final stage of ripening, the cheese's rind is given a deep orange flush by rubbing it with annatto. This used to be rubbed into the rind with the beestings or colostrum yielded by a cow just after calving; but since colostrum was seldom available and was therefore kept until stinking, modern makers have given up using it. The orange rind is quite enough to give the cheese an attractive, come-hither look.

The paste does so too, when the cheese is cut. The whole cheese is a stout wheel shape, 36 cm/14 inches in diameter, 12 cm/$4\frac{1}{2}$ inches thick. The cut paste is distinctly darker than that of other Dutch cheeses. It is distinctive to taste too; dry, salty, with a strong, acid 'punch'. It is hard enough to be grated and may even be crumbly; and as it ages it picks up the flavour of the seeds in its paste.

Wrapped in foil, it will keep for a fortnight if refrigerated, but will degenerate into a sweaty mass if allowed to get too warm.

The Dutch drink beer with it, but it is likely to go equally well with a spicy red wine from Sicily or California.

DENMARK/NORWAY

SAMSOE

We do not think of Denmark as a country with a serious and honourable cheese-making past, but we should. It began long, long ago when primitive Finnish and Lapp herdsmen trekked south with their sheep, goats and cattle, probably over the narrow sound into the green island where Copenhagen now stands. Like most such peoples, they almost certainly made soft cheeses and fermented milks, and may have developed a fair degree of skill.

Between the thirteenth and fifteenth centuries, the Cistercian monks, who lived by farming, spread all over northern Europe, and penetrated into Denmark and Sweden. One of their major activities was cheese-making. It was often left to lay brothers who cared for the flocks and herds at granges (barns and sheds) some way from the main abbey, or to small farmers who rented land from the abbey and paid the rent in produce, including cheeses. The monks, who were vegetarians, taught them the method to follow, using plant juices for curdling, and sometimes ripened the cheeses for them in the abbey cellars. They also claimed some of the cheeses as payment of the taxes levied by the Church.

Some of the farmers, among them the islanders of Samsoe, became expert cheese-makers. However, it cannot be said that they loved the Church, their teacher.

In the early sixteenth century, King Christian II, elected king of Denmark, allied himself with the Church under one Archbishop Trolle to defeat the Swedes and make himself their king. However, he really wanted to diminish the power of the Church and the nobles, and raise the status of the peasants. He is known to have done a lot to improve their dairy farming by bringing in Dutch cheese-makers. He also took it on himself to permit the eating of cheese during the most sombre church fast of Lent by issuing letters of dispensation (no doubt in return for cash) to would-be cheese-eaters. That improved the peasant's cheese sales as well.

By this time, cattle had replaced goats and sheep as the main milch animals in much of Europe, including Denmark. But the Danes got little chance to profit by the change in the next 200 years as they were so heavily embroiled in European wars.

Luckily, first-class agricultural progress was made in the eighteenth century, under the Kings Frederick V and Christian VII. Then, like other dairying peoples, the Danes started experimenting with copying foreign cheeses for the home market around 1800. A landowner called Constantin Bruun called in Swiss cheese-makers to make Emmental from the total milk yield of his dairy herd. The idea and the execution were fine. Only the grand, great cheeses were not really needed in the small country, and so Danish Emmental gradually became smaller and more graceful, with a character, and in the end a name, of its own – Samsoe.

Cheeses were then only made on small farms and on the estates of landowners like Bruun. But in 1882 the first Danish co-operative dairy factory was established in Jutland, and within a few years the movement away from farm cheese-making was in full swing.

Samsoe today is made in two large forms. First, there is a true cartwheel shape with sharp edges which weighs about 14 kg/30 pounds. Then there is a square, rindless block also 14 kg/30 pounds in weight.

In substance, the product is a firm full-cream cheese made from pasteurised cow's milk, with regular, cherry-sized shiny holes (enough, although fewer than Emmental) scattered in the paste. These are made by pressing the warm, stirred curd underneath the whey at the bottom of the vat by means of a cheese press, then running off the whey, and cutting the curd into suitable blocks for moulding. Pressing the curd in this way avoids air traps occurring, and the holes are formed only by the bacterial gas during maturation.

The paste is creamy coloured, firm and sliceable. The flavour is sweet and nutty while the cheese is still young, and the rindless blocks are sold at this stage, after six weeks. The round cheese is ripened for twenty weeks, and when fully mature its flavour is generous although never harsh. Its rind is dry and yellow, coated with wax and bearing the imprint of its name.

An attractive small cheese for gifts is a mini-Samsoe, matured for one month before sale and capable of another month's life. It weighs 225 g/8 ounces, has a fat content of 45 per cent and is jacketed in red wax. It is mild and popular for picnics and with children, leaving the stronger, more redolent cheese for their elders. Once cut, the big cheese should keep well for ten days, but not much longer. Use it for cooking if you wish – it is great for a pizza – or eat it on brown bread (warm for choice) with mild pickles, celery, pepper rings and Beaujolais wine.

A Note on Danbo and other Samsoe Derivatives

Samsoe has been called the 'grandfather' of all Danish cheese types. But the square Danbo is known as 'the cheese which every Dane has in the fridge' as a standby and an ever ready snack. It is yellow-rinded (and normally yellow or red waxed on top of that), but the rind has little or no aroma and flavour of its own – it is rather a vehicle for the imprinted name of the cheese and its fat content of 45 per cent. The firm, natural-coloured paste has scattered regular round holes, a firm slicing quality, and a flavour which is mildly aromatic – and seldom, in this popular cheese, gets the chance to grow stronger. If it *does* stay in the ripening cellars, old Danbo is called Gamme-

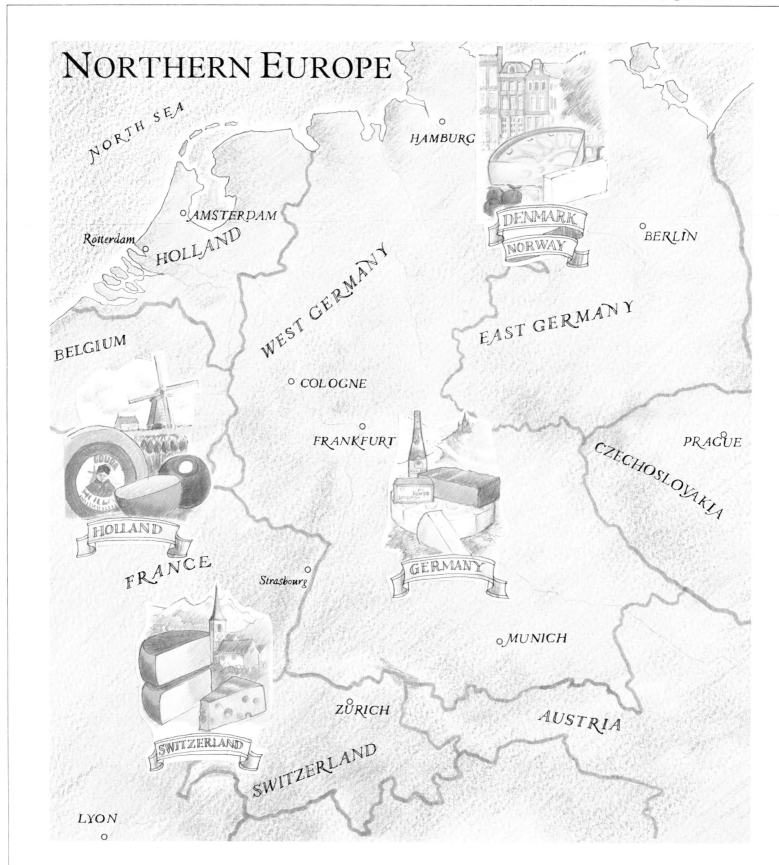

NORTHERN EUROPE

NORTH SEA

HAMBURG

AMSTERDAM

Rotterdam

HOLLAND

BELGIUM

WEST GERMANY

COLOGNE

FRANKFURT

DENMARK
NORWAY

BERLIN

EAST GERMANY

PRAGUE

CZECHOSLOVAKIA

GERMANY

HOLLAND

FRANCE

Strasbourg

MUNICH

SWITZERLAND

ZÜRICH

AUSTRIA

SWITZERLAND

LYON

SHRIMP-BROCCOLI 'STRUDEL'　　　　**Main dish**

Serves 4 to 6

puff pastry, thawed if frozen	400 g/14 ounces	1 pound (scant)
frozen broccoli spears (two 227 g/8 ounce packets)	454 g/1 pound	1 pound
salt as needed		
canned shrimp in brine, drained (one 198 g/7 ounce can)	125 g/4½ ounces drained weight	¾ cup drained weight
egg whites	2	2
Sbrinz cheese, finely grated	75 g/3 ounces	¾ cup
ground nutmeg	pinch	dash
white pepper	sprinkling	sprinkling
cayenne pepper	a few grains	a few grains
egg yolk, beaten with a few drops of water	1	1

Roll out the pastry into a rectangle about 3 mm/⅛ inch thick. Trim neatly; reserve the trimmings. 'Rest' the pastry in the refrigerator while preparing the filling.

Simmer the broccoli in slightly salted water until tender. Drain well. Cool. Cut off the stout ends of the stems. Arrange the broccoli heads in two rows down the centre of the pastry, stem ends outward. Cover with the shrimp. Whisk (beat) the egg whites stiffly. Fold in the grated Sbrinz cheese, nutmeg, pepper, cayenne and a little salt. Spread over the shrimp and broccoli.

Fold the two uncovered portions of pastry over the filling so that they meet in the centre and overlap slightly. Brush the edges of both portions with egg yolk. Press the edges together, making a raised, sealed centre rib. Seal the short ends of the 'roll' too. Roll out the reserved pastry trimmings, cut into leaf shapes and arrange on the pastry. Brush the whole surface with egg yolk. Place the 'strudel' on an ungreased baking sheet. Bake at 220°C/425°F/Gas 7 for about 20 minutes until the pastry is cooked through and golden. Garnish if you wish with lemon wedges and watercress.

Serve with a crisp celery salad.

Freezing The baked strudel freezes well for up to 3 weeks. Reheat from frozen in a low oven or microwave.

lole after one year; then it well deserves its reputation as a pungent collector's speciality cheese.

Fynbo is a more domestic little cheese, smaller than Samsoe. It comes from the island of Fyn (Funen), the largest of the Danish islands and the home of Hans Andersen. Its vital statistics are similar to those of Danbo, except that it has fewer, less regular holes. The mild Elbo has a firmer paste and large 'eyes', while Tybo is half the size, a nutty, friendly compact cheese if you find it. The firmer Maribo has a slightly different, firmer personality, because it is made by crumbling and kneading the curd before it is salted. It is therefore, open-textured with many small irregular holes in the paste. Its flavour is pleasantly nutty, with a distinctive aftertaste.

All these cheeses are made with pasteurised milk, and are presented without any added colouring except the (almost inevitable) coloured wax rind. They are all good, everyday cheeses, worthy of lager or a quaffing wine, although the purist seeking cheeses of character will lament the fact that some of them – Maribo in particular – are made with differing fat contents for different markets.

HAVARTI

One of the world's great cheese-makers was a woman called Hanne Nielsen. She was born in Denmark in 1829, a country girl who, in due course, married a country farmer but, by all accounts, long before she did so she had become beguiled by the idea of making basic country products. That was not perhaps unusual. Nor was it, perhaps, strange that a young woman of that period should have persuaded her husband to rent her the farm dairy to manage on her own account.

But it certainly was strange that, at a time when most women are busy raising a family, Hanne packed her bags, and – with hardly any knowledge of foreign tongues or currency – set off to study cheese-making in other European countries. It is tempting, if absurd, to think of her in a crinoline and bonnet, with elastic-sided boots and a sturdy gamp, preparing to conquer the cheese-makers of Europe with a note-book, a quill pen, a reticule of small change and a tape measure.

Yet conquer them she did. She visited at least six countries; Norway, England, Holland, France, Prussia and Switzerland, and unerringly pin-pointed a different type of cheese to study in each place. Goat's cheese. Hard English Cheddar. Semi-hard Edam and Gouda. Surface-ripened Camembert and blue-mould Roquefort. Pliable Tilsit and grand Emmental with its big round eyes. The list reads like a programme for a commercial cheese-making course. And so perhaps it was. Hanne's interest was quite probably not so much in the creative excitement of making those cheeses at home but in developing a cheese which could be turned into hard cash.

She did that too. She returned home to the farm and began experimenting with the cheeses she had been taught to make by all those foreign cheese-makers. (She had even been helped by the redoubtable Joseph Harding in Somerset, although she

did not copy his Cheddar in the end.) From all her experiments, Hanne created a cheese more like Prussian Tilsit than anything else, but perfectly geared to the Danish love of fairly mild, cookable, munchable cheese. Within quite a short time, her farm was turning out great quantities of cheese, some of it being sold to the royal palace.

Hanne Nielsen did not stop even there. She started teaching young dairymen cheese-making as well. In this way, her influence spread and created a whole new industry, because in the 1880s when cheese-making became a co-operative and then a commercial creamery industry, the cheeses tried out were based on those first experiments she had made in adapting foreign cheeses.

Denmark paid its due tribute to Hanne Nielsen. The cheese she developed as her own was called after her own farm, Havarti. It is still so called today.

This cheese is now made in three forms, with average fat contents of 30, 45 and 60 per cent although as a rule the 30 and 60 per cent are not exported. It is always a semi-soft, pasteurised whole-milk cheese, with small irregular holes in the paste, and it is always the natural colour of the good, rich milk. Both 30 and 45 per cent Havarti come in loaf-shaped or cylindrical form weighing as a rule 4.5 kg/10 pounds. Both shapes have a thin moist rind, are yellow-waxed, a supple smooth-to-cut consistency, and a flavour veering from mild when young to distinctly aromatic when fully aged at twenty weeks old.

The richer 60 per cent Havarti may be shaped like a long bread loaf, a large Mortadella sausage or be presented in a little carton. Its weight varies from a mere 200 g/7 ounces to a grand 4.5 kg/10 pounds. The paste is more supple, and the taste gentler and more subtle than its 45 per cent fellow, being slightly acidulous, yet creamy. The cheese is packed in a vivid red cryovac jacket.

Havarti is not 'just another' holey, adaptable, easy-to-eat cheese. It has a definite, individual personality, one worth seeking for inclusion on a cheese tray. Serve any type like this, offering wholemeal crackers or pumperknickel as a 'carrier' and Chianti as a drink. Why not?

DANISH BLUE

Danish blue, or to use its internationally protected name Danablu, looks deceptively mild. It is a semi-hard pasteurised and homogenised cow's milk cheese 'blued' with *Penicillium roqueforti*. Its white paste, delicately veined and speckled with mould, gives the unwary consumer no hint of its power. Nor does the production date on the label of every exported cheese, because it ripens surprisingly fast, in just thirty-five days. It is therefore a surprise to anyone trying the cheese for the first time to find that, under its buttery texture, its flavour is piquant, quite salty and tangy on the tongue.

There cannot, in fact, be many cheese-eaters in Europe or America who have never tasted this well-known cheese because it has been famous, and extensively advertised, since before the First World War. It began life when the Danes, seeking to make a blue-veined cheese, experimented with making an adaptation of Roquefort using homogenised cow's milk. A well-known cheese-maker called Marius Boel, using a bread culture at first, devised the present Danish whole-milk cheese with its 50 to 60 per cent fat content. (Nowadays a microbial culture is used.)

Lacking minerals, Denmark's flat countryside is almost wholly given over to crops, cattle and pigs, and to the processing of their products. The export of cheese is therefore of major importance in Denmark's economy, and very considerable care is taken to make sure that the highest possible standards of quality and consistency are maintained. Every cheese is strictly examined before an export license is granted by government-appointed inspectors. This license carries with it the right to use a label bearing the logo of four interwoven horns on it, and also carries the cheese's fat content and production date.

The Danish Blue we usually see is in the form of a cylinder 19 cm/$7\frac{1}{2}$ inches across and 11.5 cm/$4\frac{1}{2}$ inches high. The whole cylinder weighs 2.7 to 3.2 kg/6 to 7 pounds. Pre-packed portions are also widely available, and are popular, while rectangular and square blocks are sold for certain markets.

Whatever its shape, though, and wherever it is sold, Danish Blue should be wrapped in foil once cut, and should then be refrigerated and used within seven to eight days. This is easy because it is a popular, safe party choice, one which almost everyone will recognise and accept. (If you are one of those who tend to find its flavour a bit overwhelming, do as the Danes sometimes do and blend it with butter on the plate.)

With butter or without, eat it on oatcakes or wholemeal crackers, and drink a hearty wine with it such as Cahors or Chateauneuf de Pape.

SAGA

What's in a name? Where modern soft cheeses are concerned, plenty, because there are so many similar ones. However good a cheese is, it will claim more attention, and even seem to taste better if it has an arresting name. Saga is the best known of the soft blue and white mould cow's milk cheeses made by the Danish firm of Tholstrup outside their Castello range, and heartily deserves the plaudits it receives.

This Danish Saga can be bought as a whole round, 20 cm/8 inches in diameter and 4.5 cm/$1\frac{1}{4}$ inches thick, weighing 1.2 kg/2 pounds 10 ounces. More often, however, you will find it in pre-packed portions, eight to a round. Each weighs 150 g/5 ounces approximately. A portion will keep for about six weeks after dispatch from the factory, a whole round probably rather longer. But since the cheese is rich, with a fat content of 70 per cent, it must be refrigerated until an hour before use at a temperature of 4 to 6°C/39° to 42°F.

Saga is made by the addition of a blue mould culture to the

fine, pasteurised cow's milk of which it is made. When the cheeses have formed and have been aerated by piercing with steel needles to make space for the blue mould to develop, a white mould culture is applied to the surface. After ten to twelve days, a velvety white coat has covered the cheese which now has a light blue mould aroma and flavour. It is then ready to be packaged and sold.

When Ramon Tholstrup founded the firm which bears his name in 1890, he had no idea how its range would grow. Soft blue cheeses with white-mould coats were then a thing of the future; but now the three best-known cheeses which the firm makes are of this type, and although Blue Castello (page 121) is the 'flagship' of the Tholstrup 'fleet' and Blue Creme with its layered blue and white mould has its addicts, Saga is probably the most generally beloved. The cheese-master who created it maintained his watch over the first thirty years of its life or more, a care which not many modern cheeses can claim. Moreover, it is still, as it has always been, a care based on constant sampling and tasting, without the use of any chemical correctives.

Once the packaging is broken and the paste cut, the cheese should be eaten quickly. It is good with wholemeal crackers, excellent as a stuffing for cucumber or celery, or with grapes as a sophisticated 'dessert'. I would suggest a full-bodied white wine with it, say a Sicilian Corvo.

JARLSBERG

Norway deserves a big hand for developing her few natural resources with a patient skill and flair for success. Only 3 per cent of her land can be cultivated but she has made the very most of it and of her pasturage. She also made the most of hydro-electric power when it came in, not only to develop her manufacturing industries, pulp, paper, timber and canning, but her dairies too. Norway had northern Europe's first co-operative dairy plant way back in 1856. Today, there are more than 200, and an improved road system has been developed to link them with the farms which supply them with milk. Now, cheese factories are also part of the same system, making Norway's traditional cheese types and new varieties as well.

Since the earliest times, the women in small farmsteads have made cheeses as a valued food to add to the salted preserves they had to live on in their long, snow-bound winters. Jarlsberg is thought to be one such. It is certainly named after an old estate on the west bank of Oslo Fjord in south Norway where the Vikings first settled; and cheese is one of the few agricultural products the old warriors really focused on. Be that as it may, Norwegian farmers long ago learned to skim their milk for salty butter, and to make the remaining milk into cheese. By the start of the nineteenth century, they were making a large-holed cheese not unlike modern Jarlsberg.

The cheese was almost 'lost' when commercial co-operatives took over most Norwegian cheese-making, but a

FESTIVE PORK NOISETTES — **Main dish**

Serves 4

soft round white rolls	4	4
Swiss Gruyère cheese, rindless, grated	100 g/4 ounces	I cup
salt and freshly ground black pepper to taste		
eggs, beaten	2	2
butter for frying	I tablespoon	I tablespoon
pork noisettes, 50 g/2 ounces weight each, about I cm/$\frac{1}{2}$ inch thick	4	4
Swiss Gruyère cheese slices, 7.5 cm/3 inches square	4	4
227 g/8 ounce can of pineapple rings, drained (optional)	I	I
red maraschino cocktail cherries	4	4

Pork noisettes are small round steaks cut from boneless pork fillet or tenderloin. In this vivid recipe, they are veiled in melted cheese and can be capped with wreaths of golden pineapple. First, make patties to put them on.

Split the rolls, and crumble the top halves finely. Combine with the grated cheese, and season. Bind with enough egg to make a mixture which can be moulded into 4 patties the same size as the remaining roll halves.

Heat the butter in a large frying pan or skillet. Add the cheese patties and pork noisettes to the pan. Fry over fairly high heat for 2 minutes. Reduce the heat, turn the patties and noisettes over, and fry for 3 to 5 minutes until golden brown underneath; the meat should be almost tender. Transfer patties and noisettes to soft kitchen towelling.

Place the bottom halves of the rolls on a buttered baking sheet, cut side up. Cover each with a cheese patty, then a noisette. Drape a cheese slice over each noisette, and top if you wish with a pineapple ring. Bake at 220°C/425°F/Gas 7 for 5 to 6 minutes or until the cheese slice melts enough to run down and cover the meat. Top each helping with a red cocktail cherry just before serving.

Freezing You can make and freeze the patties ahead of time. But it is not wise to freeze the fried foods.

SWISS CHEESE FONDUE (NEUCHATEL FONDUE) — **Main dish**

Serves 4

garlic clove, peeled	I	I
dry white wine, warmed	275 ml/$\frac{1}{2}$ pint	I$\frac{1}{4}$ cups
fresh lemon juice	I teaspoon	I teaspoon
Emmental Switzerland, coarsely grated	200 g/7 ounces	I$\frac{3}{4}$ cups
Gruyère Switzerland, coarsely grated	400 g/I4 ounces	3$\frac{1}{2}$ cups
small glass of Kirsch	I	Mixed together
cornflower (cornstarch)	I heaped teaspoon	
ground nutmeg	good pinch	$\frac{1}{8}$ teaspoon
freshly ground white pepper	grinding	grinding
French bread batons (long sticks)	about I kg/2$\frac{1}{4}$ pounds (or half baton per person)	2$\frac{1}{4}$ pounds

Use a Swiss caquelon or a heavy-bottomed saucepan. Rub round the inside with the garlic clove. Add the wine and the lemon juice (which will help to bind the wine and cheese together). Stir in the cheeses. Still stirring, bring the contents of the pan to the boil over fairly high heat. Continue stirring until the cheeses have melted.

As soon as the fondue is creamy, mix in the kirsch and cornflour, and season to taste with nutmeg and pepper. Stir round, and then transfer the pan to a spirit burner on the dining table. The diners should be ready, waiting, with their plates piled with bread cut in cubes. Each diner spears a cube on a fondue fork and dips it in the creamy fondue, giving the fondue a quick stir (this keeps it creamy until it has all been eaten). Dipping and eating goes on until then.

(This recipe has been supplied by *Cheeses from Switzerland*.)

few farmers persisted in their work. The Royal Norwegian Agricultural College then worked in the 1950s to develop the cheese into a consistent, commercially viable product, under the direction of a Professor Ystgaard, and it was rechristened with its original name. This consists of two basic Norwegian words, *jarl* meaning earl or lord and *berg* meaning a hill or small mountain.

Once named and repackaged, the cheese became an instant commercial success and is now made in factories all over Norway. It is one of Norway's most popular eating cheeses; Norwegians eat 12 kg/25 pounds of cheese per head per year, at all their meals including breakfast (when they mostly eat whey cheeses such as Gjetost (see page 128)). It is even more popular as an export, however, especially to the United States.

Jarlsberg, as it is now made, is a pasteurised cow's milk, semi-hard cheese with a dry rind, made in the form of a thick wheel 30 cm/12 inches in diameter, and 10 cm/4 inches high. It weighs 10 kg/22 pounds and has the usual minimum fat content of 45 per cent. The paste with its natural cream colour and sizeable holes reminds one of Emmental, but cuts a little 'softer'. It has an attractive lactic aroma, and a flavour which is nutty and sweet, more creamy than Emmental yet in no way bland.

It is first class in salads and sandwiches, but less helpful for cocktail snacks since the large holes make it hard to cut into cubes. As an after-dinner cheese, serve it with two others: one mild, blue-veined type, say Mycella, and one goat's cheese such as Sainte Maure. To drink with it, choose a medium-light red wine or a dry white; for instance, a Chardonnay.

WEST GERMANY

TILSITER

The south coast of the Baltic Sea in northern Europe edges a belt of fine farming country, from Tilsit (now called Sovetsk) in the east to the Netherlands border in the west. From the early Middle Ages for several centuries, the farmers in the east produced and exported surplus grain to Scandinavia and Flanders. But the western farmers probably sold the butter and cheese from the milk of their fine, local Friesian black and white cows in the ports and other towns of their own area, to feed the local and foreign merchants who thronged them; for this was also Europe's greatest trading centre where the writ of the Hansa merchants ran. The local farmers joined in the constant traffic in foreign goods of all sorts including cheeses which crowded the waterways and highways.

The farmers noted red-coated Edam, French Port Salut, Belgian Limburger and a dozen more cheeses, scratched their heads, and in time began copying some of them. It was the common, accepted practice; there was no copyright in cheeses.

Tilsiter (or Tilsit) is one such cheese which, through widespread copying, has almost ceased to be a particular cheese and is really only a variously-labelled cheese type.

It was first made, it is said, in nineteenth-century Tilsit (at that time in the kingdom of Prussia) when an expatriate Dutch housewife tried to make her native Gouda; but without success because in her damp cellar, the raw-milk cheese softened and went sour. Nonetheless it was pleasant enough to be repeated. Now, more or less the same cheese is made, above all, in Switzerland (where it is called Royalp, and made in large quantities). It is also made in the Soviet Union, Norway, Denmark (as Havarti), Sweden (as Svensk Tilsiter), Austria, Poland (as Ser Tylzycki), Australia, East Germany and West Germany (where it is sometimes called Ragnit).

The making of the West German cheese is supervised by the German version of the British Milk Marketing Board under similar rigidly high standards. This German cheese may be made with whole or skimmed milk; the skimmed version is flavoured with caraway or anise. The curd is scalded lightly then drained and pressed, is ripened for a month, then matured for three to five months more. It emerges from this treatment as a not-quite-standard Tilsiter. It is a semi-hard cheese with a few irregular little holes in the pale cream-coloured paste, and a fat content varying from 30 to 50 per cent, depending on the type of milk used. Its texture is yielding, although it is firm enough to cut smoothly and to grate. Its natural washed rind is delicate and yellowish without much aroma, and sometimes dipped in wax.

The cheese is marketed in either a grindstone shape or as a loaf for commercial cutting. In one or other shape, it is possible to find almost any standard weight from 1.5 kg/3¼ pounds to 20 kg/44 pounds. The aroma and flavour of the cut paste are however unvarying. The scent is lactic, with a hint of the cellar; the taste is mild, buttery yet with a slight sharpness to prevent it being dull. It is an immensely popular munching cheese, wherever it comes from; the German type is as near as we can get to a cheese from its original home.

Wrapped in foil, a cut piece will survive in the refrigerator for two weeks at least. Give it a minimum of one and a half hours at room temperature before serving it. Drink with it a not-too-dry German or English white wine.

LIMBURGER

Like many traditional popular cheeses, Limburger has been so widely copied that it has become a type of cheese rather than a specific one, simply because every maker varies the recipe slightly. It is always, however, the strongest smelling of the surface-ripened types on the cheese counter.

It was born in the Middle Ages in the monasteries near the town of Limburg in Belgium, where it was marketed for centuries. Then in 1830, when the Bavarian cheese producer, Karl Hirnbein, thought of expanding the making of cheese in the Allgau region (already well-known for making a not very successful Emmental) he was advised by the Belgian cheese specialist Grosjean to try Limburger. He did; and his cheese was an instant success; so much so that many people think of Limburger as a German cheese by origin.

It is now produced in at least five other countries besides Germany and Belgium. But in the others (Austria, France, Israel, Switzerland and the United States) the strength of Limburger only appeals to a limited section of the population. In Germany, it is a subject of national pride.

The enthusiasm of the German people for strong cheeses is much debated. They seem to be in two minds about cheese. Since time immemorial, they have made a lot of light, fresh and sour-milk cheeses, and their main imports through the centuries have been mild Edam and Emmental types. Yet they have also made the pungent, hand-moulded Handkäse and, along with Limburger, they took over the little 'stinking cheese' of Belgium, Romadur and the Alsatian Munster. One theory about this love of assertive cheeses is that it has come down from the old tough inhabitants of East Prussia, whose desolate terrain enforced a diet of strong-flavoured foods such as pickled cabbage and strong, smoked meats and fish, along with fierce herbal ales; and that German palates, there and further south, had also, since ancient times, enjoyed the game foods of their enveloping forests, the boar, birds, hare and venison, and cheeses of the same ilk.

Germans distinguish seven types of Limburger, and one of them at least is not all that strong. It is the little, round breakfast cheese, or Frühstuckäse, which ripens in its package and is eaten almost fresh. The other types, classified by their fat content, are: Halbfettstufe (20 to 30 per cent), Dreiviertelfettstufe (30 to 40 per cent), Fettstufe (40 to 50 per cent), Vollfettstufe (45 to 50 per cent), Rahmstufe (above 50 per cent), Romadur, now classed with the Limburgers, (60 per cent) and Doppelrahmstufe (up to 85 per cent). The size of the cheese varies a good deal but it is usually a fairly small rectangular block.

Limburger of any type is technically difficult to make (which is why all the foreign copies vary). The difficulty lies in preserving the red bacterial flora called B. *linens* which give the surface of the developing cheese its highly distinctive smell and taste. It has to be watched with immense care because it falls victim so easily to variations in temperature and moisture.

The cheese is made with fresh pasteurised milk, warmed to 33 to 36°C/90 to 96°F, and renneted to coagulate in forty minutes. The curd is broken into cubes $\frac{1}{3}$ inch in size, is stirred, reheated and then pressed overnight without weights in rectangular forms 70 cm/27$\frac{1}{2}$ inches long, 13.5 cm/5$\frac{1}{2}$ inches wide and 20 cm/8 inches deep. The moulds are drained, with frequent turning to get rid of all the whey, after which the contents are cut into variously sized blocks, and given a brine bath. Bathing takes twenty-four hours for big cheeses, seven to twelve hours for smaller ones, and two to four hours for the little Romadurs, depending on the fat content.

To turn them into Limburgers, the cheeses are given a mechanical wash or rub with a bacterial solution of the surface flora, after a brief start has been made to ripen them; they are washed every other day, up to eight times, while being ripened for three to four weeks in all. By that time, their surfaces are ochre-coloured without cracks but covered with sticky flora. The paste is white to yellow and crumbly with a softer core (it is firmer in the low fat cheeses). After four weeks (only two for Romadur) the flavour of the surface, and to a lesser extent of the paste changes from spicy to distinctly piquant. The flora are then scraped off and the cheeses are packaged in foil to retain their pungency unimpaired.

Limburgers proper have several near cousins. Weisslacker Bierkäse (good with beer) gets a brine bath of two to three days although it weighs only 60 g/2$\frac{1}{4}$ ounces; it can be stored for up to a year. The Allgauer Gaiskäsle is made in two types; first an orange one using 60 to 80 per cent goat's milk and 20 to 40 per cent pasteurised cow's milk. It develops a fine orange surface with the same B. *linens* flora as the Limburgers; the paste is pale yellow, smooth and spicy to the nose — not to say goaty after three weeks. Second, there is a white type, made with the same goat's and cow's milk mix, but treated with whey and *Penicillium camemberti* after its bath. It develops a white coat, and behaves more like a mould-ripened cheese. It is milder, develops a few holes and gets a mushroomy scent.

If you are brave, you may tackle a Limburger surface. Whether you do or not, rye bread or pumperknickel makes a good 'bed' for the cheese, and a green salad (undressed) a fair companion. Drink with it beer, schnapps, or very dry cider.

CREAMY BLUE CHEESES
Bavarian Blue, Cambozola

I want to treat these two cheeses together because they illustrate in two, quite different ways the same innovative modern handling of mould-ripened cheeses – and with it, the emergence of sophisticated creative cheese-making (and eating) in Germany.

Now, mould-ripened cheeses as we know are ripened in two different ways. Some are ripened by mould spores sprayed on the surface of the curd; these cheeses grow a white downy mould on their surfaces. Other cheeses are ripened by mould spores which grow along minute air cracks in the paste, making blueish or greenish veins. The down and veins are made by different kinds of *Penicillium* moulds. Both kinds have been known, and used on or in cheeses, for a very long time. But not together intentionally!

It has been said that the idea of using them together took hold when scientists discovered that a very small quantity of (let us say) *Penicillium roqueforti* could be mixed into the milk or curd for a very creamy, cow's milk cheese and would 'blue' the curd just enough to give it a good flavour. They put some curd containing a 'blueing' mould into a Camembert-style hoop, and after it had 'blued', sprayed its surface with a mould which makes white down grow. After many experiments – because the surface-ripening mould seemed to prevent 'blueing' ones' growth – there emerged a crop of what we call 'blue Bries'.

Interesting and good to eat as these are, they are still all-blue cheeses under the lightly flavoured white coat – and this is where Bavarian Blue, like some of the Danish soft cheeses, is unusual.

Bavarian Blue, first produced in 1973, is a cow's milk, soft, partly blued cheese with a white washed rind, described by its makers as a blue and white mould cheese. It is made in the Bergader Waging factory a few kilometres north of Salzburg in the south Bavarian Alps. In shape, it is a thickish disc 18 cm/7 inches in diameter, 5 cm/2 inches deep and weighing 1.3 kg/2¾ pounds in the piece. It has a high fat content of 70 per cent; but what is more interesting is that its outside layers appear to consist of Camembert-ripened curd while the centre layer contains *Penicillium roqueforti*. If, as we think, they ripen together it is pleasing to record that, so far from being sterile, the union results in a beautiful cheese, gentler in flavour even than standard 'blue Bries', with just a light semblance of greyish-blue mould across the centre to underline its cellary flavour.

Once cut, it will keep in a refrigerator for ten days, but its subtlety makes it essential to take it out into a warm room to 'breathe' two hours before eating it, with a delicate, not too dry, white wine.

Cambozola is much better known by name than Bavarian Blue because its name is more dramatic. It also hints at mystery. Where did the name come from? The makers are cagey, divulging only that it is a 'blue Brie' with a flavoured rind. It has been suggested that it is a Camembert-Gorgonzola combination which seems plausible, or perhaps a Roquefort, Gorgonzola and Camembert 'mix' which seems less so; and it is sometimes confused with Bavarian Blue – understandably since it comes from the same area. But it can claim no pride of ancestry, nor even known parentage.

What it can claim is a quite outstanding flavour. It is, as John Arlott has said, indisputably a distinguished cheese. He goes on to point out that German technological excellence is such that it can not only copy successfully the cheeses of other nations but can originate its own surprises – and in the case of Cambozola has certainly done so.

The cheese is a full-fat (70 per cent) soft, blue cow's milk cheese, made in 2 kg/4½ pound wheels and similar weights, and also sold in 135 g/5 ounce portions. It comes from Kempten, the 'cheese town' in the Allgau Alps close to the Swiss and Austrian borders east of Lake Constance. It is, therefore, almost undoubtedly made from the milk of the low-built, attractive brown Bavarian cows with their flat-keyed bells. It is almost undoubtedly too, nurtured by the skilled Kempten affineurs in the damp atmosphere the blue and white mould cheeses require.

Cambozola arrived in Britain in 1977, and despite its lack of official 'papers' has proved a welcome immigrant. It is certainly rich, but its seeming blandness hides a flavour which expands on the palate into generous but not cloying blueness.

Keep it wrapped in foil in the refrigerator for as much as a fortnight if you must; but you will probably want to eat it sooner. It will go well with a rosé wine, or say, the 'seewein' (lake wine) of the area which is the traditionally pink-tinted Weissherbst – white wine pressed from red Spätburgunder grapes.

MEDITERRANEAN

FETA/FETTA

My cousin's husband, Dimitri, would not eat a main meal without a salad crowned with the black olives of his home in Greece nestled in snow-white, sheep's milk Feta cheese. But then Dimitri was a Greek to his fingertips besides being a poet and philosopher; and Greeks eat more cheese in their home-land than any other people in Europe – an astonishingly high average of 15 kg/33 pounds a year per person, so we are told. Greek cheeses include Kasseri, Kefalotyri, and several others (along with Myzittra and its local variants which are whey cheeses). However, notable and most popular among them is Feta or Fetta (spell it as you will).

This weight of cheese eaten per person each year is only slightly less astonishing when one realises that Feta, like the whey cheeses, is very moist indeed; it is ripened in its own whey mixed with brine, and so the load of cheese which a healthy Greek ingests is more than fractionally a load of liquid.

Dimitri, being a poet, could quote from the first great classic poet, Homer, the story of how Polyphemus, the one-eyed giant, son of the sea-god Poseidon, made sheep's cheese in the cave where he lived. Almost all the ancient cheeses of Greece, like the modern ones, were made from sheep's milk or sheep's and goat's milk mixed, for the very good reason that most of the land was too poor to supply grazing for cattle. Such cattle as the Greeks possessed pulled the plough, unless they were beautiful enough to be treated as sacred sacrifices; to call a girl 'cow-eyed' was a huge compliment. Besides this, goats, and especially sheep, provided hair or wool, high protein, rich milk and meat – to say nothing of kids and lambs; and shepherds were almost as common in Greek mythology as sheep's cheeses are on Greek dinner-tables today.

There are three main types of these Greek cheeses. The type of cheese Polyphemus made in his cave sounds like a *fresh* cheese. One translation runs: 'He curdled half of the white milk and stacked it in plaited baskets; the other part he put away in barrels to drink from.' This is much like the making of fresh cheeses today; the milk is hung in a bag made of the skin or vell of a dead beast, either in the sun or near a fire where it curdles quickly, and the solid curd is then skimmed off into small baskets in which it drains. Being only lightly renneted, it must be eaten within a day or two, unless heavily salted – and then you only taste salt.

The method would not be much more complex if Polyphemus were making a *pickled* cheese such as Feta. Modern sheep's milk Feta, as the Greeks like it, is made from soured pasteurised milk, renneted, curdled and partly drained; then cubed, pressed, moulded and drained some more. It is cut into tidy pieces and salted by hand or in a brine bath, is dried in small moulds for just a short while, and is finally matured in sealed moulds in a mixture of its own remaining whey and added brine for two to three months. (The moulds have to be opened from time to time in case pressure builds up inside; otherwise there might be a rather messy explosion.)

The remaining type of sheep's cheese made in Greece is a hard table cheese. The Greeks make two such table cheeses which are known beyond their borders: Kasseri, which is a firm white, well-aged cheese, good for grilling; and Kefalotyri, whose main claim to fame for westerners seems to be its name which is a combination of two words meaning 'skull' or 'cap' and 'cheese'. (One wonders if Greek schoolboys use it as a taunt – 'You kefalotyri, you!' has a good, expletive sound to it.) Both these cheeses are often called by local names in their homeland, and they are made elsewhere in the Balkans with yet other names.

Feta – or what passes for Feta – is made in many countries outside Greece too. In fact, after Cheddar, 'Swiss' and Brie it is possibly the commonest bastard cheese in the world. It is most often made with cow's milk, when it is yellowish or (worse) is artificially decolourised. It has cream added to simulate the richer content of the smaller non-copyable fat globules in sheep's milk. It is generally sold vacuum-packed in flat slabs which have a tough, rubbery consistency (I must admit this is a fault one encounters in some real sheep's cheeses so perhaps one should not be too rude about it). Finally it has no particular taste, not even that of the pickling brine, certainly not the piquant, sourish interesting taste of real Feta. On the whole, such copies of Feta do not seem to have much going for them.

But genuine, Balkan sheep's milk Feta, crumbled over a lettuce, onion and potato salad, spiked with pine nuts and topped with shiny black olives – that is quite something. (You can cook with Feta too.)

What you drink with your cheese will depend on how you eat it. Try a Balkan wine if you can, red or white according to your type of meal.

MANCHEGO

I call Manchego the 'three-in-one' cheese because when I last tasted it – admittedly at a party – I thought I was being offered snack cubes of three distinctly different cheeses; and different they certainly were. In fact there are *four* different types of this seemingly ever-varying sheep's cheese, depending on how long it has ripened for. There is Manchego *fresco* (fresh and young), Manchego *curado* (three to thirteen weeks old), Manchego *viego* (more than three months old) and Manchego *en aciete* (up to a year old). The very name of this last cheese has a sigh of age about it, and its grey-black rind has an elderly look – although that, in shepherds' cheeses, is due to preservative immersion in olive oil.

More Manchego is made than any other Spanish cheese. All the milk comes, by law, from the pastures of four provinces in south-east central Spain (Toledo, Cuenca, Albacete and Ciudad Real) and from the Manchego breed of sheep which feed there. Originally, the rind bore the impressions of the beautifully plaited rush baskets in which the shepherds had pressed the curds by hand, and of the flower they placed on top. Now the factories copy it.

The cheese is made of whole sheep's milk, with its natural 50 to 58 per cent fat content. Pasteurised or not, it is heated to about 30°C/86°F and held for forty-five to sixty minutes to ensure firm curdling. The drained curd is cut into 5 to 10 cm/2 to 4 inch cubes, then stirred and reheated to up to 40°C/104°F before moulding.

The cheese emerges from this as a solid wheel 25 cm/10 inches in diameter and 8 to 12 cm/3½ to 4½ inches high, with a hard, corn-coloured rind, usually now waxed. The fairly fatty, firm paste sometimes has small 'eyes' in it. A fresh cheese is flavoured only with the milk used to make it, but thereafter the flavour strengthens progressively as the cheese ages, and the colour darkens slightly from pale cream to near yellow.

Provided you are prepared to try a sheep's milk cheese, you will like Manchego at some stage of its development, but I suggest training on the milder ones before you graduate to a 'grandfather' cheese. I'm afraid you will not come across an oil-bathed cheese, but the waxed ones supply fine tasting experiences. Eat your cheese piled into pitta breads with stoned olives and anchovy fillets or (when old) just cubed or thinly sliced, on rye or coarse brown bread. Obviously you will not insult it by drinking a foreign wine. Suit the age of the Rioja you choose to the age of the cheese (or, if you have a well-aged cheese, try a pungent dark, dry oloroso sherry).

OLD DUTCH COBBLER

Main dish

Serves 4 to 6

Dough

self-raising (self-rising) flour	225 g/8 ounces	2 cups
baking powder	1 teaspoon	1 teaspoon
salt	pinch	dash
unsalted butter	50 g/2 ounces	$\frac{1}{4}$ cup
milk	150 ml/$\frac{1}{4}$ pint	$\frac{2}{3}$ cup
Dijon mustard	1 tablespoon	1 tablespoon
Mature Edam cheese, grated	50 g/2 ounces	$\frac{1}{2}$ cup

Base Mixture

cod or other white fish fillet	450 g/1 pound	1 pound
milk	425 ml/$\frac{3}{4}$ pint	2 cups
unsalted butter	75 g/3 ounces	$\frac{1}{3}$ cup
onion, chopped	1	1
plain (all-purpose) flour	40 g/1$\frac{1}{2}$ ounces	5 tablespoons
Mature Edam cheese, grated	225 g/8 ounces	2 cups
frozen peas, thawed and drained	225 g/8 ounces	$\frac{1}{2}$ pound
chopped parsley	1 tablespoon	1 tablespoon
dry mustard powder	$\frac{1}{2}$ teaspoon	$\frac{1}{2}$ teaspoon
salt and white pepper to taste		
egg, beaten	1	1

Make the cobbler dough first to give it time to chill. Sift the flour, baking powder and salt into a bowl. Cut or rub in the butter. Mix with milk to a soft dough. Knead lightly. Then roll out into a 250 by 200 mm/10 by 8 inch rectangle. Spread with the Dijon mustard and cheese. Roll up like a Swiss roll (jelly roll). Chill.

Poach the fish in the milk until tender. Drain it, reserving the liquid. Skin and flake the fish. Set it aside.

Melt half the butter and fry the onion in it until soft. Add it to the fish.

Put the flour, remaining butter and the milk from cooking the fish in a saucepan. Beat over fairly high heat until the sauce thickens and smooths out. Take the pan off the heat and stir into the sauce the fish, onion, cheese, peas, parsley and mustard powder. Season to taste. Mix well.

Butter the inside of a 1.7 litre/3 pint (3$\frac{3}{4}$ pint) baking dish about 5 cm/2 inches deep. Spoon in the fish mixture.

Cut the roll of chilled dough into 1 cm/$\frac{1}{2}$ inch slices. Arrange the slices, cut side down, in an overlapping line around the dish. Brush with the beaten egg. Bake the dish at 200°C/400°F/Gas 6 for 25 minutes until the cobbler dough slices are golden brown. Serve hot.

Freezing The cobbler dough can be frozen before baking. It would be a good way to make use of 50 g/2 ounces ($\frac{1}{2}$ cup) leftover cheese, whether you use it later on this fish cobbler or some other dish. Don't risk freezing the fish mixture.

PART III

GLOSSARY OF CHEESES AND CHEESE TERMS

I am well aware that this list of cheese names and terms is cruelly selective. Everyone who reads it will fault it for omitting the *one* cheese they have always wished to know about or the term they most want to clarify. I can only plead the restrictions imposed by space and time, that is by the number of pages I can spare and by my publisher's deadline.

AFFINÉ: French word denoting 'ripened' as compared with 'fresh' (French-*frais*). Thus *Gournay frais* means fresh Gournay cheese while *Gournay affiné* means ripened Gournay cheese.

AMERICAN CHEESE: Loose term for American Cheddar and similar, locally-made cheeses such as Brick, Colby.

ANGELOT: Medieval Norman cheese, named after a golden coin and therefore, presumably, golden-rinded.

APPELLATION CONTRÔLÉE, APPELLATION D'ORIGINE, APPELLATION D'ORIGINE CONTRÔLÉE: A French designation phrased in various ways which applies to certain cheeses. It is similar in intent to the 'Appellation contrôlée' quality label attached to certain wines. The international Stresa Convention laid down that imitations of established cheeses might not use the parental name, and the appellation acts as a kind of 'keep off' notice.

APPENZELL SWITZERLAND: A semi-hard Swiss cheese made from cow's milk, pressed and cooked, with a 45 to 50 per cent fat content. It is smaller than the other famous Swiss cheeses, but made with the same strict care. Being less heavily cured, it is milder, but its flavour is unique because it is washed, during its curing, with diluted and seasoned white wine or cider.

APPLEWOOD: Said to be a favourite wood for smoking cheese in ancient Rome. See also Smoked Applewood.

ASIAGO: A strong-smelling grana Italian cheese, named after its birthplace in the province of Vicenza. It is now made in many parts of north Italy, mostly from a mixture of skimmed and full cow's milk; also made in the United States.

Some Italian Asiago (and its derivative *Pressato*) is eaten after about sixty days as *Asiago di taglio* (slicing cheese). The semi-skim *Asiago d'Allievo* is matured for longer and is well known as a grating cheese.

There are three forms of American Asiago: fresh (soft), medium and old cheese. Fresh Asiago is cured for about sixty days, medium Asiago for about six months and old Asiago for as much as a year.

AUSTRALIAN CHEESES: Britain's decision to enter the European Common Market posed the Australian dairy industry a formidable challenge to find new markets. At the same time, the home market was widened by an influx of immigrants from various countries and by urban Australians developing more sophisticated tastes.

The industry responded swiftly and effectively. Besides its established range of brand-named Cheddars of varying degrees of maturity, it now produces medium to excellent copies of many other cheeses ranging from hard to semi-soft, such as Tilsit, Samsoe, Danbo, Edam, Gouda, Stracchino, Pecorino (fresh and matured) and Parmesan (table and grating). Soft cheeses, too, are finding a growing market, in particular Mozzarella (pizza cheese) and flavoured cottage and cream cheeses. Several goat's cheeses are now being made, as well as cow's milk cheeses such as Brie and Camembert; and a start has been made on producing sheep's milk cheeses.

Besides these, Australia already produces several local types of 'blue' cheese, ranging from the strong indigenous Gippsland Blue, which is rightly esteemed, to Brie-style lightly 'blued' creamy cheeses.

Among the familiar Cheddars, some well-flavoured, mature cheeses are made and sold under brand names such as Millel, Mersey Valley and (Tasmanian) King Island, Bega, Trafalgar and Brown-Rinded. Rinded Cheddar is becoming popular again. Cheddar-type cheeses also include some reduced fat cheeses such as mini-chol (whey cheese). The giant, semi-autonomous Kraft combine produces six Cheddar-type cheeses and twelve others, such as Colby, Haversham, Swiss and Romano and its internationally famous packaged blocks and slices. Such packaged cheeses are still sold much more widely (eg in supermarkets) than cheeses sold by weight, such as the local Emmental-style St Clair or the speciality Haberfield Cheddar with port wine. These are only available in a few city speciality and department stores.

An Australian curiosity is the local fruit cheese, normally a soft cheese mixed with assorted chopped, dried and preserved fruits; very popular with children. Sweet, smooth compound 'cheeses' flavoured with strawberry, chocolate, coffee etc are also sold by weight or in cartons.

BAGNES: Swiss cow's milk cheese used for making raclette, but also a pleasant table cheese.

BAKER'S: American cow's, skim-milk cheese, like cottage cheese but softer and more acid. It is normally only used commercially, although if cream is added it can be eaten like 4 per cent fat cottage cheese.

BANBURY: English sixteenth-century thin, pressed cheese known to Shakespeare. Probably a cow's milk cheese. Also said to have been popular in the early nineteenth century as a rich cheese shaped into a 'log' an inch thick.

BANON: An attractive small cheese from southern France, made from sheep's milk in spring, goat's milk in summer through autumn and from cow's milk year-round (in creameries). Its fat content and flavour obviously, therefore, vary a good deal. Its stable distinguishing feature is that it is wrapped in chestnut leaves tied with raffia, usually dipped in the local *eau de vie de marc*. The marc-flavoured cheeses are matured in earthenware jars for two weeks to two months (when they are very strong-flavoured indeed).

BARAKA: A French cow's milk soft cheese in the shape of a horseshoe about 11 cm/$4\frac{1}{2}$ inches long and wide, and 3.5 cm/$1\frac{1}{2}$ inches thick. It is made, specifically for the tourist and for celebrations, in a creamery close to where a good Brie de Coulommiers is made. It has itself much the character of a Brie. Although it can be eaten fresh, and is perhaps best that way, it can also be allowed to ripen slightly to achieve a downy white rind. Don't keep it after this moment.

BEAUMONT: A commercially-made Savoy cheese similar to Saint Paulin, developed by the firm of Girod et Cie. It has a smooth yellow, supple rind and a delicate, bland paste with 50 per cent fat content. A flattened disc 20 cm/8 inches in diameter and about 3.5 cm/1½ inches thick, a whole cheese weighs about 1.5 kg/3 pounds 5 ounces.

BEAUVOORDE: Hexagonal Belgian cheese with a firm yellow paste, named for the local château, and for many years made only by one family. Post-war expansion and initiative on the government's part has meant that it is now made in a modern dairy at Passchendaele. It has a natural grey rind, and when cut the paste has a delicate, almost feminine flavour.

BEENLEIGH BLUE: A full-flavoured, naturally crusted cheese made from unpasteurised sheep's milk. It is matured underground for seven months in 1.8 kg/4 pound drums. It is made in South Devon, in the south-west of England. *Harbourne Blue* is a similar cheese produced by the same maker from unpasteurised goat's milk.

BEL: French multinational producer of cheese such as Bonbel, Baby bel, Kiri and La Vache Qui Rit in Europe, and Albany in the United States.

BELLE BRESSANE: A modern French, soft cow's milk cheese with blue veining, made in a 20 cm/8 inch wheel with a 7.5 cm/3 inch hole in the centre. It was invented by cheese-makers of Grieze, a cheese centre in the rich dairying area of Bresse, to cash in on the popularity of its predecessor, Bresse Bleu. Belle Bressane is made from pasteurised milk, and has a fat content of 50 per cent. It has a fine smooth rind, a supple creamy texture and a mild, 'cellary' flavour not unlike that of Gorgonzola, although lighter. If foil-wrapped it will keep for a week in a refrigerator, but it is not really a good keeping cheese, and unless eaten soon, should be made into a pâté or mousse for eating with salad (in summer) or as a 'floater' on a spicy soup (in winter).

BELLELAY: Alternative name for Tête de Moine.

BELLSHIRE: Modern English, semi-soft cheese flavoured with chives and onions.

BERGADER BLUE: A German, cow's milk softish 'blue' cheese with a natural rind which develops a slight white surface mould. It has a white paste with branching blue veins made by *Penicillium roqueforti* – a fact which led to it being given, originally, a German name ending in 'roquefort'. An eight-year court case resulted in the change of name – a happy one, since its new name means 'mountain vein', which is pictur-esque, and describes the view from the dairy where it is made. The cheese is a low cylinder in shape, 17.5 cm/6¾ inches in diameter and 8 cm/3⅓ inches high, and has a fat content of 50 per cent.

BERGKÄSE: Austrian cheese, traditionally made during the summer months in the mountains. Even today, to qualify for the name, the cheese must be made above 800 metres. It is a hard cheese with a brown rind, and the golden-yellow paste is full of small 'teardrop' holes. It is matured for at least eight months.

BERKELEY: The best cheese-making area in Gloucestershire, in the south-west of England, has been since early times the Vale of Berkeley on the south bank of the Severn River. From the time when cheeses became recognised by 'area' names until the 1930s, Single and Double Berkeley cheeses were sometimes sold under their own 'labels', although made and marketed like the more common Single and Double Gloucester cheeses. The name of Double Berkeley has been revived in a small way in the 1980s; and the cheese is described in the profile of Gloucester cheeses on page 36.

BIERKÄSE: German and Belgian cheese usually called Weisslacker. Also made in Wisconsin, USA, where it is translated as 'Beer Cheese'.

BLENDED BRITISH CHEESES: See compound product, page 140.

BLEU: The French word for 'blue', used in cheese parlance for cheeses with visible blue-green mottled or branching mould in their paste. Cheeses mottled with mould may alternatively be described in French as *persillé*.

BLEU DE BRESSE: Although only about forty years old, Bleu de Bresse is already considered a 'classic' French blue cheese and one of the best. It is a cow's milk cheese, sold in solid 'drainpipe' shapes of various sizes and weights, from tiny 'logs' weighing 120 g/4½ ounces to massive ones weighing almost 2 kg/4½ pounds; it has a 50 per cent fat content. Pipo Crem', a popular export, is a copy made at the well-known cheese town, Grièges.

BLEU DES CAUSSES: An ancient and respected French cow's milk blue cheese, made from full, unpasteurised cow's milk. Bleu des Causses is made and ripened in much the same way as Roquefort, without artificial aids. It has a 45 per cent fat content.

BLEU DE HAUT JURA: Name legally restricted to certain regional types of French blue cheese made at an altitude of at least 762 cm/2,500 feet. Well-known cheeses which qualify are Bleu de Gex and Bleu de Septmoncel. Bleu de Sassenage is another.

BLUE BRIE(S): Several countries now make one or more creamy, surface-ripened cheeses into which mould spores which create a light interior veining have been introduced. They tend to be rich double-cream cheeses. The French Brie au Bleu for instance has a minimum fat content of 63 per cent and Danish Saga of 70 per cent.

BLUE CHEESE: An American-made cheese ripened with the help of *Penicillium roqueforti* and akin to French Roquefort, except in being made from cow's or goat's milk rather than ewe's milk. Cured for about three months.

BLUE STUART: Scottish cheese made for a short time in the 1970s by a well-known cheese-maker for the North of Scotland Milk Marketing Board.

BLUE VINNEY: This English low-fat hard blue cheese from the milk of Dorset and Gloucester cattle was christened Blue Vinney (or Vinny) long ago, probably when *vinew*, an old local word for mould or veining was still in everyday use. The cheese itself was common enough as a by-product of butter making until the mid-nineteenth century when rail transport made it more profitable to send the fresh milk to the towns than to process it. But some Blue Vinney was still being made in the 1930s although by the time World War II broke out and put an end to it 'for the duration', machine skimming, which leaves milk too thin for cheese-making, had already sounded its death knell.

The English cheese expert Patrick Rance, who has researched the subject meticulously, says in *The Great British Cheese Book* that a few Blue Vinney makers recaptured their craft after the war although most attempts to re-create the easily spoiled, very low fat cheese failed. At one time in the 1970s there seemed to be no genuine Blue Vinney, only some so-called Dorset Blue from an unknown source. Then, in the early 1980s, a few dedicated makers were brought to light; and in 1984, a modern disease-resistant Blue Vinney came on the market, although not easy to obtain.

Anyone who wants to know more about Blue Vinney should read the detailed story in the 1988 edition of Major Rance's *The Great British Cheese Book*.

BONBEL: See Bel.

BONCHESTER: Soft Coulommiers-type cow's milk cheese, made from unpasteurised Jersey milk in the Scottish border country. The cheese is made in 450 g/1 pound rounds, with a natural white mould crust.

CHEESE AND PARSLEY BAKE · **Light dish**

Serves 4 to 6

Esrom cheese without rind, finely sliced (see method)	150 g/5 ounces	5 ounces
large square slices of white bread with crusts cut off	10 to 12	10 to 12
butter for spreading		
salad celery stalk, finely chopped	25 g/1 ounce	2 tablespoons
chopped parsley	2½ tablespoons	2½ tablespoons
milk	175 ml/6 fl oz	¾ cup
egg yolks	2	2
salt and pepper		
Parmesan cheese, finely grated		

If possible cut the cheese into paper-thin slices with a continental cheese slicer. Keep it aside. Use an oblong or oval baking dish about 18 cm/7 inches long and 5 cm/2 inches deep.

Spread one side of each bread slice lightly with butter. Cover the bottom of the dish with a layer of bread, buttered side up; cut the slices into pieces which fit closely without gaps between them. Cover the bread all over with a layer of cheese, using about a third of the slices. Then cover the cheese with about a third of the chopped celery and parsley. Repeat these layers twice more, ending with the last of the vegetables.

Measure the milk in a jug, add the egg yolks and seasoning, and beat well to blend them. Trickle the milk into the dish, pouring it in down the side in two or three places. Cover the dish thickly with Parmesan cheese.

Bake for about 30 minutes at 190°C/375°F/Gas 5. The top crust should be firm and golden, and the pudding underneath creamy but not sloppy.

Freezing Freeze the prepared dish for up to a month before baking if you like. Cook it from frozen, allowing enough extra time to cook the bread in the centre of the dish. If frozen, keep the dish loosely covered for the first 15 minutes of the cooking time.

HAVARTI VEGETABLE BAKE · **Main dish**

Serves 4

small onions, peeled and sliced	2	2
butter	75 g/3 ounces	⅓ cup
courgettes (zucchini) sliced into thin rounds	225 g/8 ounces	½ pound
tomatoes, sliced	225 g/8 ounces	½ pound
dried mixed herbs	1 teaspoon	1 teaspoon
salt and black pepper to taste		
plain (all-purpose) flour	50 g/2 ounces	½ cup
milk	575 ml/1 pint	2½ cups
Havarti cheese without rind, grated	175 g/6 ounces	1½ cups
soft white breadcrumbs	50 g/2 ounces	1 cup
parsley sprigs to garnish		

Fry the sliced onions in 2 tablespoons of the butter until soft but not coloured. Place half the courgette slices in a 1 litre/1¾ pint (2¼ pint) ovenproof serving dish, in an even layer. Cover them with half the fried sliced onions, and all the tomatoes. Sprinkle with the dried mixed herbs, and a little salt and black pepper. Then add the remaining sliced onions, and cover with the rest of the courgettes.

Place the remaining butter, the flour and milk in a medium-sized saucepan. Heat, whisking (beating) constantly, until the sauce thickens. Remove from the heat. Add 100 g/4 ounces (¼ pound) of the grated cheese, and seasoning to suit your taste. Pour the sauce over the vegetables. Combine the remaining grated cheese and the breadcrumbs, and sprinkle them over the dish.

Bake the dish at 180°C/350°F/Gas 4 for 30 to 35 minutes. Serve garnished with parsley sprigs.

This dish is hazardous to freeze.

(Recipe by courtesy of the Danish Dairy Bureau)

BOULETTE D'AVESNES: Mashed, kneaded cow's milk curds flavoured with parsley, tarragon and pepper, made in Hainaut (Flanders). Strongly flavoured, after three months' curing; fat content about 50 per cent.

BOULETTE DE CAMBRAI: Fresh cow's milk curds, mixed with parsley, tarragon and chives and hand-moulded into balls. Made in Flanders. Has a mild flavour; 45 per cent fat content.

BOULETTE DES MOINES: Fresh cow's milk curds, flavoured with herbs, formed into 8 cm/3 inch balls by the monks of La-Pierre-qui-Vire in Burgundy, France.

BOURSIN: A small French triple-crème cheese made in factories from enriched cow's milk, and named after the owners. A popular supermarket cheese, sold with various coatings or flavourings.

BRESSE BLEU: Another name for Bleu de Bresse. See also Belle Bressane page 117, and Pipo Crem' page 133.

BRICK: Creamy-yellow, brick-shaped, semi-soft cow's milk cheese with irregular 'eyes'. The cheese originated in Wisconsin, USA and is still made there, in Oregon and across the border in Canada. Its flavour has been likened to a mild Cheddar with a hint of Limburger. The name may refer to its shape or to the bricks used to press it; or it may be derived from an old English Wiltshire cheese called Brickbat.

Brick cheeses are usually about 30 cm/10 inches long, 12.5 cm/5 inches wide and 7.5 cm/3 inches thick; this size of cheese weighs about 2.3 kg/5 pounds. The fat content is about 50 per cent of dry matter.

BRICQUEBEC: Trappist monks make this French cheese near Cherbourg, and market it as *Providence*. It is a cow's milk, pressed but uncooked cheese cured in humid cellars for two months. The shape is a flat wheel 21.5 cm/8¾ inches in diameter. It weighs about 1.4 kg/3 pounds. The washed rind is smooth and yellowish, the flavour and texture akin to St Paulin.

BRIE AU BLEU: French double-cream cow's milk soft cheese, made commercially by the firm of Le Roitelet. The cheese is only very lightly 'blued' under its natural white flor rind. It is made near Mâcon, north of Lyon, and is a fairly new cheese created in 1978 to exploit the popular love of creamy cheese with the fashionable hint of blue-mould flavour.

BRIE CHEESES WITH FLAVOURINGS: A modern development. Several European manufacturers have specialised in the production of Brie-style cheese with herbs or black peppercorns layered in the paste, or with a covering layer of mixed-colour peppers. Strictly they are usually double-cream cheeses, having a fat content of 62–70 per cent.

BRIE DE COULOMMIERS: See Brie, page 57.

BRILLAT-SAVARIN: A French, Norman cheese with no less than 75 per cent fat in the dry matter, it was invented between the wars by arguably the most skilled European cheese-man of our time, Henri Androuet. Surface-ripened, its flavour is always delicate, and – not surprisingly – creamy.

BRIQUE, BRIQUETTE: French name for brick-shaped cheeses.

BROUSSE: Old French Provençal word for stir, beat, which features in the names of several cheeses of the south.

BRUDER BASIL: Based on an old monastery cheese type, this German Bavarian smoked cheese was created to mark the 75th anniversary of the Bergader Company under the guidance of the daughter of the firm's founder. This lady, conscious of its monastic association, christened it Brother Basil, using her father's name. One day, perhaps, an aura of healing power may surround it. For the moment, it is just a semi-hard, smooth-pasted cow's milk cheese, naturally smoked over Alpine oak, with a lightly piquant pleasant flavour.

BÛCHE: French word for 'log', hence for cheese shaped like a log.

BUN: Shape of cheese popular in New Zealand, flat underneath and domed on top.

BURRINO: An alternative Italian name for Manteca cheese.

CABECOU, CABICOU: Alternative spellings for Chabichou.

CABRALES: A naturally-made Spanish blue cheese from mountain ranges in Asturias. It consists of raw whole cow's milk with some ewe's and goat's milk added. Lightly pressed after cutting the curd, the cheese drip-drains in natural caves with mould-covered walls, and may ripen for up to six months. The flavour of the cheese when ready for eating is strong, and its greyish-white, blue-speckled paste has a pungent aroma. It is not normally exported, but travellers in Spain who like Roquefort will find it rewarding.

CACETTA, CACIETTO: An Italian, cow's milk, medium-fat cheese of the 'plastic curd' type and similar to Caciocavallo. Hung on strings (sometimes to be smoked) it develops the same 'saddlebag' shape. An unsmoked cheese, it has a pale natural rind, generally waxed, and the very smooth, almost white paste of most of its kind.

CACIOCAVALLO: Italian plastic curd (pasta filata) cheese akin to Provolone but with less fat. The cheeses are tied in pairs and hung over a pole to cure, so they are pear-shaped rather like saddlebags; hence their name, derived from *cacio a cavallo* meaning 'cheeses on horseback'.

Caciocavallo is now generally made from cow's milk, skimmed evening milk being mixed with whole morning milk. It is made like Provolone, and can be eaten after curing from two to four months. Its fat content is 42 per cent.

CAMBRIDGE OR YORK CHEESE: Soft English domestic cheese made from unskimmed cow's milk. The renneted curd is set in small oblong moulds for 24 to 36 hours and must then be eaten almost at once. The cheese is usually made with an annatto-tinted golden strip through the centre.

CANADIAN CHEESES: In the early 1600s, cattle were introduced into the vast territory destined to become Canada. By 1670, the finest milking cows from Normandy and Brittany had been imported into what was then New France. Their arrival gave rise to cattle breeding (perhaps the Canadienne breed) and certainly heralded the start of Canadian cheese-making. The French colonists began by making soft cheeses such as they had known in France.

With the arrival of the British came the production of hard cheeses because they introduced the making of Cheddar cheese, which was to become a major food item for home consumption and export alike.

During the nineteenth century, exports from the provinces of Ontario and Nova Scotia increased rapidly. In 1864, the first official cheese factory called 'Pioneer' was established in Ontario. Then in 1893 the Trappist fathers of Oka created the cheese which bears the same name, (see Port Salut, page 52). As waterways grew and railroads spread in the territory, Canadian cheese-making expanded and it became a promising industry.

By 1904 Canadian Cheddar was already the top-selling cheese and it has not stopped there. During this century, Canadian Cheddar has been a major import by the United Kingdom. At the same time, especially since World War II, the types of cheeses made in Canada have grown to sixty or more due to the many and varied immigrants. Italians have introduced Ricotta, Mozzarella and Parmesan. Greeks have brought a taste for Feta, while French-speaking Canadians have increased their eating of Brie and Camembert. All these cheeses and many more are now made in Canada. Ethnic restaurants have played their part in making them ever more popular. Between 1975 and 1985 the production of these fine cheeses doubled and is expected to double again before AD 2000.

Most of the fine Canadian cheeses are well known but some (perhaps sometimes copies of cheeses with 'protected' names elsewhere) are unique to Canada. Among her fresh cheeses, *Tuma* is unusual and pleasant, based on a Sicilian cheese. Semi-soft cheeses include *Trecce*, an Italian spun-curd cheese shaped like (and named after) a braid. Among surface-ripened cheeses, there is *Serra*, a Portuguese mountain cheese, and various Oka types are made.

Canada has many other cheeses ranging from soft to hard, but the various categories of Cheddar dominate them all. Canadian Cheddar, young or old, is accompanied on the cheesemonger's shelves by variations such as marbled and wine-cured cheese, and by unpressed curds. However, of them all, a plain medium Cheddar, aged for six to nine months, and ready for use as a table cheese is probably still the most popular at home and abroad.

CAPRICE DES DIEUX: Double-cream, soft-ripened modern French cow's milk cheese made in an oval shape by the firm of Bongrain et Cie. Very popular outside France.

CAPRICORN: An English, goat's milk cheese from the West Country, surface-ripened and suitable for vegetarian use.

CARRÉ: The word for 'square' in French, applied to various cheeses which are square and generally flattish in shape. One of the best known is *Carré de l'Est*. A popular type in America is *Carré Frais* also called *Double Creme Carré*, a small rich cheese of Neufchatel type, eaten fresh; it has a minimum of 60 per cent fat in dry matter.

CASTELLO: Popular brand of exported Danish cheeses, of which the best known is the creamy blue and white mould speciality, Blue Castello, which is a popular export. Like the other seven Castello cheeses it is made by the family firm of Tholstrup. It is sold in 150 g/5 ounce wedges and as a 1 kg/2 pound round. See also Saga (page 105).

CENDRÉ: French term for cheese ripened in ashes or coated with ash during storage. One reason is that an ash coating slows down the maturation process and the resultant cheese is slightly softer than an untreated version. Some cheeses are packaged in ash to prevent them going over the top.

Cheeses are most often ripened in ashes in wine-growing regions.

CHAMOIS D'OR: Modern French commercially-made cow's milk cheese with a high fat content (62 per cent) and a flavour almost as bland as pure cream under its thin white flor rind. It is designed to suit all tastes and all wines, even the lightest. It would make a good dessert base, for, say, a strawberry cheesecake or chilled sweet cheese with Melba sauce.

CHAMPANET: A Brie-style modern French cow's milk cheese which needs to be treated with the same respect as Brie. It has a high fat content of 52 per cent, so is vulnerable if allowed to stand in warm surroundings, although made from pasteurised milk. Available in speciality delicatessen, usually among others of much the same type.

CHARNWOOD: Modern English speciality cheese made from medium moist Cheddar, smoke-flavoured and coated with paprika.

CHEESE MARK: In 1983 the English National Dairy Council introduced a Quality Selected Cheese Mark, as a symbol of high-standard cheese. The Cheese Mark is a registered trade mark and manufacturers/packers must be registered by the NDC and satisfy its rigorous requirements to use it. About 80 per cent of English and Welsh cheese is covered by the scheme. Stilton is not included. The Cheese Mark is unique among quality schemes in having a post-production, product-monitoring procedure which lets consumers comment on the product at point of sale. (Adapted from *Prodfact 1988. British Food Information Service.*) See also Scottish Cheese Mark, and Northern Ireland Cheese Mark Schemes.

CHENNA, PANIR: Terms used by some Indian cooks for drained curds or curd cheese. In making *chenna*, milk is curdled with tartaric acid or lime juice dissolved in sour whey, and the resulting curds are drained in a cloth. In making *panir*, the chenna is drained still more, under a heavy weight, until it is firm enough to be cut into cubes.

CHESTER: French version of Red Cheshire, or what passes for it, made in large cylinders as a cooking and melting cheese. A similar cheese of the same name is found in East Germany and also in Latin America.

CHEVIOT: Composite cheese (strictly a compound product) made from white Cheddar and chopped chives. Mild.

CHÈVRE: French word for 'goat'. It defines by law French cheeses made of goat's milk; the term *pur chèvre* means cheeses made wholly of goat's milk.

CHEVRET: Small goat's cheese from the Jura mountains, made in the form of a flat disc, small square or rectangular loaf. It has a natural, delicate bluish rind with pink spots, and a smooth texture. Usually only 9 cm/3½ inches by 2.5 cm/1 inch high, it has an average weight of 150 g/5 ounces and a fat content of 45 per cent. The aroma of the matured cheese (four to five weeks) is mild, its flavour nutty.

CHEVROTIN: A word for goat cheeses; used in particular for several small Bourbonnais cheeses with local names, made on farms.

CODEX ALIMENTARIUS: Food standards criteria listed by the Food and Agriculture Organisation of the UN and the World Health Organisation acting together. Volume xvi includes Individual Standards for Cheeses.

COEUR: French word for 'heart', used as a label for certain heart-shaped soft cheeses such as *Rollot Coeur*, or *Coeur de Bray* (see Neufchatel, page 132). *Coeur à la Créme* is a well-known dessert of cheese curds drained in a heart-shaped mould, then turned onto a plate and covered with cream and sugar.

COLBY: One of America's most popular cheeses, Colby gets its name from Colby, Wisconsin. It is very like Cheddar and made in the same way except that, as in stirred-curd or granular cheese, the curd is not matted and milled. Colby has therefore a softer body and more open texture than Cheddar, and contains more moisture. Obviously therefore, it does not keep as well.

This popular cow's milk cheese, made from raw or pasteurised milk, is now made in factories more or less world-wide. It is not made in the United Kingdom.

COLWICK: An ancient English, unripened soft cow's milk cheese like Cambridge cheese. It is made from whole raw milk, in open-ended metal cylinders lined with muslin which is knotted over the partly drained cheese to make a depression in its centre. When fully drained (on soft mats) the cheese is unmoulded and salted. It must be refrigerated, and eaten within a week.

CONCHES: A Swiss cheese very similar to Bagnes, Conches is also a good melting cheese used for making raclette. In fact, its alternative name is *Fromage à Raclette*. With 45 per cent fat content it is a cow's milk, pressed, cooked, hard cheese with a brushed rind, ready for eating (or for cooking with) after three months' curing.

COON: An American Cheddar, cured by a special patented method at a temperature and humidity higher than usual. Good quality cheese is therefore needed to prevent mould growth.

Coon is a dark-coloured cheese, with a sharp, tangy flavour.

CORSICA: Better known perhaps as *Niolo* after a plateau in its island homeland, this

Left: Jarlsberg; *right*: Gjetost

NORWEGIAN COCKTAIL PASTRIES   **Snack**

Makes 20 small savouries

frozen puff pastry, thawed	113 g/4 ounces	$\frac{1}{4}$ pound
Jarlsberg cheese without rind	50 g/2 ounces	2 ounces
paprika (mild) for sprinkling		
single (light) cream for brushing		

Set the oven to heat to 230°C/450°F/Gas 8. On a lightly floured surface, roll out the pastry into a rectangle 25 × 20 cm/10 × 8 inches in size. Leave to stand for 5 minutes. Meanwhile grate the cheese finely. Sprinkle $\frac{2}{3}$ of it over the pastry except for 1 cm/$\frac{1}{2}$ inch around the edge. Sprinkle the cheese lightly with paprika, and press the surface of the cheese to make it adhere to the pastry. Brush the uncovered pastry edges with cream, then fold the long sides over to meet in the centre of the rectangle. Sprinkle the remaining cheese over the cut edges, and dust with paprika. Brush the edges of the strip of pastry all round with a little more cream. Now, carefully, fold the long outside edges of the strip to the centre, making a tubular shape filled with curled-up pastry. Cut it across into about 20 equal-sized slices. Lay them flat, cut side down on a baking sheet covered with baking parchment. Bake for 8 to 10 minutes. Serve warm or reheated.
Freezing The pastry roll can be frozen before or after slicing, or the baked savouries can be frozen for a week or two. Reheat from frozen before serving.

excellent sheep's milk cheese has long been popular there. It is matured for at least three months during which time its rind becomes cream-coloured, flecked with grey and russet, and its paste develops a semi-soft texture and a full, delicious, almost spicy taste. It is made in 450 g/1 pound, slightly convex-sided discs, 10 cm/4 inches across and nearly 5 cm/2 inches high. A very good buy if one can find it by either name.

COTHERSTONE: This English, north-eastern cheese began as a farmer's version of the old monastic Wensleydale cheese. From the seventeenth century, it was made from cow's rather than sheep's milk, and was looser in texture than Wensleydale, so 'blued' more readily. It was, therefore, in much demand locally for many years, although not much known south of Yorkshire. It is now a very rare treat indeed.

COTSWOLD: English cheese, consisting of Double Gloucester with chopped chives and onions blended in.

COTTAGE CHEESE: In its simplest form, cottage cheese just consists of soft, uncured cheese curds made by adding a lactic starter to fresh or ripened skim milk. There are several forms of it, with different local names. Large grain, low-acid cheese for instance is made by adding rennet to the milk, cutting the curd into large cubes and washing it well to reduce the acid taste. In its home in the United States, it may be called sweet-curd cottage cheese, low-acid cottage cheese or 'popcorn' cheese from the size of the curds. Cheese with smaller particles may be called farmer's cheese, country-style or pot cheese.

Cottage cheese made at home yields about 450 g/1 pound cheese from 4.5 litres/1 gallon skim milk. In factory conditions the yield is of course higher, especially if cream or flavouring materials such as chopped chives, onions, sweet peppers or pineapple are added to the milk.

Cottage cheese in any form, natural or flavoured, has a very short shelf life, and should be eaten as soon as possible after it is bought or made.

COULOMMIERS: See Brie.

CREAM CHEESE: In America, cream cheese is a soft, mild, uncured rich cheese made from cream or cream and milk, homogenised, pasteurised and cooled to between 75° and 85°F before having lactic starter added; sometimes rennet is added too. The cheese may be made in different ways, and may have flavouring additions like cottage cheese; its fat content also varies a great deal from the minimum 33 per cent. It is one of the most popular cheeses in the US.

In Britain, such soft cheese is only called cream cheese if it has a fat content of between 45 per cent and 65 per cent. If it contains more than 65 per cent fat, it is officially called double cream cheese. In France, cheeses are called 'cream' cheeses if they have a minimum fat content of 55 per cent, 'double-cream' cheeses with a minimum of 60 per cent, and 'triple-cream' cheeses with a minimum of 75 per cent fat. Many cheeses, not only French ones, have the word 'cream' or 'crème' (or a variation of it) in their names but it is wise to check the fat content on the label before accepting them as genuine cream cheeses.

CRÈME DE POLDER: Fairly new Dutch cow's milk, semi-soft cheese ranking as a double cream cheese by virtue of its 60 per cent fat content. It is a solid wheel, 25 cm/10 inches across and 8 cm/3¼ inches deep, black-wax rinded and weighing 4.7 kg/10 pounds 6 ounces. The paste is smooth and golden with a few 'eyes' at intervals.

CRESCENZA: Also called *Crescenza Lombardi* or *Stracchino Crescenzo*, this cheese is a mild, creamy, uncooked, fast-ripening Italian cheese made from whole cow's milk. An American cheese billed as a 'Crescenza type' is also made.

CROWDIE: The word 'crowdie' derives from the lowland Scots word for curds which is 'cruds'. Crowdie is of ancient origin; a low-fat, lightly salted cow's milk cheese now revived under the name of *Highland Crowdie*. One version is mixed with cream cheese or Caboc, others have assorted flavourings or coverings such as toasted hazelnuts.

CURD CHEESE: Low fat smooth, soft cow's cheese sold by weight in the United Kingdom as an alternative to cream cheese. Used a good deal for cheesecakes, and by slimmers for salads, stuffings and sandwiches.

DANABLU: Sometimes used as a name for Danish Blue cheese, the best known of the various Danish blue-mould cheeses. See page 104.

DANISH WHITE MOULD CHEESE: A very rich cheese, like a 'supreme', with 70 per cent fat content and a gentle white floury crust.

DAUPHIN: A heart or crescent-shaped version of the Flanders cheese, Maroilles. The name is said to have originated when Louis XIV and the Dauphin visited Flanders. It is a soft cow's milk cheese with a washed rind, flavoured with herbs and spices.

DEMI-SEL: A rich cow's milk and cream mixture coagulated with rennet, and well salted to preserve it after it is drained. It is eaten fresh. See also Petit Suisse.

DEVON GARLAND: This is a mild-tasting cheese, made in North Devon in England's West Country from the unpasteurised milk of Jersey cows. It is a wheel-shaped, semi-soft cheese with a garland of fresh herbs through the centre which give it a slightly sharp taste.

DORSET BLUE, DORSET BLUE VINNEY: See Blue Vinney, page 117.

DOUBLE BERKELEY: An old name for Double Gloucester made in the Vale of Berkeley south of the city of Gloucester. See Gloucester cheese, page 36. A modern version of Double Berkeley is now made, which has a marbled paste of mixed plain and annatto-tinted curds.

DOUBLE CREAM CHEESES: See Cream Cheese, page 124.

DOUBLE GLOUCESTER: See Gloucester, page 36.

DOUCEUR D'AUVERGNE: See Tomme Blanche, page 138.

DUNLOP: The first Scottish full-cream hard cheese except for Orkney is said to have been made by a cheese-maker called Barbara Gilmour who settled in Dunlop, Ayrshire with her husband, who was a dairy farmer, in 1688. Her cheeses travelled well, and thus spread the fame both of her cheese and the Dunlop cows. By 1800, both were renowned, and Dunlop became a 'national' cheese. During the nineteenth century however its quality declined, and many cheese-makers, instructed by Cheddar-makers such as the famous Joseph Harding, went over to making their own type of Cheddar. Dunlop was still being made successfully however in some areas up to World War II.

Like all speciality cheeses, Dunlop vanished during the war. It revived briefly, but when *Paxton and Whitfield*'s export 'arm' sought Dunlop cheeses for export to America, they were only being made for dairy shows.

In 1987-88, a new-character Dunlop was being made at a creamery on the Isle of Islay. The rindless cheese was a hard cheese like Cheddar, produced in 19 kg/40 pound blocks, matured for up to six months for a mild flavour, or longer for a stronger one.

DUNSYRE BLUE: Scotland's only blue cow's milk cheese made on any scale. It is made by the same firm as Lanark Blue, and may be called a cow's milk version of that cheese.

EDELPILZKÄSE: German full-fat cheese, made wholly or mostly of pasteurised cow's milk (occasionally a little ewe's milk is mixed in). A culture of *Penicillium roqueforti* gives the cheese faint spots of blue in its very creamy paste. It is most notable however for its mouldy flavour, unique among cheeses.

ELBO: Danish variant of Samsöe. It is shaped in a rectangular block, has a very mild, smooth plastic paste and is covered with red or yellow wax. A good slicing cheese for breakfast.

EDELSCHIMMELKÄSE: Another German cheese sometimes confused with the one above. This one is treated with *Penicillium camemberti*, which is added to skimmed pasteurised milk soured with lactic acid. The cheeses are pale gold, with (usually) a white floury rind. The taste is distinctly sharp.

EMILIANO: A very hard, Italian cow's milk cheese of the grana type, made in the province of Emilia. It is like Reggiano, but its quality is variable. It is made in large cylinders, and has a light yellow paste under a dark, oiled surface. Its curing period (for a grating cheese) is one to two years.

EMMENTAL, EMMENTHAL: This cheese, now made in many different countries, takes its name from the River Emme which flows through central Switzerland. For Emmental Switzerland as it is called, see page 81 in the Profiles. See also Swiss, page 137.

EMMENTAL FRANCAIS (FRENCH EMMENTAL): Is sometimes regarded as a sub-type of Gruyère in France because Gruyère is seen as the generic Swiss cheese. However, French Emmental is now coming to be thought of more and more as a separate variety. It dates from about 100 years ago when poverty forced some Swiss Emmental cheese-makers to cross the border into the French Haute Savoie, Franche Comté and Burgundy. Today more Emmental is made in France than even (so they say) in Switzerland, and the French eat it all. It is made by co-operatives and creameries from raw, pasteurised or irradiated milk. The cheeses are made from pressed cooked curds, and have a fat content of 45 per cent. They are cured either in cool cellars for six months, or at a warmer temperature for only two or three months. Cheeses aged for three months can be identified because the convex sides of the large wheels bulge more than usual. The cheese has a brushed, oiled rind, less dry than that of a Swiss cheese. Its paste is smooth and non-rubbery with quite large, well scattered holes. The aroma and flavour are both quite mild, but are brought out finely when the cheese is used in a cooked dish.

ESROM: Danish cheese named for a long-lost monastery, made from the 1930s until 1951 as a near-copy of Port Salut, and bearing the same name. It has, however, developed a gentle but distinct flavour of its own, said to be nearer that of Tilsiter or even (some say) with a hint of Pont l'Evêque about it. When ripe, both the rind and paste can be definitely aromatic.

EXCELSIOR: Triple-crème Norman cheese with 72 per cent butterfat, invented at the end of the last century. Downy-rinded, mild-flavoured and sold in small, uneven cylinder shapes.

EXPLORATEUR: An overtly modern cheese from near the home of Brie, in France, it was christened for the space rocket Explorer. It is a soft, triple-cream cheese with a white surface down and an almost soufflé-like texture, despite its 75 per cent fat content.

FARM CHEESE (FRANCE): A similar cheese to cottage cheese, but even simpler to make. Most French farm cheese (called 'ferme') is made from whole or skim curdled milk which has soured naturally. The whey is drained off, or the curd is drained in a cloth under a board and weight. Salt and sometimes cream are mixed into the curd which is then moulded. It must be eaten while still very fresh.

FARM CHEESE, FARMER CHEESE (USA): A very variable pressed cheese made on farms from whole or skim milk. Buttermilk or another lactic starter is added, sometimes along with rennet (if the milk is not soured naturally). The curd is cut into more or less coarse particles and stirred, drained and salted, then pressed in bags or cloth-lined hoops. It may then be eaten fresh, or it may be dipped in hot paraffin and cured in a cool cellar. See also Cottage Cheese, page 124.

FERMIER: French term for a farm-made cheese eg *Camembert fermier*. A creamery-made Camembert is called a *Camembert laitier*.

FIOR DI LATTE: Italian term for Mozzarella cheese, made from cow's milk instead of the traditional buffalo's milk.

FIORE SARDO: Sheep's milk, Italian (traditionally Sardinian) cheese of good repute. It is eaten as a table cheese when fresh, or after maturing as a piquant cheese. Later still it can be used for grating. It is made in wheels weighing anything from 1.5 kg to 6 kg/$3\frac{1}{2}$ to 13 pounds. Its natural yellow crust covers a pale off-white paste.

FONDU: French term for some types of processed cheese.

FONDUE: Dish made with melted cheese, generally kept warm and semi-liquid while being eaten. Also, by extension, used for meat dishes in which small pieces of raw meat are dipped into hot fat or liquid by the diner before eating them. The heating is done over a spirit burner.

FONDUTA: Version of a classic Swiss cheese fondue which includes eggs. Made in various parts of France, and in Italy. An Italian fonduta should be made with Fontina cheese, white truffles and milk instead of white wine.

FONTAL: The name given to Fontina-style cheeses made in parts of Italy other than the Val d'Aosta, and in France and Denmark. In the USA a version called Fontinella is produced.

FONTINA: Classic and ancient Italian mountain cheese from the Aosta Valley (Val d'Aosta) in Piedmont. Originally a sheep's milk cheese, its supple texture and delicate flavour are now said to be due to the raw milk of the mountain cattle and the co-operative local manufacture. The name Fontina is restricted by law to these raw-milk valley cheeses. They are flattish and round with a smooth brownish rind and a white or cream-coloured paste.

FOOD FROM BRITAIN: Food from Britain is the government and industry sponsored organisation working with the UK food and drink industry to encourage professional marketing and to identify and develop opportunities for British food and drink in the UK and overseas.

FOOD FROM BRITAIN QUALITY MARK: 'In March 1985, the organisation *Food from Britain* launched a national quality assurance scheme. This scheme takes in many kinds of British-produced foods that reach and maintain specified national standards. The red, white and blue triangular symbol called the *Foodmark* tells a consumer that produce bearing the mark meets not only its own sector standards but those of an overall national authority.' (*Prodfact 1988. British Food Information Service.*)

FOODMARK: See Food from Britain Quality Mark.

FORMAGGIO: Italian word for cheese.

FORMAGGIO DI PASTA FILATA: See Plastic Curd cheese (page 134).

FOURME: French word meaning shape or mould, derived from the Latin *formas casei*, from which also comes the French word for cheese, *fromage*.

FOURME D'AMBERT: An imposing French blue cheese from the mountainous central area, Fourme d'Ambert is nearly twice as high as it is wide. It is made from cow's milk, and has a dark grey rind generously mottled with red and yellow patches. An *Appellation Contrôlée* cheese.

ALLGAU MARBLES   **Snack**

Makes 24 snacks

Limburger or Romadur cheese with all rind removed	225 g/8 ounces	I cup
butter, softened	2 to 4 tablespoons	2 to 4 tablespoons
beer or medium-dry sherry	I tablespoon (approx)	I tablespoon (approx)
fine dark rye breadcrumbs for coating		
finely chopped (minced) parsley for coating		
paprika pepper for coating		
finely chopped shelled peanuts for coating		

Shred or mash the cheese in a bowl and beat in the butter until smooth; if the cheese is a soft one 2 tablespoons may be enough. Beat in the beer or sherry, depending on the drinks you will serve. Chill until firm enough to handle. At this stage, test by taste and feel whether you need to add extra butter; it may depend on whether you serve the 'marbles' at room temperature or chilled. When the cheese paste is the consistency you want, shape it into small balls. Roll in one of the coatings suggested above; for instance offer 8 green marbles (rolled in parsley), 8 red ones (rolled in paprika) and 8 tan ones (rolled in peanuts). Serve on cocktail picks or nestled in lettuce leaves. Use as snacks, or as a garnish for a mixed hors d'oeuvre.

Freezing Freeze without coatings for up to I month. Thaw and coat. Chill but do not freeze again.

BATEAUX D'ANGELOT   **Starter**

Serves 4

medium-sized avocado pears	2	2
egg yolks	2	2
lemon juice	I teaspoon	I teaspoon
salt to taste		
grinding of black pepper		
Pont l'Évêque cheese	175 g/6 ounces	$\frac{3}{4}$ cup
golden fried breadcrumbs	2 rounded tablespoons	2 rounded tablespoons

Halve the avocado pears lengthways. Discard the stones. Scoop most of the flesh out of the skins, leaving 5 to 7 mm/$\frac{1}{4}$ to $\frac{1}{3}$ inch shells. Beat together the egg yolks and lemon juice. Sieve the avocado pear flesh into the egg yolk mixture, and blend it in smoothly. Season to taste. Cut any rind off the cheese, then cream the paste with the back of a spoon until soft. Divide the paste between the avocado skin 'boats'. Cover with the avocado-egg mixture. Sprinkle all over with crumbs. Place in a shallow, lightly greased baking dish, cut side up. Bake at 180°C/350°F/Gas 4 for 20 minutes. Serve hot as a first course at dinner.

The dish is not suitable for freezing.

See picture of cheese on page 50

FRAIS: French word for 'fresh' (unripened).

FROMAGE: French word for cheese.

FROMAGE BLANC: Smooth low-fat French 'white cheese' used like cottage cheese or quark.

FROMAGE À LA CRÈME: Soft, rich cream curds eaten fresh with sugar and extra cream. Also a simple type of soft rich, fresh cheese made by renneting whole fresh milk or milk and cream, coagulating it with mild heat, then slicing, draining and kneading it. It may be enriched and lightly salted before being put in small wicker moulds.

FROMAGE FORT: French 'cooked' cheese, made from melted skim-milk curd, pressed, drained in ashes, then grated and ripened for about ten days. After being seasoned, flavoured and enriched, it is ripened again.

FROMAGE FRAIS: French term for soft, un-ripened cow's milk cheese with the con-sistency of thick cream. Now sold with various fruit flavours in small pots as a supermarket product.

FYNBO: This Danish variant of Samsöe takes its name from the island of Fyn, where Hans Anderson came from. It is a semi-firm, smooth-textured cheese like Samsöe with regular small holes. Made in a thick wheel, it is covered with yellow or red wax. The paste has a mild flavour and gently aromatic scent.

GAMMELOST: One of Norway's best-known cheeses, partly because of its strong aroma and flavour. Gammelost is a semi-soft, blue-mould cheese made from soured, skim cow's milk treated with two and sometimes three different moulds. It is made mainly in the areas called Hardanger and Sognz. The method of making differs slightly in each, but the curing method is the same.

GÉRÔMÉ: Gérômé, also known as *Gerard-mer* (after its birthplace) is a softish cheese very like Munster. It comes from the Vosges Mountains in France, and is made mainly of cow's milk, sometimes with goat's milk added. The fresh whole milk is ren-neted, the curd is cut in large cubes, and after draining, put in hoops. These are piled on one another for several days, the cheeses being turned frequently. The cheeses are then dried, and transferred to curing rooms where they are given a brine-washed rind. They are cured from six weeks to about four months, depending on their size and weight.

GERVAIS: The name of a French factor who built up a thriving business to sell the double-cream fresh cow's milk cheese (60 per cent fat) called Petit Suisse.

GIPPSLAND BLUE: The best known, and deservedly the highest priced, of Australia's indigenous firm blue cheeses. Not unlike a creamy Dolcelatte, it is certainly worth trying by anyone visiting its homeland. Quota restrictions prevent its being impor-ted into the UK.

GJETOST: A Norwegian goat's or mixed milk whey cheese, cooked, unripened and of a caramel flavour and colour. It is sold in rindless blocks, and is a popular breakfast cheese in Norway because its completely smooth paste slices thinly and easily. Its flavour comes from long stirring of the whey to expel all the water, and then the addition of lactose and milk or cream. These days most Gjetost is made from the whey obtained from a mixture of 90 per cent cow's and 10 per cent goat's milk; when made entirely from cow's milk whey the cheese is called Mysost, and if from whole cow's milk, Gomost.

GLAMORGAN: Glamorgan cheese from South Wales vanished long ago but its name survives in a savoury cheese-herb mixture fried in sausage shapes, called – not surpris-ingly – Glamorgan sausages.

GOLD 'N RICH: American, semi-soft cow's milk cheese made in a loaf shape. It was originally derived from Port Salut.

GOMOST: See Mysost (page 132).

GOURNAY: French, soft cow's milk cheese of Normandy, sometimes sold fresh for im-mediate eating, and sometimes ripened, when it has a white downy rind and smells lightly of mould. It is only ripened for about a week.

GRADING OF CHEESE (BRITAIN): Most British cheeses are graded for quality before sale. Some large English creameries employ their own graders, while many small and medium-sized ones use graders from the Creamery Proprietors' Association; in Scotland, the Company of Scottish Cheese-Makers Ltd administers the grading scheme.

GRADING OF CHEESE (FARMHOUSE): Most grading of English and Welsh farm-made cheeses is carried out by the Milk Market-ing Board graders for Farmhouse Cheese-makers' Ltd; the cheeses are graded as superfine, fine, graded or no grade. Cheeses made by members of the co-operative and graded as superfine or fine are entitled to display a special 'Farmhouse' logo on their products. Manufacturers of farm cheeses who grade their own cheeses may not use it, nor may cheese-makers whose cheeses do not merit the top two grades. The Farm-house logo thus guarantees that the cheeses which bear it are farm-made by traditional methods and are first-class of their kind. But the many farm cheese-makers who, for various reasons, do not belong to the co-operative have no comparable 'voice'.

See also: Food from Britain Quality Mark (page 125).

GRANA: Italian term for 'grain' used to describe the 'feel' and texture of very hard grating cheeses such as Parmesan and Swiss Sbrinz. These cheeses (almost all Italian) are characterised by their sharp flavour and good keeping and carriage quality as well as by being hard and grainy. They are among Europe's oldest cheeses.

There are two main groups of Italian grana cheeses, defined by where they are made. One lot are classed as *Grana Padano* cheeses (see below). They are made mostly in the province of Lombardy. The others are labelled as *Grana Reggiano* cheeses, being made mostly in and around Reggio in the province of Emilia. There are several variations within each group which cling to local names such as Grana Lodigiano (cheese made at Lodi). However the name one sees most often is Parmigiano-Reggiano because it is by law an alternative name to Grana Reggiano for any grana cheese made in certain districts around Reggio such as Bologna, Mantua and Parma.

A great deal of grana cheese of both groups is exported to other parts of Europe and to the United States as Parmesan or Reggiano Parmesan. Both names are also used for grana cheeses made in the United States.

GRANA PADANO: Name embracing all the grana cheeses made, roughly speaking, in the valley of the river Po, ie the cheeses formerly known as Grana Lombardo and Grana Lodigiano. This grouping, accord-ing to André Simon, was meant to provide a united opposition to the producers of the Parmigiano-Reggiano cheeses. The term Grana Padano was given official status in a decree of 30th October 1955.

GRANULAR OR STIRRED-CURD CHEESE: Type of cheese similar to Cheddar or Colby, made from raw or pasteurised cow's milk.

The method of making it is like that of Cheddar except that (as in the making of Colby) the curd is not matted or milled. It is stirred continuously, or with intermittent draining, until it is dry enough to salt. After salt is stirred in, it is pressed in hoops like Cheddar.

GRATIN: A dish which is covered with fine breadcrumbs, sometimes mixed with grated cheese, before being cooked, so that the crumbs form a thin golden crust on the cooked dish. In modern cookery, grated cheese alone may be sprinkled on the uncooked dish, or cheese sauce sprinkled with grated cheese may be substituted for breadcrumbs.

GREEN CHEESE: Unripened or immature cheese. The term is sometimes used to mean blue-mould cheese in which the veins or speckling is more green than blue, or a cheese with green streaks or patches such as Sage Derby or Sapsago.

GUBBEEN: A fine washed-rind Irish cheese, made year-round by traditional methods, both for local use and export. An attractive oak-smoked version is also made from unpasteurised milk. Gubbeen is made in two sizes weighing 1.5 kg/3¼ pounds and 0.5 kg/1 pound. Both are round like grindstones, with a full yet amenable flavour. Eat it with brown ale, cider or a dry Madeira.

HALLOUM, HALLOUMI: Originally a Middle Eastern Bedouin cheese of sheep's and perhaps goat's milk, Halloum is a long-keeping, tough, salty cheese. Being a good traveller and cooking cheese, it has been exported all over the Middle East, to Greece and Cyprus and as far afield as Australia. In the Lebanon it is known as a kebab cheese, being cubed, skewered and grilled over charcoal on street stalls. But in the expatriate communities in the West it is more often used for grating.

HAND: Popular among Teutonic peoples, this small, sour-milk surface-ripened cow's milk cheese is too pungent to appeal to many others. It has various names depending on where it is made, but mime and the question 'Handkäse?' will probably lead to identifying it anywhere in Germany or Austria.

HERB-FLAVOURED CHEESES: Herb-flavoured cheeses have been made for as long or longer than cheeses containing seeds or spices. Besides the various plant juices and flowers he suggested for curdling milk, the first century Roman Columella mentioned adding thyme or other herbs to the milk for cheeses to be eaten fresh, and his contemporary Pliny also recorded it. The tradition persisted. By the Middle Ages, fresh herb cheeses called *spermyse* cheeses were popular with the well-to-do of most of Europe. Many different herbs were chopped and added to these cheeses, but sage was always one of the most popular. (See Sage Derby, page 25). It is still so today, being used to flavour both the time-honoured British 'territorial' hard cheeses and the host of modern soft ones made in most European countries. Garlic, chives,

onion, parsley and savory are other popular herbal flavourings in cheeses, such as Scottish Hramsa. (See below; also the glossary entries for Margotin Herb, Sapsago and Tartare.)

HIGH MOISTURE JACK: See Jack.

HRAMSA: A rich, smooth fresh Scottish cheese; a modern version of the traditional crowdie flavoured with wild garlic.

HUNTSMAN: A modern composite cheese produced in the English Midlands; it consists of layers of Double Gloucester and Blue Stilton.

ILCHESTER: Hotelier Ken Seaton developed Ilchester cheese in the early 1960s from a mixture of Cheddar, garlic and beer. This was the first of the modern type of compound products (generally called composite or blended cheese) made in the UK; its marked success led to many others being created. It resulted in the development of Smoked Applewood, for instance, by Mr Seaton himself, followed by a Cheddar with port and flavourings and a herb or pickle-flavoured Double Gloucester. These are now marketed by the Ilchester Cheese Company in 4.5 kg/10 pound drums.

INCANESTRATO: Italian word meaning 'basketed' – cheeses drained in wicker baskets, and retaining the imprint of the weave on their surface.

One such cheese made in Sicily from ewe's milk is called Pecorino Incanestrato (see Pecorino, page 92).

ISLAY: The Islay Creamery Company on the Scottish island of Islay produce large blocks of rindless Dunlop, called Islay Dunlop, a post-war commercial 'revival' of the traditional drum cheeses. It is similar to Cheddar but has a flakier texture, and a pleasant, less forceful flavour.

ITALICO: A term created by a decree of Mussolini in May 1941, applying to a range of similar, soft cheeses hitherto known by various fancy names. They are all full-fat, raw cow's milk cheeses, clotted at a fairly high temperature for ten to eighteen hours and matured for between twenty and forty days. They are usually flat cylinders about 20 cm/8 inches in diameter, with a straw-coloured yellow paste; smooth, compact and creamy. The thin rind is ochre or rosy, the flavour mild. Besides Bel Paese, their names are: Cacioreale, Bell-Alpina, Bella Milano, Bel Piano Lombardo, Bel Piemonte, Fior d'Alpe, Pastorella, Savoia, Vittoria and Bick.

JACK: The name of a Colby-style, American cow's milk cheese from California, now

usually called Monterey, except for the version of whole milk cheese called High Moisture Jack. See Monterey Jack.

KAAS: Dutch word for cheese.

KÄSE: German word for cheese.

KASKAVEL, KASHKAVEL: The Romans (probably) introduced sheep's milk cheeses very like Caciocavallo to the Balkans. The cheeses are still made with raw sheep's milk as in centuries past, although methods have been modernised. Kaskavel (the Bulgarian spelling) is a plastic curd cheese. The curd is cut and stirred, pre-pressed and heated, moulded and salted, and finally ripened for fifty to sixty days. Inevitably the method, like the spelling, varies from place to place; but always the cheese is salty and has an aroma and flavour which calls the sheep to mind.

KASSERI: Another plastic-curd, sheep's cheese from the Mediterranean, this time from Greece. It is not unlike Provolone, is fairly mild and keeps well. In Greece itself it is eaten as a table cheese, or is sometimes sliced and broiled over charcoal, so it makes a good barbecue cheese. It may also be floured, fried in oil and dressed with lemon juice as fritters. A cow's milk type of Kasseri is made in the United States.

KEFALOTYRI: A factory cheese made all over Greece and in Syria from goat's and sheep's milk, often having a local name, a dialect spelling and a regional use. The name is said to come from the name of a man's hat called a *kefalo*. It is a hard cheese something like Parmesan, and is much used for cooking.

KERNHEM: A modern cow's milk cheese developed from a monastery recipe by the Netherlands Institute for Dairy Research. It is a lightly pressed, washed-rind cheese with a soft, creamy paste and red-brown crust.

KNEADED CHEESE: See Pasta Filata.

KOSHER CHEESE: Kosher cheese is made from curd coagulated without animal rennet because Jewish dietary rules do not allow meat to be mixed with dairy products. The milk is allowed to sour naturally, or a starter based on vegetable juices is used.

KUMINOST, KUMMINOST: Scandinavian seeded cheeses, usually made with skim milk for home consumption but exported (eg to America) with a 50 per cent fat content. Cumin and caraway are the usual seeds mixed into the curd before it is pressed.

LA BOURRINE: Modern French, creamery cheese from the Perreault firm now absorbed by the Bongrain group. It has a light

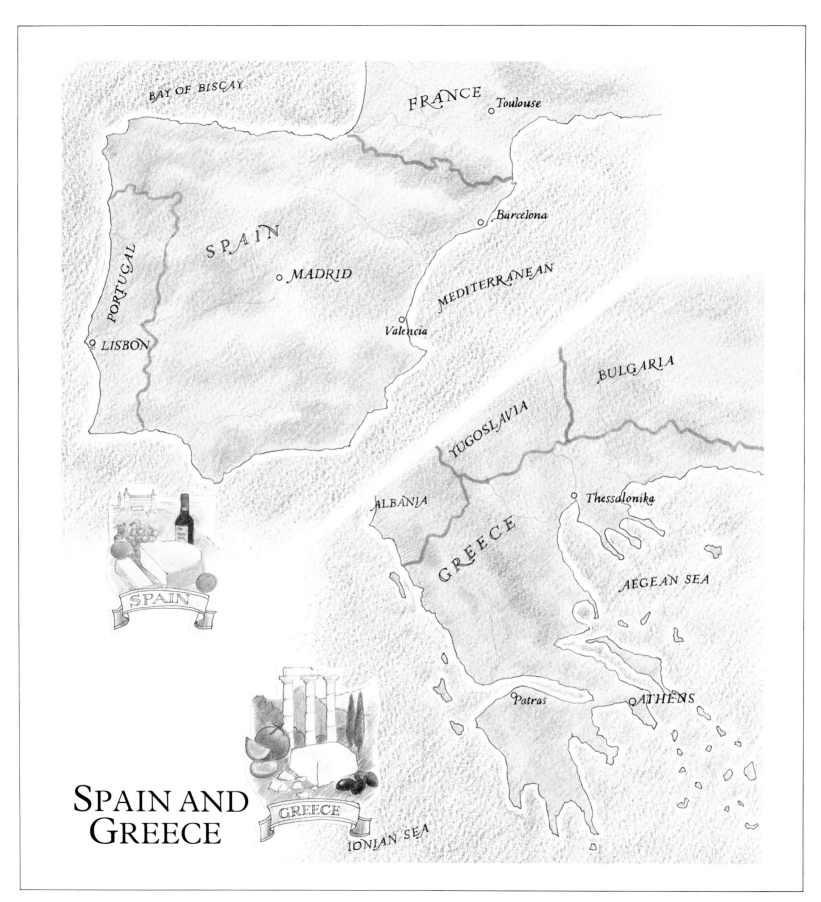

BAY OF BISCAY

FRANCE

Toulouse

Barcelona

PORTUGAL

SPAIN

MADRID

MEDITERRANEAN

Valencia

LISBON

BULGARIA

YUGOSLAVIA

ALBANIA

THESSALONIKA

GREECE

AEGEAN SEA

SPAIN

Patras

ATHENS

SPAIN AND GREECE

GREECE

IONIAN SEA

fawn crust dusted with white, and a cream-coloured paste with small eyes which tastes slightly fruity, although gentler than its quite 'earthy' fragrance suggests.

LABNA, LABNEH: Throughout the Middle East, soured milk or yoghurt is drained of its whey to make a light creamy curd cheese usually moulded in small balls and preserved in olive oil. In most Middle Eastern countries, dairying and cheese-making are unimportant, but Labna is relatively popular. The cheese varies in flavour with the type of milk used and its fat content.

LAGUIOLE: An ancient Gallic cheese has given rise to this modern French cow's milk pressed, uncooked cheese from the Rouerge area said to be as good or better than Cantal. It has a grey rind which thickens with age, a supple to firm texture and a distinct tang on the palate. It is a good cooking cheese, being used for instance in the local truffade, a kind of potato hot-pot.

LAITIER: French word for creamery-made cheese.

LA-MOTHE-ST-HERAY: Small round goat's milk cheese from the Poitou area of France. It used to be wrapped in leaves, but the commercially-made cheeses are now boxed. They have a white, downy rind and a 45 per cent fat content so the texture is tender, although the flavour can be somewhat strong.

LE CHEVROT: A fine, little goat's cheese made entirely of raw, unpasteurised milk from Poitevine goats. Its manufacture is based on an old secret farmhouse recipe, but it has been modernised enough to be made by a co-operative and to have won a silver medal for goat's milk cheeses – no mean achievement in France. It is only 6 cm/2¼ inches in diameter and 3.5 cm/1¼ inches high, weighing about 160 g/5¼ ounces, so it is easy to eat at a sitting once cut, in spite of its richness (50 per cent fat). It is also easy to eat because it has an unusually delicate, fresh flavour for a ripened goat's milk cheese.

LE FOURNOLS: With its washed golden rind, this 29 cm/11½ inch flat disc of soft cow's milk cheese is a grand sight. Its creamy paste made from pasteurised milk by a method not unlike that of Pont l'Évêque (page 52) is however much milder. The Société Fromagère du Livradois, which created it, is one with great initiative and an immense 'feel' for its cheeses, centred as it is in the cheese-making mountain area of the Auvergne. Occasionally exported, always worth enquiring for.

LE ROI: Almost solid cream, this 7.5 cm/3 inch cylinder of French pasteurised, en-riched cow's milk cheese has a lusciously rich texture and a mild flavour with a strong after-taste. Made like Boursault it is a novelty, but increasingly easy to find.

LEYDEN: See Leiden, page 100.

LIEDERKRANZ: This 'all-American' cheese is one which commands respect far beyond the bounds of its native Ohio. Yet it had a modest beginning in the efforts of a Swiss-born cheese-maker, Emil Frey, to produce a cheese which his business partner could sell in New York to newly-arrived German immigrants. They wanted a strong cheese like the Limburger which they had enjoyed at home.

After three years, Frey produced such a cheese, and his partner sold it with increasing success as his 'own brand' cheese, without a trade name. It was only christened a year later when the renowned singing club, the New York Liederkranz, gave it a 'big hand'.

Liederkranz is a soft, surface-ripened cow's milk cheese very like a mild Limburger. It is made with pasteurised milk, with added starter and rennet, drained in 1 cm/½ inch cubes and then in metal forms. After salting, the cheese is cured for three to four weeks at 45°F, while surface-applied organisms ripen it from the outside inward. The small cheeses, only weighing 150 to 175 g/5 to 6 ounces are wrapped in foil for marketing. They are sold mainly in special delicatessen.

LIPTAUER: Not a cheese, but a cheese spread based on a Hungarian sheep's cheese called Liptoi. The spread is heavily seasoned with paprika, caraway, capers and other flavourings. It is often served in a decorative cone or mound garnished with small items such as anchovy fillets or sliced, stuffed olives.

LLANBOIDY: An old-style, full-fat hard cheese made in Wales from milk of a rare breed of Red Poll cattle. They are grazed on pastures free from chemical interference. The cheeses, too, are natural, free from artificial preservatives, and are hand-pressed. They are natural-rinded and matured for two months in 4.5 kg/10 pound wheels.

LODIGIANO AND LOMBARDO: Two very similar Italian grana cheeses made in the same area, and in much the same way. Lodigiano takes its name from its 'parent' city Lodi. It is slightly larger than Lombardi, and is cured for longer, up to four years. Even so, it is slightly less strongly flavoured than other granas.

MAASDAM: A yellow-waxed cow's milk cheese with a 45 per cent fat content. The paste has fairly large 'eyes' and a mild nutty flavour. The cheese is a wheel weighing 4 to 12 kg/9 to 27 pounds.

MANTECA: Also called Manteche, Burrino, Burro, etc, Manteca is a mild pasta filata Italian cheese made from buffalo's or (usually) cow's milk, and enclosing a lump of fresh butter. The cheese itself has been called by André Simon a flask-shaped, normal Provolone; but it has also been described as a special kind of Mozzarella or as the same kind of curd as Scamorze. Probably any kind of mild pasta filata curd can be used depending on the type of milk supply and butter available. Whatever it is, the enclosing cheese paste prevents air reaching the butter which, therefore allegedly, stays fresh for a long time.

The butter is usually whey butter, often a by-product of the cheese-making.

MARGOTIN HERB: A modern (1967), creamy little cow's milk disc, strongly redolent of herbs and especially of garlic. A fresh cheese, its shelf life is short even before it is cut, and once cut it should be eaten at once. As it only weighs 100 g/4 oz this should be no problem despite its 58 per cent fat content.

MARIBO: A similar Danish cow's milk cheese to Havarti (page 104). Not often found in the United Kingdom.

MAROLLES: An alternative name for Maroilles (see page 56).

MASCARPONE: Also called Mascherpone, this fresh cream cheese is so like Devonshire clotted cream that some authorities say it should not be classed as a cheese at all. It is made mostly in Italy, from whole cow's milk, and it is often sold with candied fruit mixed in, or with a lemon juice or spice flavouring; so it may well have influenced the making of Australian fruit cheeses. It is also used as the basis of some well-known, rich desserts.

MEAUX, BRIE DE: A brie de Meaux fermier, as sold by Paxton and Whitfield, is arguably, according to John Arlott, the finest cheese it is possible to eat. Its special characteristics are described under Brie de Meaux on page 57.

MERSEY VALLEY: Well-known Australian brand of Cheddar-type cheeses.

MELUN, BRIE DE: See Brie, page 57.

MIGNON: A small version of Maroilles.

MILK MARKETING BOARDS: There are five Milk Marketing Boards in the United Kingdom. They are: the British Milk Marketing Board of England and Wales; the Scottish Milk Marketing Board; the North of Scotland Milk Marketing Board; the Aberdeen and District Milk Marketing

Board, and the Milk Marketing Board for Northern Ireland. Their joint body is the Federation of UK Milk Marketing Boards.

These bodies were set up in 1933 to provide a mechanism whereby farmers could market their own dairy products including cheese. Between them they handled in 1987 the consumption and use, in cheese-making, of 6835 million litres of liquid milk, and the sale of milk and milk products. The Boards normally act autonomously, each being a very powerful body in its own area.

MIMOLETTE: A Dutch cheese (a form of Edam) by origin, which is now also made extensively in northern France and Flanders. It is a pressed, reheated cheese with a deep orange paste, and is shaped like a flattened sphere. It is entirely factory-made, from cow's milk, has a 45 per cent fat content, and a brushed rind. It is not strongly flavoured, but makes a pleasant lunch-time cheese, being reasonably fruity.

MITZITHRA, MIZITHRA: A pot cheese spelt in several different ways, eg Mezithra, Myzithra. It is popular all over its homeland of Greece, being used as a salad and dessert cheese when fresh, and even as a grating cheese when it has hardened with age. It is comparable to the Italian ricotta when fresh, but it is made from goat's or sheep's milk, and whey which has been drained off when making feta cheese. See page 112.

MONASTERY CHEESES: Cheeses – and great cheeses – were being made in Europe's Rome-based monasteries almost as soon as those monasteries became established. It was not surprising. Benedictine monks were supposed to feed themselves by farm work, and the Benedictine diet rules demanded (officially, at least until the fourteenth century) total abstinence from butcher's meat and often miserably small meals, to discourage lust. Cheese was both a comfort and much-needed concentrated nourishment at first, and later, a means of making luxurious, interesting dishes. Later still, monks such as the Trappist brothers of Entrammes discovered that the sale of cheeses could make excellent profits for their foundation as well.

MONSIEUR: A rich, French double-cream cheese from Normandy with 60 per cent butterfat content. It was created early in this century by a local farmer named Fromage, so it is sometimes called Monsieur Fromage. It is a small cylinder, with a short shelf life.

MONT CENIS: A firm, blue-veined cheese similar to Bleu de Gex made from mixed cow's, goat's and sheep's milk on the French side of the Franco-Italian border in Savoy. On the Italian side, it is called Montecenisio. It is made by old-style methods using skimmed evening and whole morning milk, is moulded and pressed, then brine-washed during three to four months curing.

MONTEREY JACK: Indigenous US cow's milk cheese first made in California about 1892. The name Monterey, from its birthplace, has largely replaced the name Jack except in the variety called High Moisture Jack.

Monterey is of three kinds: there is whole-milk, semi-soft Monterey; grating type or dry Monterey, made of semi-skimmed or skimmed milk, matured for six months or more; and a whole-milk, high-moisture type.

The cheese is made by a method similar to that for making Colby but quicker, and the cheeses are pressed between boards or in a hoop. They are about 26 cm/9½ inches in diameter, and weigh between 2.7 and 4 kg/6 and 9½ pounds. Semi-soft Monterey is cured for three to six weeks, and the grating-type for six months. See also Teleme, page 137.

MONTRACHET: Popular, widely exported French goat's milk 'logs'.

MUENSTER, MUNSTER (US): This American cheese is made on the same pattern as its European namesake. It is a semi-soft, whole milk cow's cheese, made from pasteurised milk. The curd is heated then moulded in cloth-lined forms, and curing includes frequent turning and salting. The cheeses may be cured for only a week or so and are fresh and mild, or may be left for six to eight weeks before sale. Their fat content is not less than 50 per cent in dry matter.

MYCELLA: Pasteurised cow's milk semi-hard cheese from Jutland in Denmark, Mycella won the Chris Hansen Perpetual Challenge Cup for the Best Blue-Veined cheese at the Nantwich International Show in 1988 out of 52 competitors. It is milder than its compatriot Danish Blue, and is based on Gorgonzola. Its name derives from the *Penicillium mycelium* (mushroom filament) spores used to produce its greenish veining. It can be bought in rindless pre-packed portions. A very attractive buy.

MYSOST: A caramelised cow's milk whey by-product of making other cheeses, Mysost is made in Norway, Sweden, Denmark and in the United States (in small quantities). It varies a good deal depending on the proportion of buttermilk or whole milk included. Some is made entirely from whole milk and is then called Gomost.

The cheese consists mostly of caramelised lactose with the fat, protein and minerals present in the whey, and usually with sugar and spices added.

NATIONAL DAIRY COUNCIL (ENGLAND AND WALES): This organisation founded in 1920 devises and implements the dairy industry's generic advertising and promotional activities in England and Wales. The Council works on behalf of the Milk Marketing Board (MMB), which is the organisation of dairy farmers, and the Dairy Trade Federation (DTF) which represents processors, manufacturers and distributors of milk and dairy products.

NEUFCHÂTEL: The name of a soft white and creamy cow's milk cheese made in the dairying district of Normandy in France known as the Pays de Bray. The town of Neufchâtel-en-Bray is where one of the oldest markets for Normandy cheese is held, selling especially the cheeses which bear its name. Since the Middle Ages, it has sold them in various shapes such as squares, briquettes and hearts, the last (Coeur de Bray) being by far the most popular.

All the cheeses weigh between 100 and 300 g/3½ and 11 ounces and gain a soft white fluffy rind within a few days of starting to ripen. They are cured for about three weeks, but when ready must be eaten within three or four days even if kept whole and refrigerated. Their fat content is 45 per cent, the flavour lightly savoury when at their peak.

American Neufchâtel, developed in 1892, is made from a mixture of cream and milk, in much the same way as commercial cream cheese.

NEW ZEALAND CHEESES: New Zealand is one of the world's major Cheddar exporters, besides sending out massive quantities of other dairy products. Their uniformly high vitamin content and quality is due to the fact that her cattle graze on fresh pasture year-round, are kept outside, and so have more natural carotene in their milk than elsewhere.

Given her gigantic investment in ultra-modern plant, the loss of her British cheese market following the UK's accession to the EEC looked like a dangerous blow to New Zealand's economy. She had begun to take part in the growing colonial sales of Cheddar to Britain back in 1900 when she supplied 4000 tons. From then on, especially in World War II, she had steadily modernised and automated her cheese-making plant and equipment, largely to give Britain mass-quality, uniform cheese.

Her response to the new situation was to open up new markets and offer them new cheeses. Her first original cheese type, *Egmont*, had already been developed in the 1960s for the emergent Japanese market, and in 1975 was recognised in the Codex Alimentarius of the United Nations Food and Agriculture Organisation as a separate cheese variety. Egmont is a sweetish 'children's cheese' when young, but with maturity it strengthens and develops (so its makers say) both Cheddar and Gouda characteristics; it is a smooth, slicing cheese with a few scattered 'eyes'.

Many other cheeses have followed Egmont, not only for export but for home use by increasingly sophisticated New Zealand palates. In 1985, a private New Zealand company signed a ten-year technology transfer agreement with the French Compagnie Francais des Fromages. They got a French cheese-maker and some half-dozen French cheeses, ranging from a gourmet Bleu de Bresse to a Poitevin ripened with the local, naturally occurring rind flora. All have been consumer-tested in a French market.

New Zealand has its copies of Dutch, Swiss and German cheeses but its own modern new ones are more interesting. Perhaps the ultimate in modernity is a brine-salted, sweet-curd cheese called *Riverlea Red* made entirely automatically by press-button, from a central computer control room. Flavour and texture characteristics develop from the actions of the starter bacteria during maturation.

Then there are cheeses with mellifluous Maori names like *Tupihi* (meaning *thin* or *lean*) which is a skim-milk, reduced-fat cheese, or *Waitemata* which is like a full-fat, creamy Havarti; it is washed daily with red wine during its six-week ripening time, so its soft paste is distinctly tangy under its red rind. Cheeses are also made for vegetarians; *Kapiti* is one, which is exported to North America. Finally one must applaud the imaginative enthusiasm and skilled craft which has led to the production of a New Zealand Wensleydale and a best-selling semi-soft companion cheese called simply Farmhouse. New Zealand Cheddar, important as it is, does not have things all its own way these days.

NIOLO: See Corsica, page 121.

NOKKELOST: Norwegian, cow's skimmed milk cheese copied from Leiden and generally containing the same seeds and spices.

NORTHERN IRELAND CHEESE MARK SCHEME: 'The rigid standards which apply to the England and Wales Cheese Mark Scheme also apply to NI territorial cheeses that bear their own Quality Mark (a circle with the words Selected Quality Cheese and in the middle a round cheese with a wedge cut from it).' (*Prodfact 1988. British Food Information Service.*)

NUTWOOD: This cheese has been called 'a meal in a mixture'! It is a cheerful mélange of Cheddar cheese, raisins, hazelnuts and cider, with a surprisingly smooth texture, somewhat heavier than that of most Cheddars. It cuts almost like halva, but its flavour is much more virile. The tang of the Cheddar and nuts comes through the sweetness of the dried fruit and 'apple wine' to make a very 'English' sturdy flavour.

The cheese is packed in wheels 2.5 kg/5 pounds 9 ounces in weight or in half-moons. The paste is mottled due to the raisins and hazelnut skins in it – which also make it beige-coloured rather than golden.

OKA: Canadian, cow's milk cheese similar to Port Salut, with a mild aroma and softly piquant flavour. It has been made since 1881, first by the monks of La Trappe in Quebec, later commercially; but production is deliberately limited so it is not available here.

OLIVET BLEU: A French cheese from Orleans which sounds like a blue-veined cheese. However, Olivet is a smooth, straw-yellow cow's milk cheese, mildly fruity in flavour, with not a hint of blue mould in the paste. Its aroma of blue mould comes from its rind, blueish-tinted by curing in local chalk caves for about a month. It is a naturally-made small disc, 12 cm/5 inches diameter, with a 45 per cent fat content, which is sometimes eaten fresh (and therefore unblued), as well as half-ripened for ten days to a fortnight.

OLIVET CENDRÉ: Olivet cheese is sometimes allowed to ripen in cases filled with wood ash for about three months. Cheeses ripened thus are savoury in flavour. They are, as Pierre Androuet says true preserves, made and put aside when milk is plentiful for times when cheese as portable food is greatly needed, eg during haymaking and harvest.

Visitors to France, especially to the Orleans area, will find either Olivet Bleu or Olivet Cendré a pleasant cheese to buy.

OST: Term meaning cheese in Norway, Sweden and Denmark. Often used as a suffix.

PANT-YSGAWN: An attractive, Welsh goat's cheese, soft and mild, made from pasteurised milk with a three-week life. It is pre-packed for sale in 114 g/4 ounce rounds and 1 kg/2 pound logs. It can be bought unflavoured, or with various flavourings such as herbs, black pepper, honey and spice, or black cherry and brandy. Obtainable from a few speciality shops outside its own area, it is good for party use, although not a connoisseur's cheese.

PASSENDALE: A semi-hard cow's milk cheese in the shape of a bun loaf, made in Belgium. It is about 10 cm/4 inches high and 20 cm/8 inches in diameter, weighing about 3 kg/6½ pounds. Made from the pasteurised milk of local herds, it has a dark, hard rind with a light down on the surface, and a consistency similar to Tilsiter almost too soft to grate, with small 'eyes'. The flavour has been likened to that of a mature Gouda.

PASTA FILATA: Italian name for the type of cheese called 'plastic curd' cheese in English. Another name is 'spun paste' cheese. See Plastic Curd Cheeses, page 134.

PAVÉ D'AUGE: General name for several French cheeses which are called *Pavés* because they are flat and square, rather like the old paving stones. Such cheeses, made in Normandy, are akin to Pont l'Évêque, and need the same type of handling.

PAVÉ DE MOYAUX: One of the best known *pavé* cheeses. It is 11.5 cm/4½ inches square and 6 to 6.5 cm/2 to 2½ inches high, weighing about 800 g/1¾ pounds. An ochre rind hides a spicy, supple paste.

PETIT-SUISSE: A famous French unripened cream cheese, either a 'double-crème' or 'triple-crème' according to whether it contains 60 or 75 per cent fat. It is said to have been created by a Swiss dairyman working in Normandy in the last century, and to have been given its name by a well-known cheese industrialist named Gervais.

'PICKLED' CHEESES: Cheeses cured and often stored in salted milk, whey, oil or water. Usually white Mediterranean cheeses, such as Greek feta (soft) and Cypriot Halloumi (hard).

PINEAPPLE CHEESE: A nineteenth-century American product consisting of American Cheddar-style cheese pressed in moulds which give it the shape of a pineapple. The cheeses are dried and cured for several months hanging in loose-meshed nets, during which time they are rubbed with oil several times, or are shellacked to give them a hard surface.

Some sources say that the cheese originated in Berkshire, England, in the early nineteenth century. It may well have done so independently, then or earlier.

PIPO CREM': First available in 1961, Pipo Crem' was created to meet the popular demand for blue cheese created by Bleu de Bresse in France. It is a soft, full fat, rindless cow's milk cheese made in a long roll, 28 cm/11 inches in length and 11 cm/4½ inches in diameter. Its own popularity now matches and even exceeds its predecessor's, and it is available in England from most good delicatessen. Its paste is very white, its blue veining delicate, and its flavour matches both, being creamy, mild and modest.

PLASTIC CURD CHEESE(S): These cheeses are sometimes called in English 'kneaded' cheeses, which describes how the malleable curd is achieved. The drained curd is soaked in hot whey two or three times until it is firm but elastic. Then it is kneaded and pulled by the cheese-maker into long threads – which accounts for the Italian name, *pasta filata* (cheese in threads). The pummelled and pulled curd is moulded into balls and soaked once more in hot whey, which makes it as malleable as warm putty and ready for moulding into whatever shapes the cheese-maker chooses. Some well-known plastic curd cheeses are the Caciocavallo family, also Mozzarella and Provolone.

POIVRE: Used of cheeses, this French word for 'pepper' usually means a coating of crushed black peppercorns.

POIVRE D'ANE: Quaintly named cheese, meaning in English 'donkey's pepper'. It is made in Provence, the southernmost French province, from any milk available. The soft, lightly cured cheese is formed into small balls or discs, rolled in fresh savory sprigs, and sold unwrapped. Under the savory sprigs, the rind is whitish and the cheese itself has a pleasantly aromatic, mild smell and taste. The fat content is 45 per cent and it is 7.5 cm/3 inches in diameter, 2.5 cm/1 inch high. It weighs about 100 g/3½ to 4 ounces.

POT CHEESE: One of the names for home-made curd cheese, usually drained in a muslin bag or sieve. May be made with rennet, acid herbs, naturally soured milk or buttermilk. See Cottage Cheese, page 124.

POTTED CHEESE: A preparation sometimes called Everlasting cheese, made in several countries. It consists of almost any kind of leftover cheese, grated or shredded and then blended with softened butter, liquor (usually brandy or sherry) and seasonings. The cheese must not be 'off'. It is beaten with all the other ingredients until smooth, then put into a jar or crock, covered and left in a cool place for at least two days. (It will keep for a long time if refrigerated.) It must be brought to room temperature before

being served. The usual proportions are 175 to 225 g/6 to 8 ounces of cheese, 2 tablespoons each of the butter and liquor and a pinch each of cayenne pepper, black pepper and ground allspice. Care must be taken not to leave airholes when filling the pot; it should be tapped on the tabletop several times while filling, to 'knock down' and settle the cheese spread.

PRÉCLOS: A modern French cow's milk semi-soft cheese, made by the Fromageries Perreault of the Bongrain Group. It has a mild lactic flavour, a smooth resilient paste and a rind covered with toasted wheat flour. A useful cheese for sandwiches and for cooking.

PRINCE DE CLAVEROLLES: A modern wax-rounded Pyrénéan cheese.

PROCESS, PROCESSED CHEESE: See List of Cheese-making Terms, page 141.

PROVIDENCE: American as it sounds, this is an old French Trappist cheese, made from cow's milk in Normandy. It is sometimes called Briquebec from the monastery of that name which makes it. It is a traditionally-made cheese with 45 per cent fat, cured for two months and with a washed rind. It is akin to other monastery cheeses, and some say to Port Salut.

QUARK: German name for smooth, soft cheese, similar to cottage cheese in the way it is made and in its flavour. Quark, however, belongs in several different categories, depending on its fat content. It may be virtually fatless or as rich as any medium-fat cheese. Quark is also made with various added flavours.

QUEIJO: Portuguese word for cheese. Queijo Fresco, as its name suggests, is a fresh cheese, often home-made and therefore differing from household to household – but similar always in that it dries out if left lying, shrinks and crumbles. When brine treated, Queijo Fresco becomes Queijo Seco; dryish, pale yellow and – obviously – salty. Harder, longer-cured cheeses are Queijo da Ilha from the Azores, and Cabreiro, matured for three months in brine. Portuguese cheeses are not exported.

QUESO: Spanish word for cheese. The Spanish cheese best known in Britain is Manchego (page 113); both the young and the older, hard cheeses are delicious – and quite different. Popular cheeses in Spain are Cabrales (page 120) and Roncal (page 135). Mahon from the island of Minorca is a widely eaten cheese there.

Queso is also the word for cheese in Spanish-speaking Latin and Central America.

QUESO ANEJO: Cow's milk Mexican cheese. Skimmed milk is used to make a crumbly, salty cheese used for cooking.

QUESO BLANCO: Soft, white cheese from cow's or mixed milk, popular throughout Latin America. The curd is coagulated with acid, drained, salted and pressed in moulds. It can be sold after twenty-four hours.

RACLETTE: Originally, Raclette was the name of a cheese made only in the Swiss canton of Valais, and noted for its quick melting quality. However, due to very heavy demand, the name Raclette is now used as a generic term for several quick-melting Swiss and French cheeses which can be used to make the famous Swiss dish of melted cheese over hot split potatoes described below. Bagnes, Conches and Orsières are three of them, and Raclette Livradoux (see over) is another. These cheeses are now generally made from pasteurised cow's milk in modern mountain dairies, although the original cheese was made from raw ewe's milk.

To make the dish, a chunk of cheese with the rind pared off is placed on a tilted board in front of an open fire (or in these days a grilling element); as the cut surface exposed to the heat melts, the bubbling melted cheese is scraped off and with a flick laid on split hot small potatoes with onions and gherkins. It is then placed before the diner while still bubbling.

The overriding quality needed in a cheese for making Raclette (the French name comes from the word for 'scraper') is indeed 'scrapability'. In other words it must be quick to melt, must hold the heat well and must be slow to solidify.

If possible, drink with a Raclette a Swiss Fendant white wine from the canton of Valais, the dish's original home.

RACLETTE LIVRADOUX: This is a semi-hard cow's milk cheese, semi-cooked and pressed; made in a small French village called Fournols, south of Lyons. It is ripened for two to three months, the rind being brushed frequently throughout that time. As a table cheese, it is best bought in mid-France between July and November; you will enjoy its clean, nutty flavour.

REDUCED FAT CHEESES: In Britain, several firms have created low-fat versions of traditional cheeses to meet the consumer demand for them. These are, for instance, varieties which taste like Cheddar and Cheshire, but have only half the fat content, a third fewer calories and a quarter more protein; and ranges including a low-fat substitute for soft 'cream cheese' and variously flavoured reduced-fat cottage cheeses. These products, together with similar ones from smaller producers, are available in most fair-sized supermarkets.

Most other dairying countries produce similar cheeses, and especially whey cheeses.

REGGIANO: Hard, grating cheese from Reggiano, Italy. Part of the legally permitted designation of genuine Parmesan cheese (see page 85).

RICHELIEU: Canadian cheese, akin to Bel Paese.

RIGOTTE: An attractive baby cylinder, 3.5 cm/1½ inches in height and diameter, of French soft, snowy-white cheese with a natural russet rind 'helped' with annatto. Once made of goat's milk but now mainly a cow's milk cheese. A number of Rigottes are made with local names and various additions.

ROBIOLA: A stracchino type (although not a stracchino cheese), Robiola from the mountains of Piedmont and Lombardy is quick-ripening, delicate and gracious, weighing between 225 g/8 ounces and 450 g/1 pound as a rule. Once made from mixed milk, and still made by one firm from sheep's and goat's milk, it is otherwise now a cow's milk cheese. The cheeses ripen in straw or linen-lined boxes, and are rubbed with brine as their surface mould forms. There is a mild type as well as one which is decidedly more piquant, and is said to taste of truffles. Available sometimes from Italian delicatessen.

ROCAMADOUR: Tiny sheep's or goat's milk, soft cheese disc, weighing about 25 g/1 ounce. The cheeses are sometimes sold wrapped in leaves, sprinkled with brandy or wine and matured in crocks.

ROLLOT: A French, cow's milk soft cheese with a washed rind made either as a small round disc 7 cm/3 inches in diameter and 3.5 cm/1½ inches high, or in the larger, better-known heart shape sometimes called Guerbigny. The rind is light ochre yellow, and the paste is supple with a full bouquet and spicy taste. The cheese has a long and respectable history and does not seem to have 'lost out' by being made in creameries in modern times.

ROMADUR: Limburger-style rectangular cheese adopted by Germany along with Limburger, and now made in Bavaria far from its native Belgium. Somewhat milder than Limburger unless over-aged, the cheeses are usually only about 11 cm/4½ inches long and 5 cm/2 inches square in section, weighing about 450 g/1 pound. Whole milk Romadur is akin to American

Liederkranz according to the US Department of Agriculture.

ROMANO: One of the most popular, very hard Italian cheeses in both its native Italy and in the United States. It was originally made from sheep's milk but it is now also made from cow's or goat's milk, its name varying with the type of milk used. The sheep's milk cheese is Pecorino Romano, the cow's milk product is Vacchino Romano, and the goat's milk one is Caprino Romano. A Sardinian type is called Sardo.

The cheeses are generally cured for four to eight months for table use, and for as much as a year for use as a grating condiment cheese.

Some Romano cheese is made in the United States, but a great deal more is imported from Italy and Sardinia.

RONCAL: A raw sheep's cheese of Spanish Navarre, this is one of the oldest and most prestigious of Spanish cheeses. It is traditionally made from fresh milk as it leaves the ewe, using time-honoured methods of renneting, cutting, draining and moulding the cheeses, which are then matured for at least three months in mountain shelters. Such artisanal cheeses are increasingly rare and industrial production has been going on since 1974. Both types of the piquant and much prized cheese are protected by Spain's Denomination of Origin (similar to the French Appellation d'Origine).

The sheep produce milk rich in fat with a wonderful aroma and flavour from the wild mountain pasture. As a result Roncal is one of Spain's finest cheeses, well worth sampling in its country of origin. It has a hard, brown rind, and a compact texture without 'eyes'.

RONDEAU: A French, cow's milk, soft double-cream cheese with a fat content of 60 per cent, made in the shape of a ring or 'crown' (which is what 'rondeau' means in French). It is a modern cheese of the same general type as Camembert and Brie and it should be treated with the same respect.

ROUMILLAT: Another, even more modern soft French cheese first offered for tasting in 1982. It has a fat content of 50 per cent; when ripe it develops a downy white flor speckled with orange and a mild but increasingly flavoursome, creamy paste.

ROUY: A French cheese made in Burgundy from pasteurised cow's milk. It has a washed rind, and a soft paste with a pronounced tangy flavour, somewhere near that of Epoisses (page 69). A small square cheese with rounded corners, it is about 10 cm/4 inches square, 2.5 cm/1 inch thick, and weighs 225 g/8 ounces.

ROYALP: A Swiss, semi-hard cow's milk cheese, Royalp has been likened to Tilsiter, but is in fact a more individual cheese, coming from cows fed on mountain pasture and made by a Swiss lightly pressed method. It is a modern cheese by Swiss standards, although almost a century old, and it is softer than the four great traditional cheeses. It is made in a grindstone shape like a thick wheel, 23 cm/9 inches in diameter, 7.5 cm/3 inches in depth, weighing between 3.6 kg/8 pounds and 5 kg/11 pounds. The cut paste is creamy-coloured, with regular, round scattered holes. Mild in flavour, it can be used for any meal, even breakfast. Drink a light red wine with it (except at breakfast, when a cup of tea is better!).

RUTLAND: A modern English cow's milk cheese on the traditional pattern, made in drums of various weights from mere 125 g/5 ounce 'babies' to just under 10 kg/20 pound 'grandfathers'. It is a Cheddar-type cheese but (based on old stories) is flavoured with garlic, parsley and beer. Very much an Englishman's pub cheese, one would say.

SAANEN: A very hard Swiss cheese akin to Sbrinz (page 85). It is made from cow's milk and has a hard, compact paste. It is cured for at least three years, and sometimes much longer. It was once customary to make a cheese at a child's birth, and then to eat it at celebrations during his lifetime and at his burial.

SAGE CHEESES: Minced fresh garden sage (*Salvia officinalis*) has for centuries been one of the most popular herbs added to English cheeses. The traditional hard farmhouse cheeses, Derby, Lancashire, Gloucester and Wiltshire, have in the past all been made in sage-flavoured, green-speckled versions, although only Sage Derby and Lancashire are commonly found today. Sage Derby has, in fact, largely superseded unflavoured Derby.

American Sage Cheese is a sage-flavoured Cheddar or Stirred-Curd cheese, once made with sage leaves but now with sage extract; its overall green colour comes from green corn (maize cobs).

ST ALBRAY: Full-fat cheese in the shape of a flower with a centre hole for dramatic presentation. The paste with its 50 per cent fat content has a flavour between the hearty taste of a washed rind cheese and the mellow flavour of a bloomy rind one. A modern cheese from the house of Bongrain, its success has meant that it is quite widely exported.

ST BENOIT: A small French (Orleans)

cheese made from partly skimmed cow's milk and akin to Olivet. It has only 40 per cent fat. Its name is now also used for a proprietary brand of Brie.

ST FLORENTIN: The original St Florentin cheese, which goes back to the thirteenth century, is similar to Epoisses and Langres. Of raw cow's milk it is about 12.5 cm/5 inches in diameter with a brine-washed rind and is matured for two months in damp cellars. This cheese with its aromatic red-brown rind and tangy flavour is still made but not exported.

The more common St Florentin cheese today is made from pasteurised milk and is a fresh cheese edible within a week of being made. It is slightly smaller than the original, is rindless, pure white and good either for salads or as the basis of a sweet dish.

ST KILLIAN: An Irish, full-fat cow's milk cheese, with a six-week shelf life after it leaves the home dairy. It is a Camembert-style mould-ripened cheese, in an unusual six-sided shape.

ST MARCELLIN: Made in the French province of Isère, these little cheese discs, weighing about 85 g/3 ounces, used to be made from pure goat's milk, but are now (except on a few goat farms) made commercially from cow's milk by the same method as Camembert or Brie. It now has a fat content of only 40 per cent and is ready for eating four weeks after being made. It is sometimes sold in speciality shops.

SAPSAGO: A very hard Swiss cow's milk grating or condiment cheese flavoured with clover. It is in the shape of a small cone with the top cut off, and is coloured green. Its German name is Schabzieger.

SARDO: Sardo means Sardinian – made on the island of Sardinia. Informally Fiore Sardo, the ewe's or mixed milk cheese made on the island, is sometimes just called Sardo or Pecorino Sardo; this cheese has a ridged rind. Sardo Romano is also sometimes Pecorino Sardo but has a smooth rind and is similarly now made of ewe's milk and cow's milk mixed.

SASSENAGE: Firm, blue-veined French cheese from Isère, made from cow's milk with some goat's milk added, made in a large thick wheel. Related to Bleu de Gex, which is easier for travellers in France to buy.

SCAMORZE: Small, soft mild pasta filata cheese from central Italy, first made from buffalo's milk but now made from cow's and occasionally goat's milk and found widely in Italy. This little oval cheese is eaten fresh or lightly cured for four to six weeks and brine-washed. The cheeses are sold tied together like clusters of lemons. An attractive buy in Italy although not exported. (The name is also sometimes used to describe cow's milk Mozzarella.)

SCHABZIEGER: See Sapsago above.

SCOTTISH CHEESE MARK: The Scottish Cheese Mark, which only applies to Cheddar, is a distinctive logo designed to counter the substitution of cheese from other sources for genuine Scottish Cheddar and to assure consumers that they are getting a certain standard of cheese, monitored through the grading service of the Company of Scottish Cheese-makers Ltd.

SEPTMONCEL: French blue cheese from the Jura, similar to Bleu de Gex and Sassenage. Made mostly from cow's milk with a little goat's milk added. Cured for about eight weeks in cool 'caves'. Not exported.

SERRA DE ESTRELLA: The name of this Portuguese cheese comes from the mountain range where it is made. It is the most highly prized of a group of similar cheeses most often made from ewe's milk but sometimes from mixed milks. The cheeses are round, semi-soft, with a pale yellow paste and a pleasant light acid taste.

SHARPHAM: A full fat, surface-ripened English soft cheese, Sharpham looks like a Coulommiers but the raw Jersey cow's milk from which it is made and the home-grown starter culture places it firmly in the English farmhouse cheese tradition. It is made with fresh morning milk, curdled with vegetarian rennet, then settled and drained in perforated moulds. After turning, salting and spraying with the mould which will produce a white flor, the cheeses are dried off and matured in damp, cool conditions with much further turning and care. They are ready for sale in three weeks, although they can be matured if desired for two to four weeks longer, during which time the white coat deepens to ivory and the flavour strengthens. The cheeses are 20 cm/8 inches in diameter, weighing 1.2 kg/2½ pounds, and have a high fat content of 55 to 60 per cent. Drink with a light, smooth red wine.

SIR: Balkan word for cheese (Yugoslavian).

SLIPCOTE, SLIPCOAT: A rich, cow's milk cheese with cream added, made in English farmhouses and homes as early as 1698 and as late as 1914. Similar to Colwick or a rich white version of Cambridge or York cheese, but tending to lose its surface crust when ripe.

SMALLHOLDER: Name for cow's and goat's milk small cheeses made by English landowners whose livestock produce too little milk for large-scale or formal production. Various sizes and shapes.

SMOKED APPLEWOOD: An English, cow's milk firm cheese made in 4.5 kg/10 pound cylinders 20 cm/8 inches in diameter and 12.5 cm/5 inches deep. The cheeses have a deep russet rind and the Cheddar-based paste of pasteurised milk has a 48 per cent fat content. Since there is no permanent bulk supply of old apple-trees for fuel, the smoke flavour is perforce supplied by a wood smoke extract. It is said not to be affected by the paprika rubbed on the rind.

SMOKED CHEESES: A number of hard and semi-soft cheeses are 'smoked' today, as their progenitors have been for more than a thousand years. Properly smoked cheese is cold-smoked in heat no higher than 29°C/85°F. Preferably a smouldering fire is made in a pit or fire-box and the smoke is piped or filtered in controlled, constantly moving quantities over and around the cheeses hanging or resting on racks in a separate area. The smoking fuel is normally hickory twigs, shavings or dust. Oak, ash or fruit woods are sometimes used but they are more expensive and barely affect the flavour of the smoked foods, whatever sentiment or superstition may allege.

Smoked cheeses made on a large scale, especially processed cheeses, are almost always 'smoked' by adding synthetic chemical or 'liquid' smoke to the milk or curd or by flavouring the curd with smoke-flavoured salt. They smell and taste of resin but not much else as a rule.

Most cheese-producing countries have one or more smoked cheeses to offer. The oldest and most pleasing, perhaps, are Mediterranean peasant shepherds' cheeses smoked over chestnut wood. Smoked Provolone (Provolone affumicato) and Smoked Mozzarella are said to be good. Both Germany and Austria produce modern smoked cheeses in the same shape and colour as large sausages. The Austrian one is based on a locally made Gouda or Emmental and smoked over oak wood shavings. Britain produces, besides Smoked Applewood, Smoked Orkney, the smoke-flavoured, paprika-skinned Charnwood and a Devonshire Smoked Cheddar, while the United States makes several smoked cheeses based on Cheddar or Stirred-Curd cheese. Denmark, however, makes the most unusual smoked cheese, a caraway-flavoured, lightly hay-smoked delicacy from the island of Fyn, the same home as the frankly pedestrian Fynbo cheese. Unfortunately, the Danish smoked cheese does not travel, so you will have to visit Fyn to try it.

SOMERSET BRIE: This is a true Brie although made in the heart of England's fine cheese-making area in Somerset. It is even made by a French cheese-maker. It is in the shape – as is Brie – of a flat 'plate' of cheese 33 cm/13 inches across and 4.5 cm/13.8 inches high. It has the typical white flor coat of a creamery-made Brie cheese. In 1989, it won First Prize for soft cheeses at the London International Food and Drink Exhibition.

SPERMYSE: The name for herb-flavoured cheeses (almost certainly based on soft white 'cream' cheeses) in the Middle Ages.

SPICED CHEESES: These are the legion of cheeses to which spices or ground or whole seeds are added during making so that they are distributed throughout the paste. Popular spices and seeds used are caraway, cumin, pepper, cloves, anise and mustard seed. Paprika pepper is used for rubbing on the rinds of some cheeses.

The classic spice-flavoured cheeses are nearly all semi-hard cheeses made by the same general methods, and rigidly controlled as to their fat content, pasteurisation of the milk, and quantity of spice included; United States regulations are particularly strict. Modern spiced cheeses are now made by the score however; in fact, probably the majority of small, modern, exported cheeses for the mass market are made in two or three versions with different spice or herb flavourings. See Herb-flavoured cheeses, page 129.

Among the popular spice-flavoured semi-hard cheeses, Dutch Leiden flavoured with cumin is time-honoured, although the cheese may now contain clove or caraway instead of cumin. Norwegian Nokkelost has caraway in both its homeland and the United States versions. As for the modern soft cheeses, the French Boursin rolled in crushed black pepper and called Boursin Poivre is probably the best known.

SPUN CURD OR SPUN PASTE CHEESES: See Plastic Curd cheese, page 134.

STIRRED CURD CHEESE: See Granular or Stirred-Curd Cheese, page 128.

STORE CHEESE: American and Canadian term for standard local Cheddar or similar cheese.

STRACCHINO CHEESES: Stracco means 'tired' in Italian, and stracchino originally meant cheeses made from the somewhat thin milk of cattle on the long trek from summer pasture to wintering in the valleys. It now means cheeses which are relatively delicate and quick-maturing (perhaps because of the chemical make-up of the milk) and which therefore do not travel well unless the milk is pasteurised.

STRESA CONVENTION: In 1951, representatives of eight nations agreed to restrict the use of the names of certain great classic cheeses. In future the names might only be used of cheeses made where and how, quality-wise, they had been made originally. The signatories were Austria, Denmark, France, Italy, the Netherlands, Norway, Sweden and Switzerland. Some of the well-known cheeses covered by this certification of origin are Asiago, Brie, Caciocavallo, Camembert, Danbo, Edam, Emmental, Fontina, Gouda, Gruyère, Havarti, Samsöe and Sbrinz.

SUPRÊME: One of the invented names (Excelsior, Magnum and Fin de Siècle are others) used by manufacturers to describe double-cream modern enriched cow's milk cheeses with up to 72 per cent fat content. They are bloomy-rinded discs or ovals, with a creamy, stabilised paste designed for longer keeping than a normal surface-ripening cheese. Suprême des Ducs is a popular example.

SWALEDALE: A soft cow's milk cheese old in history but only recently revived in the English Yorkshire Dales, its traditional home. Pleasantly mild, it is seldom available on the open market but is worth asking for in north country stores.

SWEET CURD CHEESE: In the United States this refers to cheese made by the basic Cheddar process but with fresh, not ripened, milk; also the curd is cut, heated and drained quickly so that it is less acid than usual. The curd (not milled) is cured like Cheddar, but is rather more moist and open-textured. Edam, Gouda and Brick are sweet-curd cheeses.

SWISS: A general name for imitations of Emmental in the New World. A seeming Emmental is only genuine beyond doubt if it is stamped or labelled Emmental Switzerland or Switzerland-Swiss. See Stresa Convention. Swiss-style cheeses are made in many European countries and in the US. Some of these cheeses are near facsimiles of the original, others are distinctly different. For instance, much American 'Swiss' is semi-soft because it is sold when only four months old instead of the usual nine to ten months.

TALEGGIO: A stracchino cheese from Lombardy in northern Italy, Taleggio is a small, soft whole cow's milk cheese with a brine-washed rind which turns greyish with age. Its flavour when ripe is said to be emphatic, and its aroma hearty. One of the few stracchino cheeses exported.

TARTARE: A double-cream cheese, very soft and creamy, with a 70 per cent fat content, Tartare is a 'veritable' spreading cheese. It comes in two sizes, both flavoured with parsley and garlic more successfully than most similar stabilised, herb-flavoured cheeses. A Bongrain group cheese.

TELEME AND TELEME JACK: There are two distinctly different cheeses called Teleme. One is a brine-cured Balkan cheese originally, and still usually made of ewe's milk alone or with a little goat's milk included. As made in Rumania, Bulgaria, Greece and Turkey, it is almost identical with Feta (see page 112). A version of this 'pickled' cheese made from cow's milk in the United States is, however, much softer and more pliable.

The second cheese called Teleme is now more often called Teleme Jack. It is one of the names applied to the high-moisture type of Monterey Jack (see page 133), and it is said to have been thought up by Greek cheese-makers who had emigrated to America. The curd is heated less than for whole milk Monterey and is cooled more quickly. This makes a creamy white softish cheese slightly reminiscent of the Balkan Teleme; and it is considered by good south-westerners to be perfect cooking cheese for Mexican dishes.

TERRITORIAL CHEESE: Used chiefly in England and Wales as a general term to describe distinct cheeses from particular areas of the country. There are now many local British cheeses but only nine Territorial cheeses are recognised. These are: Cheddar, Cheshire, Wensleydale, Lancashire, Stilton, Double Gloucester, Derby, Leicester, Caerphilly.

TÊTE DE MOINE: Its name alone explains that this was once monk's or monastery cheese, made in fact at the Swiss abbey at Bellelay in the Bernese Jura. It is now, however, made at small dairies around the region, using cow's milk. The cheeses are uncooked, pressed, formed into drums as wide as they are high (10 to 13 cm/4 to 5 inches in diameter and height) and cured for about four months. The rinds are brushed with water during this time to give the cheeses a slightly sticky coat, and the paste is supple with a fruity flavour. Usually available to order from good cheese stores.

TOME, TOMME: A French word for semi-hard, pressed cheese; strictly, it means 'slice' but the meaning has been transferred to a whole cheese of this type because it is so often used as a daily slicing cheese for packed meals and snacks. Most of the many tommes – there are at least twenty-four – are medium-sized round cylinders of cheese. They are variously made from cow's, goat's or sheep's milk, whole or skimmed, and have a natural, greyish or *cendré* rind, or are black-waxed or covered with 'marc' (wine residues). A characteristic tomme is the well-known Tomme de Savoie described on page 64.

TOMME BLANCHE: 'White cheese', essentially soft and feminine in character, regardless of its type, or tender and fresh, not yet pungent. A typical tomme blanche is the creamery-made, 50 per cent fat, *Douceur d'Auvergne* made from full-fat pasteurised cow's milk in 20 cm/8 inch discs, 5 cm/2 inches high. It starts as a Brie-style cheese but is stabilised so that it ripens to a set creamy consistency all through and develops a fresh-tasting, fluffy white mantle as a coating.

A *Tomme blanche de Corse* is a sheep's milk cylinder of firm white cheese from Corsica sold in France for eating more or less fresh; many, if not most, of such cheeses make their way to Combalou to be cured in the caves there as (quite genuine) Roquefort, but a minority are sold in France just as they come from their homeland.

TOMME AU MARC: Cheese made with partly skimmed cow's milk in mountain valleys of wine-making Savoy and Burgundy. While curing, the cheese is brushed, then coated with fermented marc (see Tomme). In this way, the cheese acquires a strongly alcoholic flavour and 'nose', and a coating of wine residues in which it is packaged. It is, however, very rarely on the market, being reserved by farms for their own use.

TOME DE MONTAGNE: General name given to several cheeses made and ripened in French mountain regions, especially in the Jura. A typical one, more often exported than most, is a semi-skimmed cow's milk, pressed, semi-soft cheese with a 25 per cent fat content, now made and ripened separately in the mountain area called the Haut Livradois in the Auvergne, although its first ancestor 300 years ago was a Savoyard cheese. It is matured for up to five weeks in a traditional 'cave', to develop its dark grey, almost blackish rind and semi-hard pale yellow paste with small holes near the surface. The spelling of Tome with only one *m* is slightly unusual.

TOMME DES NEIGES: A cow's milk cheese with a white surface flor rind, made commercially in Dauphiné. It is 20 cm/8 inches in diameter and about 5 cm/2 inches thick.

TÒMME AU RAISIN: A commercial, medium-sized wheel of cheese covered thickly with grape pips; likewise, a small soft white cheese made from pasteurised milk and covered with pips is also sold, and exported.

Both can sometimes be found in speciality delicatessen. The pips add nothing to the flavour of the cheese and are best cut off.

TORTA: Properly called San Gaudenzio, Torta takes its name from the many-layered pastry gateaux of its Italian homeland. It is made of alternate layers of Gorgonzola and Mascarpone in a 15 to 18 cm/6 to 7 inch block with a distinctive, exotic flavour.

TRAPPIST CHEESES: The most ascetic Roman Catholic monks from 1664 onward were the small group of Cistercians at the Norman monastery of La Trappe who pursued a way of life even more rigorous than that of the first primitive members of their Order. Disbanded in the French Revolution, a group of twenty under the novice-master were allowed to settle near Fribourg in Switzerland. Strict as they were, postulants flocked to them, and their members established monasteries in England, Belgium, Italy, Spain and Canada. In 1817, now skilled in Swiss cheese-making, they returned to France, to a monastery at Entrammes. Their numbers continued to grow, and they continued to form new communities to which they took their cheese-making secrets and skill.

The prototype cheese made from the recipe brought back from Switzerland was Port du Salut/Port Salut. Since then many Trappist communities besides the original one at Entrammes have made and marketed a similar cheese under local labels, and commercial manufacturers use the name Port Salut quite freely for cheeses more or less matching the original one.

TRUCKLE: See Cheese-Making Terms.

TYROPHILE: Lover of cheese.

VACHERIN: A name common to several different kinds of cheese made in France and Switzerland. Vacherin Fribourgeois is a cheese with a brushed rind and firm interior, sometimes used with Gruyère to make a fondue. Vacherin Mont d'Or and some variations of this very creamy cheese are now (one hopes only temporarily) no longer on the market.

VALENCAY: A small truncated cone of goat's cheese, with a charcoal-smeared rind if from a farm, a merely white one if from a creamery. Fairly widely made and distributed. Has a fat content of 45 per cent in either case. The farm version (Valencay fermier) is, according to Pierre Androuet, quite mild, while the creamery version (Valencay laitier) is strong-smelling and slightly soapy to taste.

VERMONT: A good-quality and prized American Cheddar.

VIEUX PANÉ: Despite its name, Vieux Pané is a modern cheese from the Fromageries Perrault, renowned for generations of making St Paulin and Pont l'Évêque. It is a soft smooth cheese with a full but widely acceptable flavour, and a reddish washed rind. It is presented curiously. Two of the flat, square cheeses are packaged in a single wooden case, each double-wrapped in cellophane lined with parchment paper, labelled and encircled with a parchment strip. Each case carries a packing date with instructions on how long to keep the cheese and how to store it.

VULSCOMBE: An attractive goat's milk cheese, made in the English West Country, in Devonshire. It is made in the form of small 'cakes' and is suited to vegetarians and allergy sufferers.

WALTON: English, semi-hard blended cheese made in various shapes and weights from 450 g/1 pound to 3 kg/6 pounds 6 ounces. The blended paste is composed of Stilton, Cheddar and crushed walnuts, assembled after the cheeses have matured, and coated in more crushed walnuts for extra 'bite'. A traditional blend, the main trouble about this tasty cheese is its short shelf life; it only keeps about a week, even when refrigerated. It is none the less a popular cheese, which can be eaten with port after dinner.

WASHED CURD CHEESE: An American cow's milk cheese made in the same way as Cheddar except that the curds are washed (or sometimes soaked) before salting. The result is a semi-soft, moist cheese more open-textured than Cheddar, made in a cylinder or rectangular shape.

WASHED RIND CHEESES: Cheeses which need moisture to help them ripen properly may be washed while curing. Wine, whey, milk or water (fresh or salted) may be the moistening liquid used. The effect on the colour, flavour and texture of the rind varies in each case.

WEDMORE: The family tree of this young, vigorous cheese goes back to the end of the last century when a shortage of milk for Caerphilly in Wales led to its being made on English farms, in Somerset. Made from full cream cow's milk, it can be eaten at three weeks old or left to mature for two to three months. It has a line of chopped chives through the centre.

WEISSLACKER: A soft, ripened cow's milk cheese from Bavaria in Germany with a strong 'nose' and full flavour. When well ripened it may be called Bierkäse, and its kinship with Limburger is then quite obvious. It is, in fact, made like Limburger except that the curd is cut into larger cubes and is less well drained. The flavour takes between three and four months' curing to develop in the cube-shaped cheeses, which are between 10 and 13 cm/4 and 5 inches square, and 8 to 10 cm/3½ to 4 inches thick. Occasionally sold in speciality German-style delicatessen.

WHEY CHEESES: Cheeses made from the watery leftovers of making curds are probably as old as cheese-making itself. They are still made by many poor peasant peoples. Norwegian Gjetost is made of goat's whey, while other Scandinavian cheeses, such as Mysost are made from cow's whey. So is Italian Ricotta.

WILTSHIRE CHEESE: Wiltshire cheese, or Brickbat, no longer exists by that name; but the English county of Wiltshire is still, as it has always been, an important centre of the cheese-making industry. A lot of Cheddar, Caerphilly and other West-Country cheese is, in fact, made in Wiltshire. Also, since the 1980s a small soft sheep's milk cheese called Wiltshire White has been farm-made near Marlborough.

WINDSOR RED: A red-marbled English cheese made by infusing Cheddar cheese with British elderberry wine.

A SHORT LIST OF CHEESE-MAKING TERMS

ABOMASUM: Fourth (and true digestive) stomach of a ruminant animal; rennet is obtained from the stomach of a suckling animal.

ACCELERATED CHEESE RIPENING: A long-term English research project at the Institute of Food Research at Reading is being undertaken (1988) into the mechanism of Cheddar cheese maturation and flavour development, with a view to speeding up Cheddar ripening. Now nearing completion (1989), it will consist of an enzyme system which will accelerate the desirable processes but not those which lead to breakdown defects. The process had undergone factory trials with satisfactory initial results when this book went to press.

ACID CURD: Milk coagulated for cheese-making by lactic acid, not rennet.

ACIDITY: The amount of acid in milk; the degree of souring produced by acid. Acid development (sourness) is essential for cheese-making; in unpasteurised milk, it is produced by lactic-acid bacteria naturally present in the milk.

ADDITIVE: Any substance added to the normal constituents of cheese to enhance or change the flavour, improve the eye appeal or extend the keeping time of the finished product. Additives range from natural herbs and seeds to synthetic colourings and flavour enhancers.

AFFINEUR: French word for a specialist who cures and matures cheeses for sale in his own 'cellars', often on behalf of a farm cheese-maker who has no curing rooms.

AGE (vb): To keep a suitable cheese eg naturally made Cheddar, until it is fully mature or for even longer, to make it stronger-flavoured and firmer in texture.

AMINO-ACID: Basic constituent of proteins. The eight 'essential amino-acids' needed to build human tissue are all found in cheese.

ANNATTO: A harmless and tasteless vegetable dye produced from the seeds of a tropical shrub (*Bixa orellana*), it is added to milk to give cheese a reddish, orange or golden colour. It is also used to tint other foods.

BABY: Term used to describe a miniature cylinder or drum-shaped cheese, most often a Stilton. The size may vary considerably but is always much smaller than a normal full-sized cheese. A truckle is another term used to describe miniature cheeses, usually Cheddars.

BLOOM: A soft penicillin mould making a surface coating on many cheeses. This florescence shows that the cheese is mature.

BLUE/BLUE-VEINED: Term used to describe cheeses with internal mould growth, usually *Penicillium roqueforti*, spreading throughout the cheese as it ripens. The mould may be blue, blackish or greenish.

In the United States, the term 'blue' has been used as a noun and general label for all such cheeses ever since American research succeeded in manufacturing blue-mould cheese for commercial production.

BREAK (vb): Term used to describe the division of the cheese curd into pieces or particles by cutting, slicing, crumbling or other means. Done to release the whey.

CALCIUM: A mineral element, essential for forming bones and teeth. Cheese is a rich source of calcium.

CAROTENE: Good source of vitamin A (retinol) found in vegetable foods and milk, which also gives colour to dairy and other products. Vitamin A protects against skin and similar infections, and strengthens the eyes.

CASEIN: The chief milk protein. When acid or rennet is added to milk, the casein's bunch of amino-acids condense and form solid particles separate from the milk liquids. (See curd)

CHEESE FACTOR: Agent or representative who buys and sells products such as butter and cheese, usually on a commission basis.

CHEESE PRESS: An instrument or machine used to squash loose cheese curd particles into a shape firm and dense enough to be handled, squeezing out some or most of its moisture (whey).

CHEESE STARTER: See Starter, page 141.

CHEESE WRING: Simple cheese press or perforated bowl for draining curds.

CHEESEMONGER: Term used for the owner or manager of a cheese shop who is a specialist in buying and selling cheese and is responsible for doing so.

CHEDDARING: Term used for a stage in the making of certain cheeses. Blocks of curd are repeatedly cut and piled up, changing their position each time, to facilitate draining and to mat the curd particles. By this method, they become elastic, smooth and 'silky' to touch.

COAGULATION: The clotting (precipitation) of milk by lactic acid or rennet.

COME (vb): Term describing the solidifying of butter or cheese curd after processing, eg 'when the curd comes . . .'. Informal term for precipitation.

COMPOUND PRODUCT: A legal definition of a food containing more than 10 per cent cheese where the natural cheese has been changed after maturing (other than by being made into processed cheese) eg by the addition of herbs, as in Cotswold.

COOKED CHEESE: Term used for cheese whose curd is, literally, 'cooked' – that is heated or scalded. Although the method differs slightly from country to country, the method is a generally accepted way of making certain types of cheese.

COOLER: Shallow tray, usually on a trolley, to which newly-drained curds are transferred from the vat (bath) for cheddaring.

CURD: Coagulated milk solids (casein, fat, etc).

CURE (vb) Spec. of cheese: To bring a cheese to its peak of flavour; to ripen it. A cheese must first have time to 'set', that is to gain form and consistency through drainage and enzyme activity. It then needs time to ripen, and still more time to mature it and to let it mellow.

Technically, it is said to be 'cured' when it is edible, and before it begins to deteriorate.

EYE-HOLES: Holes in the paste of certain types of ripened cheeses created by the introduction of special gas-forming starters (see Starter). Holes may be large, eg in Emmental, or small 'teardrop' holes, as in Samsöe.

FARMHOUSE: Copyrighted logo of English cheeses made under contract to the English Milk Marketing Board's manufacturing and marketing company Dairy Crest. Formerly: farm-made as opposed to creamery-made cheeses.

FERMENTATION: The breakdown (decomposition) of an organic substance, especially a carbohydrate, by micro-organisms.

FLOR: Powdery mould on the surface of a cheese.

FRESH CHEESE: Unripened cheese (see Ripening). Also so-called 'cream cheese' which is not renneted and simply consists of gravity-drained cream.

GRANA: Italian term for 'grain' used to describe the 'feel' and texture of very hard grating cheeses such as Parmesan and Swiss Sbrinz.

HARD CHEESE: Hard-pressed cheeses with a moisture content of less than 40 per cent. Some hard-pressed cheeses are usually described as semi-hard or yielding to define them more clearly – or, in some cases, when they are sold young.

HERBAL RENNET: See Rennet.

HOOP: Alternative name for a cheese mould.

LACTIC ACID: Acid produced by the action of micro-organisms (bacteria) naturally present in unpasteurised milk, or introduced into pasteurised milk in a 'starter' culture. They act on the milk sugar (lactose).

LACTOSE: The type of sugar present in milk.

MATURE (vb): Leave to develop its full flavour – used of a cheese which, although ripened and edible, will still become richer and stronger-flavoured if required, without deteriorating.

MAW: Common name for Abomasum.

MEAL: The quantity of milk given by a cow at one milking; also the time of milking.

MOULD[1]: Container in which cheese curd is drained and shaped. Moulds range from small baskets in which some soft cheeses are ripened to large metal hoops or rings in which hard cheeses are pressed.

MOULD[2]: Airborne fungus which spreads rapidly in humid conditions. Although most moulds on foods are contaminants, all surface mould-ripened cheeses and blue cheeses are created by introducing specific mould micro-organisms during their making, either on the surface of the cheeses eg Brie, or into the curd eg Stilton.

Most white moulds on the cut surfaces of hard cheeses such as Cheddar can be scraped off, and the cheese can then be used for cooking.

MOULD-RIPENED CHEESES: These cheeses are ripened in two ways. Some are ripened by mould spores sprayed on the surface of the new cheese. The result is the production of a white downy growth all over the surface. Other cheeses are ripened by mould spores which grow along minute airways in the paste, making blueish or greenish veins. Both kinds of mould spores are made by one or another kind of *Penicillium*; surface mould are generally made by the species *Penicillium camemberti*. Internal moulds are made by various species such as *Penicillium roqueforti*.

NATURAL CHEESE: Cheese ripened for sale in the traditional or normal way for that particular cheese without any extra processing; as opposed to processed cheese.

OFF-FLAVOUR: Unpleasant or tainted flavour in cheese. May be the result of deterioration, eg an 'ammonia' flavour in Brie, or of cross-flavouring from other strongly flavoured foods such as onions. Package all cheeses carefully and store them separately from other strongly flavoured foods.

PASTE: Interior of a cheese, under the surface, inside the rind if there is one.

PASTEURISATION: In pasteurising milk, the temperature of the milk is usually raised to $72°C/161°F$ and held at that temperature for fifteen seconds before being rapidly reduced to $10°C/50°F$. This destroys any harmful organisms without substantially altering the nature of the milk. Not only are these organisms potentially very harmful to human beings, there are some which, when present in milk, will substantially alter the nature of, or destroy, the cheese that will be made from it. At the very least the quality of cheese will be variable; this will be expensive for the producer and fail to provide the consumer with a consistent, good quality product.

However, pasteurisation also takes some of the characteristic flavour out of individual milk supplies, which in the hands of expert cheese-makers can produce some of the world's best and most individual cheeses.

Until recently milk had to be pasteurised to cleanse it of infective bacteria for sale to the public, but with the success of modern medical methods and the virtual eradication of bovine tuberculosis in Britain, unpasteurised milk products there are becoming increasingly safe and also more common.

The vast majority of cheese products are still made from pasteurised milk and probably always will be because of the consistently edible cheese it produces, but it is worth keeping a look out for unpasteurised cheeses to sample their fuller flavour.

PENICILLIUM: Yeast producing fungi found in cheeses in which moulds grow as they ripen. For example *Penicillium camemberti* gives Camembert cheese its white downy surface.

PERSILLÉ: In French cheese jargon, cheeses which are speckled with mould rather than having branching veins of it. The word strictly means 'parslied' – sprinkled with chopped parsley.

PITCHING: Term used in cheese-making, denoting the settling of scalded curd on the bottom of the cheese vat, so that the whey can be drained off.

PLASTIC CURD CHEESE (PASTA FILATA): Cheese which, at a stage in its making, is immersed in hot water or whey and kneaded until it becomes malleable and easily shaped. Mozzarella is a well-known plastic curd or kneaded cheese.

PRECIPITATION: Technical term for the clotting of milk solids (ie of casein particles and fat) by lactic or other acid or rennet. Instead of being a solution, the milk is then separated into a precipitate (solid clots or curds) and liquid whey.

PROCESSED CHEESE: Natural cheese which has been broken down, emulsified and sterilised to stop further development. Various flavourings may then be added.

RAW MILK: Unpasteurised milk; not heat-treated.

RENNET: Any substance containing enzymes from the abomasum of a suckling animal; other substances which also curdle milk, such as the plant Lady's Bedstraw (*Calium verum*). There are also modern microbial and chemical rennets. Note that rennet sold for domestic use (ie for making junket) is not suitable for cheese-making.

RINDLESS CHEESE: Natural cheese which has been foil- or film-wrapped and ripened in a vacuum; this prevents water evaporation and a rind does not form.

RIPENING[1]: The processes by which a newly-made cheese becomes fit to eat and ready for sale, with its own individuality and flavour. Time, temperature, humidity and (sometimes) draining techniques all play a part in ripening a cheese. Some hard and *grana* cheeses continue to develop or mature after they are ripe; others, eg Brie, ripen, achieve their peak flavour at once, and deteriorate almost as quickly.

RIPENING[2]: Milk is often left to 'ripen' for a time before being used for cheese-making; this means it is allowed to become slightly more acid, that is it begins to sour.

SCALDING: Heating the cheese curd, either by surrounding the container with a 'jacket' of hot air or steam, or by draining off and heating the whey, then stirring it back into the curd.

SEMI-HARD CHEESES: Medium-pressed cheeses with a moisture content of 44–55 per cent. Lancashire and Gorgonzola are examples.

SEMI-SOFT CHEESES: Term used to describe cheeses whose paste 'gives' when pressed but is resilient. Edam, Port Salut and Bel Paese are cheeses of this kind.

SKIM MILK: Milk from which the cream has been removed thus reducing the fat content. Some milk is only partly skimmed; it is always so labelled.

SOFT CHEESE: Unpressed cheese, either ripened or unripened, with a moisture content of at least 55 per cent. Camembert and cottage cheese are both soft cheeses, showing how much this type of cheese varies.

SOURING: Acid development in raw milk; this gives the milk a clean, sharp flavour which is quite different from the flavour of milk which has 'gone off' due to decaying bacteria.

STARTER: A laboratory-made living bacterial culture which is added to milk for cheese-making to produce acid for forming curd in the first stage of production. It also contributes to the flavour of the cheese. See Lactic acid; Precipitation; Souring.

STERILISATION: The destruction of all micro-organisms by heat or chemical means.

SURFACE-RIPENED CHEESES: These cheeses are sometimes called Bacterial Surface Ripened Cheeses. They are ripened by bacteria added in solution to the shelves on which they ripen, or by being washed or brushed with the same solution. The characteristic organism used for surface ripening of suitable cheeses is *Brevi-bacterium linens*. It produces a brownish-red surface growth, quite different from the mould growth produced by a *Penicillium*.

TEXTURE: The texture of a cheese clearly demonstrates its type and quality. A young or rindless block Cheddar is as smooth and 'buttery' as Edam, but a well-matured traditional Cheddar is (or should be) close-textured but not rubbery, and should cut cleanly yet flake slightly if a cut side is left exposed. It should certainly never 'sweat'.

By contrast, a medium-pressed English cheese such as Lancashire should have a slightly open, friable (crumbly) texture.

TRUCKLE: Originally, 'truckle' seems to have been the name given to certain small English cheeses shaped like a bun loaf or cylinder-shaped roller or perhaps a solid wheel like Gloucester cheeses, weighing up to 5.4 kg/12 pounds. Today, it can mean a small cheese of any type, but it is most often used to mean a baby drum-shaped Cheddar.

VAT: Once the name for a cheese mould, vat now means the large 'bath' sometimes holding hundreds or even thousands of litres/gallons of milk in which the first stages of cheese-making take place.

VELL: See Abomasum.

WASHED RIND CHEESES: The rinds of these cheeses are brushed with or are bathed in water, brine or alcohol during their ripening time. A russet or golden bacterial growth normally develops on the surface of the cheeses, which usually gives the rind a strong aroma and flavour even if the cheese paste tastes quite mild.

WHEY: The free liquid separated from the curd when milk is curdled eg for cheese-making. Whey contains valuable nutrients, ie proteins, sugar and minerals. It is now mainly used for stock-feeding and in commercial processed foods, but it was once a popular human food in its own right.

YIELDING CHEESE: Informal but graphic term for semi-soft cheeses.

INDEX

Names of cheeses are in bold type; names of cheese recipes are in italics.

A

Accelerated cheese ripening, 33, 139
Adamson, Dermot, 8
Affiné (French: ripened), 116
Affineur (France), 53, 60, 68, 73, 80, 112, 139
Allgau Marbles, 127
American cheese, – blue cheese, 116
Ancient cheeses (Sumerian, Egyptian, Greek), 11
Angelot (France), 116
Annatto, 25, 29, 36, 37, 100, 139
Appellation d'origine, – controlée, 49, 53, 56, 64, 72, 73, 77, 80, 116
Appenzell Switzerland, 107, 116
Arlott, John, 41, 49, 53, 60, 61, 65, 96, 112
Ash-coated (cendré) cheeses, 121
Ash in Morbier cheese, 20, 65, 68
Asiago (Italy), 116
Australian cheeses, 116

B

Bagnes (Switzerland), 116
Baker's (US/Canada), 116
Banbury (UK), 116
Banon (France), 76, 77, 116
Baraka (France), 116, 117
Bateaux d'Angelot, 127
Bavarian Blue (Germany), 109, 112
Beaufort, Gruyère de –, (France), 68, 69
Beaumont (France), 117
Beauvoorde (Belgium), 117
Beenleigh Blue (UK), 117
Bel Paese (Italy), 89, 92
Belle Bressane (France), 117
Bellelay (Switzerland), 117
Bellshire (UK), 117
Bergader Blue (Germany), 117
Bergkäse (Alps), 117
Berkeley (UK), 36, 37, 117, 124
Bierkäse (Germany/Belgium), 117
Bleu d'Auvergne (France), 71, 73
Bleu de Bresse (France), 117
Bleu de Haut Jura (France), 117
Bleu de Laqueuille (France), 73
Bleu des Causses (France), 117
Blue Brie(s), 60, 89, 109, 117, 120
Blue mould-ripened cheese(s), 9, 10, 16, 20, 21, 29, 32, 33, 37, 44, 45, 48, 72, 73, 77, 89, 104, 105, 109, 112
Blue Stuart (UK), 39, 117
Blue Vinney (UK), 117
Bonchester (UK), 117, 120

Boulette d'Avesnes (France), 120
Boursault (France), 60
Boursin (France), 60, 117
Bresse Bleu, see Bleu de Bresse
Brevibacterium linens, 10, 109
Brick (US), 116, 120
Bricquebec (France), 120
Brie (France), 13, 16, 48, 55, 57, 113, 116 (Australia/France), 120
  – de Coulommiers, 57, 116
  – de Melun, 37, 57
  – de Meaux fermier, laitier 57
Brie, Somerset (UK), 17, 30
Brillat-Savarin (France), 120
Brillat-Savarin, Jean-Anthelme, 69, 85
British Food Information Service, 37, 121, 125, 133
Broodkaas (Netherlands), 100
Bruder Basil (Germany), 120
British cheese, early, 11–12; profiles, 21–45
Burrino (Italy), 93, 120

C

Caboc (UK), 44, 45
Cabrales (Spain), 120
Cacetta, Cacietta (Italy), 93, 120
Cacciocavallo (Italy), 93, 120
Caerphilly (UK), 10, 39, 40, 41
Caerphilly Salad, 39
Cambozola (Germany), 109, 112
Cambridge (UK), 120
Camembert (France), 13, 16, 17, 48, 49, 53, 60, 61, 104, 112, 116 (Australia), 120
Caprice des Dieux (France), 121
Canadian cheeses, 120, 121
Cantal, Fourme de – (France), 11, 69, 72
Capricorn (UK), 121
Carré cheeses (France), 121
Carré de l'Est (France) 17, 51, 60, 61
Cashel Blue (Eire), 43, 45, 48
Cashel Cream Soup, 43
Castello (brand, Danish), 121
Chabichou (France), 76, 120
Chamois d'Or (France), 121
Champanet (France), 121
Chaource (France), 61, 64
Charnwood (UK), 121
Cheddar, 10, 16, 20, 33, 113; traditional UK, 33, 36, 41, 45, 104; Scottish, 45; Australian, 116; Canadian, 120, 121
Cheddaring process, 33, 140
Cheese: as nourishment, 13; 'cooked', 10, 141; early history, 11–12; freezing of, 17, 20; grading (UK

incl. farmhouse), 36, 128; menu choice of, 17; storage in the home, 17; with additions, eg herbs, spices, 10, 12, 20, 28, 40, 61, 129
Cheese and Parsley Bake, 118
Cheese Marks: UK, 121; N Ireland, 133; Scotland, 136
Cheese Sauce, 20
Chenna (India), 121
Cheshire (UK), 11, 25; blue, 10, 29; red, 10, 22, 25, 29; white, 22, 25, 29
Chester (France), 25, 121
Chèvre (France), 75, 76, 77, 121
Chevret, Chevrot, Chevrotin (France), 121;
  Chevrotin d'Ambert 73
Cigarillos, 51
Codex Alimentarius, 121
Coeur (French cheese 'label'), 121
Colby (US), 116, 121
Colwick (UK), 121
Comte, Gruyère de – (France), 68, 69; blanc, 68
Conches (Switzerland), 121
Coon (US), 121
Corsica (France), 124
Cotherstone (UK), 124
Cotswold (UK), 124
Cottage, 10, 16, 17, 124
Cornish Fish Pasties, 35
Cornish Yarg (UK), 35, 40
Cream cheese(s), 16, 37, 44, 105, 121, 124, 125, 129
Crème de Polder (Netherlands), 124
Crottin de Chavignol (France), 77
Crowdie (UK), 45, 124
Crescenza (Italy/US), 124
Croquettes de Camembert, 51
Curworthy (UK), 37
Curworthy Chicken, 30

D

Danbo (Danish), 101, (Australian) 116
Danish Blue, Danablu (Denmark), 104, 105, 124
Danish cheeses: past history, 12; profiles 101–105
Dauphin (France), 56, 124
Demi-Sel (France), 124
Derby, Sage (UK), 25, 28
Devon Garland (UK), 124
Dolcelatte (Italy), 89
Dorset Blue (UK), 124
Douceur d'Auvergne (France), 124
Doux de Montagne (France), 79, 81
Dunlop (UK), 45, 124
Dunsyre Blue (UK), 124

Dutch cheeses: early types, 12; profiles, 96–100

E

Edam (Netherlands), 10, 12, 13, 16, 97, 100, 104, 108, 109, (Australia) 116, 118
Edelpilzkase (Germany), 124–125
Edelchimmelkase (Germany), 125
Egmont (New Zealand), 133
Eighteenth Century Potted Cheese, 22
Elbo (Denmark), 125
Emiliano (Italy), 125
Emmental Switzerland, 10, 12, 81, 84, 109, 125
Emmental Francais, 68, 104, 125
Epoisses (France), 61, 69
Esrom (Denmark), 10, 125
Excelsior (France), 125
Explorateur (France), 125

F

Farm Cheese (France/US), 125
Farmhouse Cheesemakers Ltd (UK), 128
Farmhouse logo (UK), 140
Fermier (French: farmhouse), 125
Festive Pork Noisettes, 107
Feta, Fetta (Greece), 112, 113, 120
Fior di Latte (Italy), 125
Fiore Sardo (Italy), 125
Fondue, fonduta (Swiss/Italy), 125
Fontina (Italy), 125
Food From Britain Quality Mark, 125
Fourme (French: mould, usually cylinder), 72, 125
Fourme d'Ambert (France), 125
French cheeses: early, 11; profiles, 48–81
Fresh (unripened) cheeses, 9, 11, 12, 16, 93
Fruitière (French: cheese-house), 65, 68, 69
Fynbo (Denmark), 101

G

Gammelole (Denmark), 101
Gammelost (Norway), 128
Gaperon, Gapron (France), 10, 73, 76
German cheeses: profiles, 108–112
Géromé cheeses (France), 64
Gervais (brand, French), 128
Gippsland Blue (Australia), 128
Gjetost (Norway), 128
Glamorgan (UK), 128

Gloucester, Double and Single (UK), 10, 36, 37
Gorgonzola (Italy), 10, 12, 17, 88, 89, 98, 112
Gouda (Netherlands), 10, 12, 96, 97, 104, 108, 116 (Australia)
Gournay (France), 116, 128
Grading of Cheese, UK, 128
Grana cheeses, 12, 13, 85, 88, 128, 131
Granular or Stirred Curd (US), 129
Gruyère Francais, 60, 65, 68, 69
Gruyère Switzerland, 10, 68, 69, 84, 85, 107
Gubbeens (Eire), 129

H

Halloum, Halloumi (Mediterranean), 129
Handkäse (Germany), 129
Hanne Nielsen, 12, 104
Havarti (Denmark), 104, 108, 118
Havarti Vegetable Bake, 118
Hramsa (UK), 129
Huntsman (UK), 129

I

Ilchester (UK), 129
Incanestrato, **Pecorino** (Italy), 129
Islay (brand, UK), 129
Irish cheeses: profiles, 45, 48
Italian cheeses: early, 12; profiles, 85–96
Italico cheeses (Italy), 89, 129

J

Jack (US), 129
Jarlsberg (Norway), 10, 105, 108

K

Kaskavel, Kashkavel (Balkans), 129
Kasseri (Greece), 112, 113, 129
Kefalotyri (Greece), 112, 113, 129
Kernhem (Netherlands), 129
Kosher cheeses, 129

L

Labna, Labneh (Mediterranean), 131
La Bourrine (France), 129
Lactose, 9, 140
Laguiole (France), 131
La Mothe-St-Heray (France), 131
Lanark Blue (UK), 43, 44
Lanark Slaw, 43
Lancashire (UK), 10, 19, 24, 25, 28, 41
  Acid Curd, 24, 25
  Sage, 19, 24
Langres (France), 61
La Rigotte (France), 73, 135

Lasagne Gaudenzio, 99
Layered Gorgonzola Soufflé, 90
Le Chevrot (France), 131
Leiden, Leyden (Netherlands), 20, 100
Leidse Kaas, See Leiden
Leigh Toaster, 24, 28
Le Fournols (France), 131
Le Roi (France), 131
Liederkranz (US), 49, 89, 131
Limburger (Germany), 108, 109
Liptauer (Hungary), 131
Llanboidy (UK), 131
Lymeswold (UK), 37

M

Maasdam (Netherlands), 131
Manchego (Spain), 113
Manteca (Italy), 131
Margotin Herb (France), 131
Maribo (Denmark), 101, 104, 131
Maroilles, Marolles (France), 11, 56, 60
Milk Marketing Board(s) (UK), 29, 36, 37, 45 (N Scotland), 108, 128, 131, 133 (N Ireland)
Mimolette (France), 97, 132
Mizithra, Myzithra, Mitzithra (Greece), 112, 132
Monastery cheese(s), – making, 11, 12, 21, 52, 53, 56, 64, 101, 109, 120, 132
Monsieur (France), 132
Mont Cenis (France), 132
Monterey Jack (US), 132
Montrachet (France), 132
Morbier (France), 20, 65
Mould (container), 140
Mould (fungus), 140. See also: Blue mould-ripened cheeses, White mould (surface-ripened) cheeses
Mountain Lamb Casserole, 83
Mozzarella (Italy), 93, 116 (Australia), 120
Muenster, Munster (US), 132
Munster (France), 11, 61, 64, 109
Münster (Germany), 64
Mycella (Denmark), 108, 132
Mysost (Scandinavia), 132

N

National Dairy Council (UK), 36, 121, 132
Neufchâtel (France), 132
New Zealand Cheeses, 132
Niolo (France), 124
Nokkelost (Scandinavia), 133
Norwegian Cocktail Pastries, 123
Nutwood (UK), 133

O

Oka (Canada), 53, 120, 133
Old Dutch Cobbler, 115
Olivet (bleu and cendré) (France), 133

Orkney (red, white and smoked) (UK), 45

P

Packaged cheeses and portions, 9, 13, 16, 32, 33, 36, 37, 41, 44, 45, 48, 60, 77, 89, 92, 93, 104, 105, 109, 113, 116 (Australia)
Panir (India), 121
Pannarone (Italy), 89
Pant-Ysgawn (UK), 133
Parmesan (Italy), 10, 12, 13, 85, 88, 90, 116 (Australia), 120 (Canada)
Passendale (Belgium), 133
Pasta filata(s) cheeses: See Plastic Curd cheeses
Pasteurisation, 9, 140
Pavé d'Auge cheeses (France), 133
Pavé de Moyaux (France), 133
Paxton and Whitfield, 7, 8, 9, 29, 33, 37, 44, 61
Pecorino (all varieties), 92, 116 (Australia)
Pencarreg (UK), 41
Penicillium camemberti, 109, 140
Penicillium candidum, 40, 49, 57, 77
Penicillium glaucum, 77
Penicillium gorgonzola, 89
Penicillium roqueforti, 44, 48, 80, 104, 112, 116, 140
Petit-Suisse (France), 133
Philadelphia Soft Cheese (US), 55, 75
'Pickled' cheeses, 76, 113, 133
Pineapple Cheese (US), 133
Pipo Crem' (France), 17, 133
Pipo Straws, 67
Plastic Curd (Pasta filata) cheeses, 93, 120, 121, 134, 140
Poivre d'Ane (France), 134
Pont l'Evêque (France), 11, 13, 16, 49, 51, 52, 53, 61
Port Salut, – du Salut (France), 13, 17, 52, 53, 89, 108, 120
Pot Cheese See Cottage Cheese
Potato-Carrot Casserole, 63
Potted Cheese (UK), 134
Préclos (France), 134
Prince de Claverolles (France), 134
Process, Processed Cheese, 20, 141
Prodfact See British Food Information Service
Providence (France), 134
Provolone (Italy), 17, 92, 93, 120
Pur Chèvre (definition – French), 121
Pyrenées cheeses (France), 80, 81, (See Doux de Montagne, Prince de Claverolles, Roey de Quercy)

Q

Quark (Germany), 134
Queijo Fresco/Seco (Portugal), 134
Queso Anejo/Blanco (S America), 134

R

Raclette cheeses (Switzerland/ France), 134
Raclette Livradoux (France), 134
Rance, Patrick, 24, 28, 29, 32, 36, 117
Reblochon (France), 63, 65
Ricotta (Italy), 16, 93, 95, 96, 120
Ricotta Tart, 95
Robiola (Italy), 88, 135
Rocamadour (France), 135
Roey de Quercy (France), 81
Rollot (France), 135
Romadur (Germany), 109, 135
Roman cheeses (classical), 11, 12, 28, 92
Romano (Italy/US), 135
Roncal (Spain), 135
Rondeau (France), 135
Roquefort (France), 10, 11, 21, 44, 73, 77, 80, 105, 112, 116
Rouy (France), 135
Royal Warrant, 7, 8
Royalp (Switzerland), 108, 135
Rutland (UK), 135

S

Saga (Denmark), 105
Sage cheeses, 135
Sage Derby (UK), 23, 25, 28
Sage Derby Doubles, 23
Saint Albray (France), 135
Saint Benoit (France), 135
St Christopher's Flan, 75
Saint Florentin (France), 136
Saint Killian (Eire), 136
Saint Marcellin (France), 11, 136
Saint Maure (fermier/laitier – France), 76, 77, 108
Saint Nectaire (France), 11, 72, 73
Saint Paulin See **Port Salut**
Salade d'oeufs a l'Auvergnate, 71
Samsoe, Mini –, (Denmark), 10, 100, 101, 116 (Australia)
San Gaudenzio (Italy), 99
Sapsago (Switzerland), 136
Sardo (Sardinian cheeses), 136
Sassenage (France), 136
Sbrinz Switzerland, 85, 103
Scamorze (Italy), 136
Scottish Cheesemakers Ltd, 36
Septmoncel (France), 136
Serra de Estrella (Portugal), 136
Sharpham (UK), 136
Shrimp-Broccoli Strudel, 103
Shropshire Blue (UK), 29
Simon, André, 56, 60, 72, 81, 128, 131
Slipcote (UK), 136
Smallholder (UK), 136
Smoked Applewood (UK), 136
Smoked cheese(s), 11, 45, 92, 93, 136 (and see **Bruder Basil**, 120; **Gubbeen**, 129)
Somerset Fruit Bowl, 30
Spiced cheeses, 137
Spun curd cheese(s): See Plastic Curd cheeses

Stilton, blue and white (UK), 10, 16, 17, 26, 28, 29, 32, 33, 44
– criteria for, 32
Stracchino ('tired') cheese(s) (Italy), 88, 116 (Australia), 137
Stratiacella (soup), 90
Stresa Convention, 80, 97, 100, 116, 137
Sweet Brie Cheesecake, 54
Sweet Curd Cheeses, 137
Swiss (as name for Emmental type cheeses, in US and elsewhere), 81, 84, 113, 137
Swiss cheeses: early, 12; profiles, 81–85
Swiss Cheese Fondue, 17, 107
Swiss Potato 'Omelette', 107

T
Taleggio (Italy), 17, 137
Tartare (France), 137
Teleme (Balkans and US), 137
Territorial cheeses (UK), 137
Tete de Moine (France), 137
Tilsit, -er (Germany), 104, 108, 116 (Australia)
Tome, tomme (France), 64, 65, 81, 137 (including **Tomme Blanche, – de Corse, Tome de Montagne, Tomme des Neiges**)
Tomme au Raisin (France), 138
Tomme de Savoie (France), 59, 64, 65
Torta (Italy), 138
Trappist cheeses (France), 138

V
Vacherin cheeses (France/Switzerland), 138
Valencay (France), 138
Veal Fricassée, 59
Vieux Pané (France), 138
Voyagers' Salad, 79
Vulscombe (UK), 138

W
Walton (UK), 138
Washed Curd cheeses, 138
Washed or brushed rind cheese(s), 9, 10, 20, 48, 52, 53, 56, 60, 61, 65, 69, 72, 89, 109, 121, 138
Washed rind for mould-free surface, 92, 108

Wedmore (UK), 138
Weisslacker Bierkäse (Germany), 138
Wensleydale, Blue (UK), 10, 11, 21, 24
– White (UK), 10, 19, 21, 24
Whey, whey cheeses, 9, 93, 96, 100, 112, 113, 139
White mould (surface-ripened) cheeses, 10, 16, 20, 37, 40, 41, 49, 57, 60, 64, 76, 77, 104, 105, 109, 112
Wiltshire (UK), 139
Windsor Red (UK), 139

Y
Yarg, Cornish (UK), 35, 40
York (UK) See Cambridge

ACKNOWLEDGEMENTS

Many people I know and hundreds whom I have never met have helped to shape this book. They include all the people whose books I have read and learned from, whom I have watched making cheese, and who have talked about it with love or anger. They have my thanks, every one, for all they have taught me.

Various cheese marketing groups and individuals deserve thanks by name for their kindly patience in supplying information and checking (often ill-typed) text: Anne Merrett of the Australian Dairy Corporation and Australian Dairy Industry Conference; Ann E Taylor of the New Zealand Dairy Board; Charles C Trevor of the Canadian High Commission; John Netherwood of the Danish Dairy Board; Alison Winson of the Dutch Dairy Bureau; Maurice Johnson of the Swiss Cheese Union; Anna Maria José de Sevilla of Foods from Spain; Mr B Penwarden of Galbani (London) Ltd; Mr Daniel Wiedemann of Fromages de France Ltd; and Mr N Dreyfus of Bongrain-Gerard et Cie (UK). Various large and small marketing offshoots of the British Milk Marketing Boards have been helpful; Clare Nullis of the Food and Drink Federation commands my thanks for clarifying various issues, and so does Sue Hayes of the National Dairy Council. Similarly, I should have been 'lost' without the help of the staff at the Ministry of Agriculture, Food and Fisheries Library, and the British Food Information Service of Food from Britain, whose excellent publication *Prodfact* has been quoted in several places. Welsh cheeses have been checked by Abergavenny Fine Foods, and my contacts with Irish cheeses were organised by the skill of Myrtle Allen, the hotelier and restaurateur.

Then there are the individual British and Irish farmers and cheese-makers who have written to me, corrected my errors where they could, and shared their historical and other knowledge. There are generous friends who have also shared their academic knowledge; David Johnston of Southampton University and Maureen Locke who researched the cheeses of the Ancient World for me, John Arlott, whose Cheese Club leaflets have been both an inspiration and source of knowledge, and Major Patrick Rance, the author of the *Great British Cheese Book* and the *French Cheese Book* (Macmillan), and the owner of Wells Stores, Streatley. Robert Black checked various other facts. Priscilla Bain and Ewart Wells both generously created recipes. Mireille Benson, Swiss chef and part-owner of Le Rustique restaurant in London gave me valuable advice.

I owe a great debt to two close friends in particular: Roy Cornwell who, with much specialist knowledge, supplied most of the List of Cheese-making Terms, and Daphne MacCarthy of the British Food Information Service who with kindness, wit and care corrected the English Profiles, and made me laugh at myself – and enjoy it.

I would not have been able to produce a coherent book all the same without the unflagging and sensible support of my friends at Paxton and Whitfield: Sue Cloke, who did all the groundwork and arranged the photography; Ray McGovern, the Managing Director; Debi Frost, the Sales Manager; and above all Ewen Adamson, a Director of the firm, whose research has been invaluable and who has made our weekly review sessions on the text both rewarding and a pleasure. I would have drooped long before the end but for his support. The or in character; which is partly what makes cheeses so interesting to hours to get the book typed from more than one excessively messy draft.

To all those I have mentioned the book owes a very great deal. Where it is inaccurate, the fault is largely mine, but I will plead in my own cause that cheeses are products capable of rapid and infinite change at the behest of their makers, and change they do – and will do still more by the time you read this book, in sizes perhaps, in weight or in character, which is partly what makes cheeses so interesting to study – and to eat.